Italian Journeys

Jonathan Keates is the author of two novels, *Allegro Postillions*, which won the James Tait Black and Hawthornden Prizes, and *The Strangers' Gallery*. He reviews regularly for the *Observer*, the *Independent* and *The Times Literary Supplement*. He is currently working on a life of Stendhal and a new collection of short stories.

Jonathan Keates

Italian Journeys

PICADOR
PUBLISHED BY PAN BOOKS

First published 1991 by William Heinemann Ltd
This Picador edition published 1992 by Pan Books Ltd,
a division of Pan Macmillan Limited,
Cavaye Place, London SW10 9PG

Associated companies throughout the world

3 5 7 9 8 6 4 2

© Jonathan Keates 1991

The right of Jonathan Keates to be identified
as the author of this work has been asserted by him
in accordance with the Copyright, Designs and
Patents Act 1988.

ISBN 0 330 32465 9

Printed in England by Clays Ltd, St Ives plc

Contents

To my Italian friends

Introduction

None of the following chapters is wholly fictional, but in many cases I have altered names, locations and circumstances for a variety of reasons. In at least one episode I have fused my own experiences with an anecdote related to me by friends which was really too good to leave out, and I freely acknowledge my debt to them.

This is a book full of the wildest generalizations and inaccuracies. For the latter I must make what apology I can. For the former I am unrepentant, since generalization encourages argument, and if this book makes travellers in Italy think, look and listen somewhat more carefully, then some of its object will have been acomplished. Even if it is, first and foremost, an autobiography – thus making the excoriations in the first chapter seem like a case of the pot calling the kettle black – it is also an attempt to stimulate curiosity and share enthusiasm.

Above all, it is a tribute, however clumsily paid, to what Robert Browning rightly calls 'the land of lands', a country and a people I hope I shall never have done with trying to love and understand as they have so generously loved and understood me.

1 The Lonely Traveller

In the old days when travellers went abroad, they nearly always contrived to have their portraits painted or their photographs taken in some striking attitude, with costume and accoutrements ostentatiously alluding to their recent adventures. Since all travel narrative traditionally embraces the art of lying and most travellers are in some sense or other, expert poseurs, the painter or photographer may be said to have colluded in an elaborate fraud. Here is the Earl of Mounterrant, newly returned from the Grand Tour, whom the inimitable Pompeo Batoni has caught in a *dégagé* moment, lounging amid the tumbled ruins of the Forum at Rome, a sketch of the Arch of Constantine dangling from his left hand. And here is Sir William Fitzperegrine by Vandyke, lately come from an embassy to the Persian Sophy and got up in the full rig of silk caftan and voluminous turban sporting an egret plume held by a jewelled clasp. And yonder is Colonel Globetrotter-Smyth, viewed through the lenses of late Victorian Bond Street, crouching, rifle at the ready, over a hecatomb of slaughtered game, with sundry plants arranged so as to transform the photographic studio into something not unlike the upper reaches of the Congo.

Nobody has themselves painted any more, and photos are mostly cheeky snaps and blurry action shots taken *in situ*, but the posing goes on. The spirit of the Earl of Mounterrant in the Campo Vaccino or of Colonel Globetrotter-Smyth with his elephant gun and pet pigmies is a deathless one, merely changing its shape to suit the quirks of the age. Now it is the turn of the words to create the desired image, striking attitude and all.

You must know the form. You have only to open *Granta* or one of the superior weekend supplements to catch the tone at once. The scene for a start is carefully chosen to appear grotesquely unpromising. We are in some hideous mining town in Angola, a tin hut in Panama or a festering suburb of Bombay. Europe, let it be said, is permissible only when the traveller is well away from anything which remotely smacks of beauty or sophistication and within easy reach of whatever will look good in those glum, grainy black-and-white shots which newspapers regularly include in their magazines to gag the readers on their kedgeree. North America will do, in this context, provided the backdrop is appropriately charmless and weird.

Everything has to be terminally ghastly so as to emphasize our voyager's potential for survival. He has, after all, lived to tell the tale, so what a plucky, gutsy, ballsy little number he must be – how knowing, how deft, how tough. Thus the indigenes, far from crowning him with garlands and thrusting their cattle and their daughters upon him, must be represented as seethingly hostile, casting a sinister eye, or two, or three, over his prospects as a principal ingredient in that evening's *ragôut*. Thus, inevitably, he must have fallen foul of the local police, who offer him a *mauvais quart d'heure* in a cell, alongside assorted headbangers, junkies and pederasts, from whose company he is as providentially released as Saint Peter by the angel in the Acts of the Apostles.

He is not without friends. There is a taxi-driver (there's always a taxi-driver; did you ever know a piece of modern travel-writing *without* a taxi-driver?) who has a knack of turning up, a sort of Sam Weller or Sancho Panza, to offer light relief when the narrative requires it and speaks in broken English of the 'Mistah-Kurtz-he-dead' variety. Then there's the Frenchman he meets in the hotel at the start of the book, who warns him over a late-night beer not to venture into the interior because the last mad Englishman or American who did so never came back. This character, it need scarcely be said, is a lineal descendant of the Old Man in Longfellow's once celebrated 'Excelsior', who warned 'the Youth who bore mid snow and ice the banner with the strange device' to 'try not the path'.

The assumption of such writing is that the place and its inhabitants will not interest the reader half so much as what the author did there. It does not matter that most of us, even in these days of rapid and convenient travel, will never set foot in Kinshasa or Alma Ata or Haiphong or the Diomede Islands, or that we might possess a certain banal curiosity as to the nature of life in spots so unvisited by those with the desire and ability to read and write about them. Such concerns must always seem vulgar beside the absorbing presence of the traveller himself, the looming figure in the landscape, attitudinizing indefatigably in an effort to monopolize our attention.

In the end how dull it is, how tired, how repetitive; what preening, self-regarding mountebankery, all this hard drinking and hard fighting and living off boiled bootstraps and being attacked by giant warthogs and knowing every muleteer west of the Khyber and every hustler and hooker east of Macao! Away, away with this posturing combination of Baron Münchausen, Ernest Hemingway and Biggles! Give up wishing you were

Graham Greene, put the back numbers of *Granta* in the billiard room, pile the weekend supplements in the garage, light the garden bonfire with the blessed things and clear the way for another kind of traveller altogether: the traveller as stupid jerk, as incompetent, ingenuous, ungainly, terrified wimp, keener to lurk behind the ruins than pose in front of them, nervous lest his jewelled turban unravels at the critical moment, anxious to prevent his elephant gun going off and winging the wretched photographer – longing, in short, not to be noticed.

In this connection I want you to think of one of those Italian landscapes painted during the early eighteenth century by artists working in Venice: Francesco Zuccarelli, Giuseppe Zais, Michele Marieschi or the great Bernardo Bellotto. Though their names may be unfamiliar, you will almost certainly have seen them hanging modestly between the Tiepolos, the Guardis and the Canalettos in some of the grander galleries. Their prospect is that singularly haunting one of distant grey mountains with rugged, shaggy country beneath, its rivers dashing over jagged boulders, its stumpy trees surrounding tumbledown sheds, half-ruined watermills and the thatched cabins of the very poor. A fat woman, skirts rolled halfway up her bare legs, is driving a brindled cow up the mountainside. A girl is hanging out sheets to dry on a line which runs between the houses beside the stream and two horsemen in buff coats and rhinegrave boots and feathered hats are pricking along the road, ahead of a lumbering carriage, studded and chased and finialled like some ornate wardrobe on wheels, drawn by a team of plodding, thick-rumped greys.

There is another figure in this landscape. You can hardly see him, but he is there, hovering uncertain and reluctant in the hazier recesses of the picture, whose confines he will eventually forsake to become a reality. He is a tall thin man of about forty, with a long jutting nose, big ears, bad teeth and rather beautiful green eyes with which he seldom looks directly at anybody. His body is as awkward and ungainly as it is possible to imagine, and his gait is a stooping, round-shouldered stalk. His clothes betray a nervous attention to style, and he has a ridiculous preoccupation with shoes, because somebody years ago was foolish enough to encourage him in the belief that he had elegant ankles.

When he speaks, his voice is loud simply because he cannot properly moderate its volume. He is a perfect stranger to self-control. As he talks, his hands and legs appear to move independently of their allotted functions, as if under the influence of some obscure muscular complaint, giving him the air of a religious maniac in the throes of a trance. He eats like a savage, pouncing on his food with a gluttonous fatalism implying that the tastier morsels will always fall to somebody else. He is the slave of his appetites – idle, sottish, greedy, yet invariably gloomy in his pursuit of pleasure, since he finds it so much easier to be wilfully miserable than to acknowledge a genuine happiness.

With the self-pity endemic to his kind, he has never learned to deal adequately with his own solitariness, and sometimes fancies himself to be just such a figure as appears in these eighteenth century pictures, the Wanderer, the Promeneur Solitaire, the nervous rustic moralist in the imagined landscape of some Augustan poet. Since childhood he has treasured Nahum Tate's lines in the libretto of Purcell's *Dido and Aeneas*:

> Wayward sisters, you that fright
> The lonely traveller by night,
> Or, like dismal ravens crying,
> Beat the windows of the dying

He both yearns and hates to be that lonely traveller.

An intense, omnivorous erudition makes him yet lonelier. He reads with the same haphazard, undisciplined, clumsy ferocity with which he eats or makes love. Libraries fill him with a crazy, sensuous abandon that sends him raging and moaning among the book-stacks, battening on anything to choke the insatiable vampire curiosity. Music too is a drug. Forever singing, whistling, devil's-tattooing from an immense repertoire of inaccurately recollected snatches, he wants to be the very sounds he adores, which cause him to shiver and burn in a continually renewed mortality of joy. And it is the same with pictures, whose forms and luminescences reach out to subsume him as if the frames were those of windows and he a stranger whom the figures in the canvas had asked up from the street below.

This sense of becoming anything to which his imagination clings is merely another way of banishing loneliness. He is fond of the company of children, and delights in observing how, when one of them encounters a strange child in the street, the two stare longingly at each other as though eager to exchange identities. It is so with him. In the people and the things he sees, it is their being of which he is jealous. Some part of him is always restless, wanting to slough off his own self and assume that other essence – a tree, a horse, a stone, a river, a woman leaning in a doorway, a young man on a bicycle, a boy glimpsed through the window of a train, the borrowed life with the imagined power to annihilate the bleakness of his solitude.

In Italy, more than anywhere else, he has found himself vulnerable to this illusion. He never meant to go there in the first place. India, and later Portugal, were the territories colonized by his childhood fantasies. A jumbled assortment of chances threw him down in Italy, and he goes on longing for the place to give him up and turn him loose, though he knows it never will.

A succession of Italian lovers, eloquent or merely garrulous, has encouraged him to speak their language in a fluent, ungrammatical, heavily accented fashion which takes no account of idiom but renders English expressions word for word with thoughtless arrogance. You might think this would make him less gauche and fearful in manner, but it does not. He continues to tiptoe across Italy like somebody negotiating the darkened landings and staircases of a house full of sleepers he is anxious not to wake.

Every confrontation – in the train, in the post office, in shops and banks and cafés – is a matter for sweat and trembling. Suddenly conscious of the gawkiness of his body, as if it were some flimsy structure barely withheld from collapse, he averts his eyes and talks at anything rather than the person in front of him. Yet it is not other people he is afraid of – hostility from Italians is something he has never encountered – or the likelihood that they will not understand him. What terrifies him most is the simple fact that they will start speaking English to him and reveal that they have found him out for the foreigner he is.

So he has moved nervously for twenty years through the towns and villages of northern Italy, and slowly, reluctantly perhaps, the country has embraced him, with that comforting, resigned, unselective, slightly cynical sweetness by which it early learned to deflect the aggression and barbarism of foreign invaders. It has tolerated his love, his sudden, unreasoning enthusiasm directed towards some pettifogging baroque fresco painter, some wretched one-horse *borgo* in the Bassa Padana, the tenth-rate portrait of a princess in a Torinese palace, the stucco decorations in the bathroom of a ruined villa in the Veneto, an earthquake-shattered city on the Adriatic and the stumpy little hills of the Marche, which he finds beautiful precisely because they are not Tuscany.

His aesthetic, as you see, is entirely degenerate. Cultivation has corrupted his taste like caries rotting a tooth. The English call this sort of thing 'showing off' or 'being pretentious': in England, it may as well be said, you are pretentious if you know who wrote the *Odyssey*, that Goya was a Spaniard, or the difference between a symphony and a sonata. So he goes to Italy to show off freely and be pretentious. He likes to buy obscure Italian authors (and these are easily procured), to indulge a fondness for recondite artists, and to hear the music of composers who haven't made it beyond the scholarly monograph or the historical footnote.

Reprehensible and absurd as it may seem, his guiding principle as a traveller in Italy is analogous to Jesus Christ's stupendously egotistical put-down of the unfortunate Judas Iscariot, who had priggishly (though not unreasonably) suggested that the woman who anointed his Master with spikenard might better have given the money to the poor. 'The poor,' said Christ, mixing truth with pomposity, 'ye have with you always: Me ye have not always.'

The Sistine Chapel and the David and the Uffizi and Saint Mark's and the Colosseum ye have with you always: the palace at Colorno, the paintings of Fra Galgario and Macrino d'Alba and Gaspare Diziani, the sanctuary of Oropa, the silent streets of Nocera Umbra and the flaking old cathedral of Sovana ye have not always. For the most part, in fact, ye have them never at all, since nobody who writes about Italy seems to have bothered with any of them. Being lonely among these things has made him want to speak about them, to find, as it were, a voice for their stones and bricks and colours and shapes so as to articulate that strange, symbiotic joy he experiences in their presence, a sense that he and they are indissoluble.

Of course it's me. It was me all the time, as if you hadn't guessed. I wrote it like this only because something in myself – call it unaccustomed modesty if you like – detests the puppyish obtrusiveness of autobiographical 'I's planted across the text like telegraph poles. I want to talk to you about Italy, but I don't suppose you'll understand what I really mean. Perhaps you might if I reduce the whole jumbled mass of sensations to a single experience, a moment so nugatory, so ephemeral, so essentially fugitive that it hardly seems worth mentioning save as an amazing encapsulation of everything this book is about.

One Sunday afternoon in winter I was at the Victoria and Albert Museum. Gripped by the cosy melancholy the place induces at that time of day, with the lurid finalities of sunset glimpsed through the leafless trees of Exhibition Road, I went to the restaurant to have tea. Behind the cafeteria counter was the usual scatter of noncommittal foreign students, unenthusiastically replacing the baskets of flapjacks and scones, the mingy cubes of butter, the sallow blobs of whipped cream and the red jam where real strawberries figure here and there with a po-faced told-you-so authenticity. I shuffled my tray along the shelf to receive a scalding teapot and a grudging dipper of milk, and then, because my palate revolts at piping hot drinks, I moved to pour myself a glass of cold water from a jug to one side of the counter.

Through the open door of the kitchen I could see the servers coming and going among the plate-racks and dishwashers, their features slack with time-serving boredom. One of them caught my attention, however, because she was notably more animated in her movements than the rest. In the process of shifting a tray of cups on to a trolley, she carried on a more or less inaudible conversation with someone I could not see, whose rejoinders were making her laugh.

She must have been about twenty-five, with a mop of black curls under her cap, and a face whose beauties of line were enhanced by a sensuous energy of expression, her glance both exalted and mischievous. I recognized it at once and in the same moment acknowledged its power to move me. The banal, the mundane, the late autumnal *fatigue du nord* in the atmosphere surrounding us disappeared, and a vista seemed to open beyond her in which lay possibilities of a happiness I was just then in danger of forgetting.

In that imagined perspective lay the poplar groves of Lombardy tremulous under the heat, the curious deep turquoise slick of the Mincio against the walls of the crumbling citadel of Peschiera, the dusty campanile of the cathedral at Fidenza and the grey, eternally empty station of Prato where no train has ever been known to stop for more than half a minute. There stood the bleary tower blocks of suburban Milan, the windowless, bunker-like factories of Novara and Reggio, the grimy underpasses of Genoa and the derricks and coolers of Marghera ghostly through the haze of the lagoon. I saw the zinc counters of a thousand bars, the *edicole* with their festoons of *Mani di Fata*, *Airone*, *Gazzetta dello Sport* and the volumes of the *Collezione Armony*, the knobbly hams and scabby sausages of the *salumerie*, the shelves in the cafés stacked high with wines never drunk and cakes never eaten, the spotless yet strangely cheerless apartments, so potently lacking in the occupational layers of individualizing disorder and the patches of dust and damp which give an English house its distinctive archaeology.

And then I heard her say a word, nothing more. She said '*allegri*'. It means 'happy', but of course you knew that already.

2 Getting There

One of my favourite operas is *Les Troyens*, Berlioz's drama of war, exile and betrayal which he completed in 1861 but never saw complete upon the stage. It purports to be a musical version of the story of Aeneas at Troy and Carthage as told by Virgil in the first four books of the *Aeneid*, but in essence it is something rather different, more profoundly located within the world of passions and longings created by the nineteenth century itself. Not quite hidden beneath the tale of Dido and the legend of the Wooden Horse lies a subtext, an abstract plot in which the romantic wanderer is spurred relentlessly onwards by a mysterious voice. We hear this voice from the lips of the crazed Cassandra, from the ghosts of the Trojan warriors, from the god Mercury and from Aeneas's sailors as he prepares to forsake Dido for ever; its message is always the same: 'Italie! Italie!'

Such a voice Berlioz himself had heard and obeyed and in his titanic singularity of invention he must surely have intended the inclusive metaphor which the scene so powerfully implies. For the voice delivers a summons, an ordinance, an invitation, call it what you wish, which none of us knows how to refuse, even if there are times when our response is a groan of resignation rather than a whoop of delight.

I begin to catch the premonitory echo of this offstage imperative around the beginning of March. Sitting in the classroom innocently taking a bored Fourth form through *My Last Duchess*, or trying to arouse the interest of daydreaming 'A' Level candidates in the moral complexities of *Where Angels Fear to Tread*, I feel Italy quickening to life under the ruthless insistence of associative powers. From the windows at the front of the school I can look across the river to where, beneath the deadening influence of the Prince of Wales (that most sincere and misguided of Italophiles) a firm of commercial developers is throwing together a wretched pastiche of Venice-on-Thames, with a touch of San Giorgio here, a dash of Doge's Palace there, a hint of Sansovino and a cod campanile for good measure. Behind me, through an air gradually thinning to vernal clarity, spin the rich-toned chimes of the clock of Saint Paul's Cathedral, a church whose design incarnates an Englishman's frustrated appeal to the spirits of Palladio, Scamozzi, Vignola and Dal Pozzo. Around these arise the baleful ziggurats of Eighties enterprise culture, yet their most dismal significance is less palpable than the palace in Renaissance Ferrara through which Browning's sinister duke is showing the count's ambassador, or the olive-and-cypress hillsides of Tuscany glimpsed from the morally treacherous walls of Forster's Monteriano.

So it is time to be off. Tonight I'll make a phone call or two, tomorrow (I never do anything today) I'll book my ticket, and in three or four weeks the familiar rites of passage will begin.

As the morning creaks up over Heathrow, I shall totter into Terminal Two, my absurdly overstuffed suitcases full of clothes and shoes I shall not get round to wearing but which I am too vain to leave at home. Somewhere compressed among the shirts and socks will be the exercise book in which I might contrive to write a dozen lines or so of the short story it has taken me three years to finish.

After check-in there follows the customary spell of intense, suicidal gloom I experience at airports, a variant of what the French call *angoisse des gares*. I wander to and fro talking to myself with mournful deliberateness, a mad litany consisting of snatches of inconsequential quotation, bits of Pepys and Tennyson and Gertrude Bell and *The Diary of a Nobody* flung together as formulas against my demons of restlessness. Nothing else here can subdue them – neither the Dior atomizers, the 'speciality teas' nor the traveller's electric converter plugs; neither the anaemic grapefruit cocktail, the teeth-glueing cherry danish nor the tub of UHT cream poured into my scalding coffee. The stewards and hostesses will welcome me with their usual smiling indifference, the passengers will be the statutory assemblage of plain-faced English couples and cardboard-suited Milanese businessmen, and, as always, I shall talk to nobody, hold the duty-free trolley in virtuous contempt and nibble my way as slowly as possible through the plastic luncheon.

Seen from the air, northern Italy looks correspondingly unromantic, a dead flat plain covered with relentlessly rectangular fields, their squares broken here and there by grey concrete farms where Friesian cows mooch dismally about in the muckyards. Except on the Alpine pastures, where they wear clanking bells and are permitted to keep their horns, Italian cows are seldom turned out to grass, nor indeed have they ever been, judging from some of the surprised reactions of Italians visiting England during the eighteenth century. Farming in Piedmont, Lombardy and Emilia is pure Euro-agribiz, grimly practical land-use by those without much love for ruralism and wild nature. The Italian word for farm is *fattoria*: you can see, from the air at least, how it might so easily translate as 'factory'.

The plane bumps on to the heat-shimmering runway at Linate. I am guiltily unexcited. And yet there's always something eternally not quite prosaic about stepping down on to the tarmac of an Italian airport. The air hits you with its different weight and texture and smell, and as your feet touch the ground you wonder whether, like William the Conqueror stepping on to the shingle at Pevensey, there'll be a patch of earth for you to stumble and clutch at as an omen of taking possession.

There ought nevertheless to be better ways of arriving. The whole nature of Italy's historical experience is bound up with the emotions of those who got over her mountains or clambered up her shores and did what they did thereafter by virtue of finding themselves ineluctably, irreversibly *there*. Aeneas and his sailors, Hannibal with the omnium-gatherum host of Carthaginians, Numidians, Iberians and Gauls, commanded by generals with names like Bomilcar, Himilco, Maherbal and Mago, who brought their elephants through the Alpine passes, the Huns and Goths and Gepids and Longobards, the Saracens who carried war into the snowy valleys of the Piedmontese Alps, Harald Hardrada's Vikings who landed on the coast of Tuscany, Tancred and his Normans harrying Apulia, Charles V's swaggering, thuggish *Landsknechte*, Napoleon's Army of Italy, even the Eighth Army under that catastrophic nincompoop General Mark Clark – all got into Italy without cheating, as it were.

Some of these have told us what they felt, but much more interesting is the reaction of the ordinary traveller, arriving without the neigh of horses, the clank of armour or the predatory glint in the eye. When they got down below the snow-line after padding over the passes and saw, at the end of the valley, those great green plains spreading southwards, with churches and castles blurred in the heat haze, what were the first sensations of the Irish monk Colomban, the poet from Iona who founded the monastery of Bobbio in 612, or Fredian, the king's son who became bishop of Lucca in 560 and lies buried in the great basilica raised by the Lombards in his memory? Most people, when grabbed by religion, grow insufferable – how many saints would you honestly have enjoyed as dining companions? – and it is a wretched probability that Colomban and Fredian and those countless other Hibernian vagabond missionaries of the early Middle Ages would simply have gone on pondering the nature of God as they slithered down the screes and forded the boulder-strewn rivers, and not noticed anything at all about the sensations attending their arrival.

Others have been more forthcoming. John Evelyn, taking ship from Cannes on 12 October 1644, crawled along the coast to Antibes, 'which is the utmost town in France', passed Nice, 'a city in Savoy, built all of brick' and 'Morgus, now called Monaco', to reach the territory of the Republic of Genoa at Oneglia. Under the beetling cliffs of the Cinque Terre, forsaking the Genoese galley whose protection they had sought against the King of Spain's ships, liable to dash out from the port of Finale and snatch any French vessels in the offing, the travellers ran into a terrible storm. An Irish bishop and his brother, a priest, set about receiving confessions from the despairing passengers, while the sailors, aided by Evelyn and his companion Mr Thicknesse, started a frantic bailing operation. 'And now,' writes the diarist, in a period of limpid ecstasy which revives his delight both in survival and in the anticipation of what awaited him on land,

> as we were weary with pumping and laving out the water, almost sinking, it pleased God on the sudden to appease the wind, and with much ado and great peril we recovered the shore, which we now kept in view within half a league, in sight of those pleasant villas, and within scent of those fragrant orchards which are on this coast, full of princely retirements for the sumptuousness of their buildings, and nobleness of the plantations, especially those at St Piero d'Arena; from whence, the wind blowing as it did, might perfectly be smelt the peculiar joy of Italy in the perfumes of orange, citron, and jasmine flowers for divers leagues seaward.

To smell Italy before you even touch it, and almost to die in the effort of getting there! The dreariness and incidental frustration of airports offers no genuine substitute: besides, they smell of nothing you'd ever want to remember. The entire principle of air travel is based on a species of anaesthesia, a careful lobotomy of the traveller with in-flight magazines, free champagne in the curtained sanctum of Club Class and Eurobusiness, Rolex and Dior on the trolley and an air of tranquillizing a colossal hysteria, sustained by the mimsy, fawning, smirking cabin staff – merely nurses wearing the wrong uniform.

Better to have done as they did in the eighteenth century, coming down the Mont Cenis pass to Bardonecchia and Susa from Alpine villages full of cretins and goitres and people who ate nothing but cheese. Over the other side, at Lyons or Geneva, you fixed your price with the *voiturin*, who became the *vetturino* on entering Italy and whose brief was not only to provide the horses and drive the coach but find bed and board for the traveller as well. On the mountain's steepest stretch, your carriage was taken entirely to pieces and you transferred to a chair borne by six porters (eight if the passenger was 'lusty', ten if 'extremely corpulent') and thus, with your servants and impedimenta on mules behind, you lurched, swayed, almost toppled into Italy.

There was more than a hint of romance – there may be still, though it is several years since I was patient enough to try it – about arriving by train. Nobody nowadays reads *Aurora Leigh*, Elizabeth Barrett Browning's novel in verse, an extraordinary literary one-off which she completed in 1856. Somewhere in this account of a woman's quest for freedom through the practice of her writer's art is one of the first great rail journeys in poetry:

> The next day we took train to Italy
> And fled on southward in the roar of steam . . .
>   . . . So we passed
> The liberal open country and the close,
> And shot through tunnels, like a lightning-wedge
> By great Thor-hammers driven through the rock,
> Which, quivering through the intestine blackness, splits,
> And lets it in at once: the train swept in

> Athrob with effort, trembling with resolve,
> The fierce denouncing whistle wailing on
> And dying off smothered in the shuddering dark,
> While we, self-awed, drew troubled breath, oppressed
> As other Titans, underneath the pile
> And nightmare of the mountains . . .

Of course they couldn't actually get across the Alps by train, since until 1861 there was no tunnel, so they had to take the boat from Marseilles. But this is hardly the point. What Ba Browning's lines celebrate is the thrill of covering the ground, of bundling down the curve of the continent towards Italy, eternally promising, suggesting, hinting, vouchsafing, within the embrace of mountains and seas.

For me, the first day of the journey never held any excitement. There was no special pleasure in the Victoria boat-train, smelling of disinfectant, old sandwiches and dusty moquette, rattling through those featureless stretches of southernmost England which always look like a half-hearted rehearsal for the genuine article. The crossing, under grey skies on a choppy sea, in a tub full of somnolent, lugubrious refugees, wailing children and exuberant splashes of sick across the companionways, possessed no romance: we were not decorative or louche or hunted or glamorous, simply bored to death by the whole business.

At Calais or Boulogne, or that dismallest of dismal holes Dunkirk, things could only get worse. The couchette compartment ought to have contained somebody with whom you fell instantly in love, or who, during the nocturnal whoosh into Switzerland, would try to rob and murder you, but of course it never did. Hope, youth, inexperience and the mere prospect of Italy were all that made the disappointment tolerable.

One year, I remember, produced an excruciating South African, obsessed by the topic of Italian sexual potency, who held forth on the fabled inability of Rudolph Valentino to manage an erection. 'Couldn't git it ep, could 'e? 'E trrahd and trrahd, but 'e couldn't git it ep!' Another journey was enlivened by the superannuated ex-head of an Oxford college and his bullying Xanthippe of a wife, who loudly proclaimed the merits of the Greek colonels – 'they planted trees, you know, planted them everywhere' – and declared that Italy needed a dose of the same, apparently unaware that rather too much tree-planting activity had taken place there earlier in the century. The nadir was reached with three schoolmistresses from Somerset, who set about the task of polishing off the biggest packed dinner I ever set eyes on. Archdeacon Grantly's breakfast and the picnic in *The Wind in the Willows* were nothing beside it. Between the unwrapping of the clingfilm and the opening of the Tupperware, their desultory conversation entangled its lethal banalities with my efforts to get to sleep. One observation I recall only because it stood so well for all the rest: 'D'you know the film I never care if I see again? *Witness for the Prosecution*, with Tyrone Power and Marlene Dietrich. It was on in Yeovil the week Fred died.'

Sleep in these couchettes was impossible anyway. With the blinds drawn and your toes cold from the draught of the window, you lay awake, tantalized by the luminous bits of France left behind in the night. Extreme wakefulness might make you pad out into the dim corridor, where a man was smoking. It was always the same man, whatever the train, and you knew his story without putting yourself to the embarrassment of asking him to tell you.

He was French or Belgian, trapped in an unhappy marriage from which there was no release save the occasional one-night stand at some dreary Hôtel de la Gare in one of the incurably ugly Western Front industrial towns through which the train passed. He stood there, glum and pasty-faced, anchored to his cigarette in a kind of despair. The scenario of his life, written by Simenon or Duhamel, was located somewhere amid those hideous lines of grey pebbledash houses, their sides blatant with advertisements for laxatives and herbal distillations, lurid under the unsparing brilliance of the streetlamps.

Yet the smell of that cigarette was an earnest of something good, an olive branch across the floodwaters of the unending night. I've never taken up cigarettes, simply because regular consumption of them seems such a footling and expensive waste of time, but perhaps for this very reason smoking has always held an imperishable allure for me. There's a doomed elegance in the implicit act of self-destruction, let alone in the beauty which a hand, an arm, an entire body can assume in holding and managing a cigarette. I love the smell of tobacco on those I kiss, the delightfully bogus suggestion it conveys of grown-up experience, of others having been there before me.

Foreigners – which is what English people call continental Europeans – smoke like chimneys (that's part of their glamour) and the fume of foreign tobacco is an intoxicating scent. Thus the man in the corridor had been put there as a kind of pledge that you really were journeying southwards and were about to cross the frontier into a land of compulsive puffers, whom all the government health warnings and environmental propaganda in the wide world could not seduce from Lady Nicotine.

Lying in the darkness of the couchette, you heard the train slow down as it entered a station. The journey's terrible prolixity was somehow emphasized by the subsequent pause behind the plastic purdah-curtain as passengers thumped and rollicked and stumbled into the carriage, and a tonic triad on the tannoy heralded one of those peevish French bureaucratic voices, announcing, in a tone which suggested it had been unseasonably got out of bed for the purpose, 'Metz, Metz, ici Metz'. Switzerland seemed as far off as Kamchatka.

When you finally glimpsed the Alpine landscape through the filters of dawn, after the interminable midnight halt at Basle and three or four hours' fitful dozing, it was a harbinger of joy. Hitched to the train you discovered a buffet car, and the dash through monosyllabic stations, Bex, Leuk, Visp, Brig, accompanied a solid Swiss breakfast: croissants, strips of cheese, a scatter of jams, strong, nutty coffee and white rolls like little clouds for carrying rococo cherubs. Wakeful animation made you alertly condescending towards the country you were leaving. Maybe Switzerland wasn't so dull after all, maybe the price of liberty wasn't eternal greyness, perhaps the scornful clichés were worth putting to the test – but the train, that inexorable arbiter of relevance, was interested only in speeding

you towards Chiasso or Domodossola and a last haul down
the shores of Como on to the Lombard plain. Italy, in its
earliest morning incarnation, arose to greet you from the palms
and rhododendrons and lemon trees of the lakeside, from the
needle-sharp campanili and flaking yellow stucco of the last
mountain villages, and the first Italian faces, with their keen
eyes and luxuriant definitions of profile. By the time those acres
of shanty tower blocks hove into view heralding the arrival at
Milan, you felt you had done your best to approach Italy with
the careful ceremony she deserved.

Perhaps because it involved entering the country by another
route altogether, only one railway journey has ever quite offered
the proper combination of pleasure and momentousness. It was
late July and I'd been wandering, for a smart magazine, through
Austria and Hungary. Vienna, abandoned to the tourists, with
all the best restaurants and cafés shut and nothing but a tatty
Fledermaus at the Staatsoper for entertainment, was as boring
as Swindon or Haywards Heath, and the Danube, up which I
had been programmed to sail in the steamer to Melk, was in
angry flood. A night or two at the Gellert in Budapest, larded
with ample dollops of plausible Hungarian charm, though it
played hell with the liver, restored my asinine complaisance,
and I climbed into the train at Kelety station with an absolute preparedness to enjoy even the dreariest, most jejune of
journeys.

I did not at first realize why, when I heaved myself into the
carriage, a fortress-like khaki-coloured tank, it turned out to be
impossible to walk through the connecting door, as in a normal
train, to the adjoining corridors. Getting out again on to the
platform to buy myself a sandwich, I stared along the line of
wagons, formiculating with life. Heads poked from windows,
people inside swapped food, bottles, magazines, anecdotes, and
it became evident that the whole of the rest of the train was
humming with an intense, spontaneous *camaraderie de voyage*
in which I at once longed to participate.

My own carriage, however, seemed completely empty. The
blinds of all the other compartments were drawn, and when I

tried to pull down the windows in mine, I found them locked. This, after all, was 1985, when Glasnost and Perestroika might have been the title of an opera by Glinka for all the significance the words then possessed. For of course the train had come from Moscow and my sleeping berth was provided by Soviet railways. The embattled nature of this wagon-lit, an emblem of those unquenchable terrors of an alien world which have dominated Russian life since Prince Igor saw off the invading Polovtsi, was made obvious as soon as we pulled out of the station. Once the bleary, reach-me-down suburbs of Budapest had been left behind and the locomotive started gathering speed, there were sudden stirrings of life in the corridor. People opened doors and threw up blinds, ran excitedly to and fro and greeted one another amid a chorus of guffaws. When I peered tactfully out into the passage, I found it full of fat women in cotton print dresses shrieking with laughter. Then a small, sallow man strode briskly past them in my direction, and I sat hurriedly back as if seeming to mind my own business. Pulling the door open and shut, he said, not unpleasantly, 'Keep closed please, for air conditioning.'

There was, of course, no air conditioning to speak of, at least not during our dull passage across the flat, unvarying landscape of western Hungary. The only air which apparently needed conditioning was that breathed by my Russian fellow travellers, who could not be permitted contact with so contaminating a unit as myself, and who were bound, what was more, to disappear into their burrows as soon as the train looked like stopping anywhere. I sat sweating, unsatisfied by the Kelety sandwich, whose filling consisted of a thin slice of *Schinken* and a correspondingly huge gherkin, less like a prizewinner at a village show than an aberration produced by nuclear fallout.

We came at last to Lake Balaton. On the map it scarcely looks enormous, but the train's sluggish progress made it seem as though we were following one of the longer tributaries of the Amazon. The shores were full of Hungarians enjoying themselves, pottering about their jolly little cabins under the pine trees, pushing boats out on the glittering water, playing tennis and pingpong and football, and cooking up lunch on primus stoves. I felt intolerably hungry.

While I wilted into somnolence against the frayed cotton antimacassar, the door was flung theatrically open to reveal a grotesque trio. One was dressed in an exceedingly dirty white coat, which hung open to reveal his belly flopping over exiguous black bathing trunks. Another wore a pair of filthy bell-bottom jeans and a correspondingly venerable teeshirt. The third had evidently been in a fight: his nose was purple, there was a smudgy scar on his chin and his right eye was covered by an amateurish plastered patch.

They were the Czechs who managed the dining car. '*Deutsch*?' asked the white coat. '*Nein, Englisch*,' I answered. 'Eat! Now!' he decreed, at which his fellows dissolved into laugher, crying '*Ja! Essen! Manger! Mangiare!* You eat!' and hooting with mirth at the very notion. Obediently I got up and followed them through the suddenly empty corridor over which the sallow-faced man stood guard. Beyond the door which he sullenly unlocked, we entered a world I had almost forgotten, crammed with visible, palpable beings who had no need of air conditioning but just shifted a bum or a leg out of the way to let you pass as they flopped against the open window to catch the wisps of breeze off the lake through the torrid afternoon.

The dining car was littered with the remains of lunch. Somebody must have remembered I was there, but in an odd reversal of traditional pecking order the single first-class passenger had been left until last. The three Czech picaroons unceremoniously plonked down a bottle of Budovice beer in front of me, accompanied by a plate of ham swimming in runny egg yolk and a few slices of dry bread, while they cleared the surrounding tables. Lake Balaton, meanwhile, went on and on, an infinite series of bijou cabinettes outside which a succession of fubsy families slumped in postprandial deckchairs.

When we reached the Yugoslav border, a strapping young customs officer arrived to take away my currency. I was sorry to lose those Hungarian forints, as lovingly engraved, in their vivid puce and indigo, as the illustrations to some nineteenth-century silver-fork annual, *The Keepsake* or *The Book of Beauty*, and almost as ephemeral in their value. The shadows lengthened, the landscape suddenly grew interesting and the Croatian villages through which we passed had an air of slightly vulgar prosperity. In a meadow on the shore of a wood, girls in pink dresses were turning the hay. Darkness seemed to come down suddenly after that, and we slipped into the station at Zagreb as if we had meant to dismantle it by stealth and carry it off.

For a long while the train lay berthed in a siding beside lines of trucks whose inexorably abstract oblongs, with their stencilled toponyms 'Düsseldorf', 'Warszawa', 'Klagenfurt', seemed like the archetypes of limitless, haphazard wandering across a Europe without borders. I slipped out into the corridor and discovered that I could pull the window down. Outside the air was palpable as the contours of a body, its warmth a skin across the night. Then, from the other end of the carriage, a little man appeared, carrying a glass of tea in a silver holder and a plate of cakes and biscuits. With his smudgy black eyes and iron-grey curls, he looked Georgian or Armenian. I wondered why this was the first time I'd seen him on the journey. 'I brought these for you, *signore*,' he said in Italian, 'I thought, since you cannot leave the train, you might feel hungry.'

How did he know I spoke Italian and had nothing for dinner? It didn't matter. I started desperately on the sandy, tasteless sponge-cakes and the archaeological biscuits, and burned my tongue with gulps of scalding, bitter tea. Discreetly he waited until I finished the glass, then took it away and returned with more. While he was gone, I slipped the sugar cubes into my pocket. Their wrappers were green and mauve, with a picture of a railway engine and that dashing Expressionist-poster-style lettering to which Russian design stays loyal. I keep them on my mantelpiece still.

We began to move again, this time into the station itself, and pulled up alongside a platform under cast-iron pillars and barge-boarded roofs, which must have been new when Zagreb was officially known as Agram and the stationmaster, to obtain his much-coveted post, had to take the Imperial-and-Royal examination and wear a cap badge with the double-headed eagle of the Hapsburgs. Seeing a train marked 'Sarajevo', I remembered George V's bluntly compassionate comment on the assassination of Archduke Franz Ferdinand, 'terrible shock for the dear old Emperor'. Once the dear old Emperor Franz Josef's domains had stretched from the gates of Milan to the mouth of the Danube, a scatter of Saxons, Tyrolese, Croats, Ruthenians, Slovaks, Slovenes, Lombards, Istrians, Jews, Moravians, Magyars, Poles, Gypsies, Wallachians, even the odd Greek or Albanian, swaddled cosily in the folds of the black-and-yellow flag. Peering from my window as the engine braked and the train settled itself, I wondered whether I should catch some fantasmal reminiscence of this dearest of dear old empires under the soft, pinkish glow of the station lamps.

The vision which in fact materialized was both an echo of that past and a singular foretaste of an age about to begin, an earnest of that ideal world in which frontiers and customs officers and visas and exchange controls and all the paraphernalia of suppression and exclusion suddenly fall away, and mankind returns to its origins as a single unified creation, undivided by race, language or history. For on these platforms, so dramatically lit, their shadowed stanchions and rafters like patches of cross-hatched steel engraving torn from a nineteenth-century magazine, humanity shifted and swarmed through the airless night in an unquenchable fever of apprehension, longing, wistfulness and despair. The place was a museum of emotions sharpened by that mingled sense of finality and optimism which railway stations uniquely generate. People threw themselves upon each other, hurled themselves up and down subways and steps, vaulted from carriage to carriage, tore themselves, laughing or hopeless, from one another's embraces, cumbered themselves with tents and sleeping-bags, bundles of vegetables, pairs of boots, dead chickens, live children, screamed, wailed, struggled, kicked and fought.

Since many of them were young and wore as little clothing as possible, the scene took on the guise of some apocalyptic fresco in which the artist has emphasized the physical beauty of earthly bodies awakening to new life. It became for me a stupendous affirmation of that immortal restlessness which trains and the stations so unmatchably emblematize. Zagreb, it seemed, was on the way to anywhere in the world, and something like the Day of Pentecost in the Acts of the Apostles was taking place here, with every nation under heaven flinging itself to and fro among the carriages in a frenzied display of noisy, irrepressible existence.

This image endured with a power beyond all others. Recollections of the Hofburg and the Belvedere, the Elizabeth Bridge and the ruins of Dürnstein, even of the incalculable Danube itself, were mere decorative flourishes compared with it. Yet to be a part of this epiphany was denied me; I was merely one of those figures the artist has included as an afterthought, watching from a distance so as to give depth to the painting.

Dozing to Ljubljana and beyond, I was awakened in the half-light by the infinitely reassuring sound of Italian voices as the Villa Opicina customs officers came pounding along the corridor. A swarthy Neapolitan boy waved my passport away as the ultimate banality. Beyond Trieste the dawn came up and the maize fields of the Veneto panted in anticipation of the heat. The mists were lifting from the waters of the lagoon as the Russians suddenly and quite unexpectedly came out into the corridors and began talking to me. I don't remember what we said (it was in a macaronic exchange of four or five languages), but I recall a feeling that they must have decided, even in the ten minutes or so which it took for us to slide in and out of Mestre and on to the causeway, that enough was enough, that their sallow watchdog might go to hell for a moment, and that it was worth sacrificing the air conditioning for a little common friendliness.

Shaking hands with them all, I was seen off the train by the kind steward and walked out of the station amid the huddled forms of sleeping students to what must be the most beautiful introduction to any city for the arriving traveller, the church of

San Simon Piccolo and the bridge of the Scalzi arching across the greenish-blue waters of the Grand Canal. For this was Venice, most gallantly rebellious of the Hapsburg domains and among the very earliest to fall away. They say its loss broke the Dear Old Emperor's heart.

3 Rest on the Flight

Cities, by custom, are people, or, to be more specific, women. Whoever heard of a male city? Art, superstition and cliché long ago decided between them that even the dullest urban agglomeration should be represented by the female, though not always of the same kind. American writers of the 1920s and 1930s, for instance, living in Montparnasse or off the Boulevard Saint-Germain, thought it the height of glamour and originality to describe Paris as an old whore bedizened with the tributes of former lovers, until the image grew too obviously well-worn. The government of sixteenth-century Venice, on the other hand, enjoined the painters in its employ – Veronese, Tintoretto and the rest – to portray La Serenissima as a blonde middle-aged dame in ermine-trimmed robes, contemplating her adorers with indulgent maternal resignation. As for the Athenians, did they not place on top of the Acropolis a huge marble temple, to be known as the Parthenon, 'the Virgin', a symbol of the city's chaste imperviousness to conquest?

It is easy to grow cynical about this sort of thing, especially when its religious or political purposes become apparent, but sooner or later you grasp the point and the sneer withers on your lips. A city will find you out, will know you for what you are, will assume an easy familiarity, without necessarily ministering to your moods in the way you wish. Don't therefore go to a city in search of anything. The notion that such and such a place will give you pleasure, such another will bore you to death, or yet another will make your fortune, is simply something derived at second or third or sixteenth hand from other travellers. Cities, after their own fashion, weigh and probe and sift you, and come to their own conclusions as to whether you will do or not. And if you should have the good fortune to please them, your reward will not be the one you wanted, but the one they decide you should have.

By the same token, my relationship with certain Italian cities long ago took on the dimensions of some edgy, contentious affair in which, as the Latin comedian tells us, 'love revives in the quarrels of lovers.' There was once an April weekend in Venice: anyone who knows anything about Venice in April will remind you to take gumboots and an umbrella. Armed with neither, I fetched up alone at a grim little *pensione* under leaden skies, and sat for three days mesmerized by the relentless downdrip from the gutter on the section of opposite roof which formed the view from my window. While the maids were cleaning the rooms in the morning I went and sat on a bench in the church of the Salute, nerving myself for the social and linguistic effort involved in ordering lunch. Afterwards I sploshed home and sat reading *The Vicar of Wakefield* until supper time, when the dining room surrendered to the merciless booming of an English art history teacher lecturing five morose-looking public school boys on the phases of Venetian art from Bellini to Tiepolo as they slurped their *tortellini in brodo*.

By the fourth day, in the afternoon of which I was due to leave, I felt the city had got it in for me. Depression and skulking fear were replaced by honest anger, and I wandered through the alleys of the Dorsoduro cursing Her Serenity for those seventy-two hours of slop and muck. I began (initially, of course, without realizing it) to talk aloud to the ermine-clad matron, furious in my disappointment: 'Look, it's just not on,' I could be heard saying as I crossed the Campo San Tomà, 'you've cheated me, haven't you? I'm not letting you get away with it.' A man pushing a trolley through the *sottoportego* by the Scuola San Giovanni Evangelista heard me muttering, 'You've simply got to do better than this,' and two tourists eyeing a brace of fake rococo blackamoors in an antique shop window turned in surprise as I passed them, declaring, it must have seemed, to nobody in particular: 'It won't do, you know, it honestly won't.' Then a pigeon shat on my head.

Very well, it was a banal enough gesture – Venice is, after all, a huge guano deposit – but one whose ominous significance I was content to accept at that juncture. Something else clinched the moment: along a little street on the other side of the canal that runs beside the Frari, there appeared an old beggarwoman. People in that part of Venice do not usually beg; if they stop you, it is either to ask for a light or the time of day or else they are map-foundered tourists. She was wearing a man's grey gaberdine tied with a tasselled dressing-gown cord, over a long striped cotton skirt and a dingy pair of pink bedroom slippers. Her eyes, a curious light cornflower blue, held an expression which suggested neither misery or greed. In an almost inaudible voice she asked me for '*cento franchi*'.*

I gave her the money not just because I find it difficult to refuse

* Venetians often use this term, which appears to
have come in with the Austrians during the 1800s,
in preference to *lire*.

beggars, or because of my superstitious belief that if you do not give alms you will inherit the consequences of some tremendous curse, but through a notion, however ridiculous it might appear, that she was the very creature with whom I had been communing aloud, who assumed this disguise to test the sincerity of my feelings towards her. The blue-eyed beggarwoman, however, failed to turn into La Serenissima. In fact, she looked rather cross at the fact that I had interpreted her request literally and given her only one hundred lire, and shuffled silently away in her pink slippers. Yet perhaps it was worth noting that when I next visited Venice, two years later, the sun shone and I fell in love, and thus commenced upon an entirely new epoch in my relationship with the city.

With other places the liaison has not always been so fortunate. There's a peculiar species of guilt I experience towards Rome, for example, the conscience-pricking of the flirtatious chancer who is always scorning opportunities to take everything a trifle more seriously. The city invariably does its best for me. The weather takes on a caressing blandness, as that peculiar Roman light which seems as if reflected off the ridges of the hills glimpsed from the terrace in front of Santa Trinita dei Monti ripens the colours of the buildings to a seductive intensity, and my eupeptic complacency is massaged by a dish of salty, rosemary-seasoned *abbacchio*, with a fistful of salads – *rughetta, lattughina* and the rest – and a glass or two of acidly no-nonsense Castelli wine, followed by an ice and a mouthful of fountain-water. Yet I do nothing to deserve all this, I don't carry Rome as close to my heart as I do Bologna, Modena or even, Lord knows why, Ancona, and one day I'll get hurt for such trifling.

There is one great Italian city where my failure is now consummate, and I cannot envisage a time when I shall ever be able to repair the sin of omission the place constantly embodies for me. I'm talking, of course, about Milan, somewhere you might have thought it was impossible to cold-shoulder. In the world's experience of Italy, it has lain on the Lombard plain like a looming boulder in the path, refusing to be rolled aside. Except, it seems, by me.

A simple glance at Milan's shape on the map will show you how old it is. We might place the original Celtic hut circle more or less around Piazza del Duomo, widening at length to become Roman Mediolanum, where Pliny the Younger sent his son to school and Constantine officially acknowledged Christianity with an imperial edict, and Saint Ambrose became the first man ever to read silently to himself. Beyond this little central node of streets and squares butting into each other at irregular angles, the town spreads in a series of concentric rings from which its annals might be recorded as though from the age-lines of a tree trunk.

The first circle marks the mediaeval commune which cocked a snook at the repulsive Frederick Barbarossa before submitting at last to the yoke of the Visconti, whose badge was the viper and who feasted a young English diplomat named Geoffrey Chaucer, on an embassy to beg a daughter's hand for a Plantagenet prince. The next marks the magnificent arrival of Leonardo da Vinci's patrons, the Sforza, who built the turreted citadel, and after them the solemn, black-clad Spanish viceroys morbidly obsessed with the racial purity of their family trees, and Saint Charles Borromeo whose every last pair of drawers and breeches you will find piously exposed to view in his family's gloomy old barrack of a castle at Angera on the southern shore of Lake Maggiore.

In the eighteenth century, when the Austrians took over from the Spaniards and built the final ring of ramparts, their course marked nowadays by the sombre, windy *viali* lined with asylums, hospitals and railway stations, Milan suddenly and unexpectedly became the liveliest city in Europe. The Paris of Diderot and Voltaire and Beaumarchais, that much-vaunted *ville de la lumière* of *encyclopédistes* and *philosophes*, was nothing to it. For about fifty years, until the arrival of Napoleon and his invading French in 1796, the air breathed was a rarefied oxygen of freedom, intelligence, wit and discrimination.

Bliss was it etcetera. I should like to have known Milan in those days, with its coffee-houses full of the earliest breed of café intellectual, led by the Verri brothers, Pietro and Alessandro, who founded an academy called the Accadèmia dei Pugni (the Fists) and started *Il Caffè*, a journal which, in its brief two years of life, revealed to literate Italians the possibility of being able to think, and even to articulate your thoughts, without feeling it necessary to ask a priest to do it for you.

With the Verri at your café table you could discuss anything from the fashionable new science of political economy to the opinions of Benjamin Franklin and Charles James Fox, from the latest translations of *Hamlet* and the poems of Ossian to the revolutionary concept of public happiness and the duty of the governor to promote the well-being of the governed. Should you be lucky enough to chance upon their fat, sleepy-looking friend Count Cesare Beccaria, you might engage him (or better still, he might engage you) on the subject of crime and punishment, to which he had devoted one of the most profoundly influential works ever written on the theme of penal justice and the relationship of sentence to wrongdoing.

When this *Dei delitti e delle pene* (Of crimes and punishments) appeared anonymously in 1764, the Church immediately placed it on the Index of prohibited books, a useless gesture as it turned out, since it was read and acted upon with enthusiasm by Beccaria's sovereign liege Maria Theresa of Austria and by both the Greats, Catherine of Russia and Prussian Frederick. Voltaire furnished his own commentary and Jeremy Bentham took over Beccaria's phrase 'the greatest happiness shared by the greatest number'. It was on Americans, however, that the work had the most enduring effect: Thomas Jefferson and the other Founding Fathers adopted Beccaria, in spirit if not word for word, as a guiding hand in the framing of their constitution. In its devotion to the principles of equality before the law and the need for justice to remain public and accountable, America is a true child of the Milanese Enlightenment.

Reading Beccaria's book – it is not very long, it hardly needs to be, so fundamental are its assertions – or Pietro Verri's *Osservazioni sulla tortura* or the vinegary little sequence of satirical poems on the decadence and superficiality of an aristocrat's daily existence, called *Il Giorno* and written by the

Lombard poet Giuseppe Parini during the 1760s, the hair on the back of your neck stands up as you catch the authentic voice of liberal common sense, merciless in the unruffled clarity with which it exposes humanity's supine submission to fear, superstition, tyranny and cant. Theirs is the always justifiable contempt for the suppositious validity of received wisdom. Merely because things are, say Beccaria and Parini, does not mean that they have to go on being so without offering a decent account of themselves to the world.

Yet, wonderful as all this lucidly brilliant cant-scouting and crap-cutting over the chocolate cups and ice-cream glasses must have been, it was essentially Milanese in its cool practicality, for Milan, though it shelters and publishes poets, is not a poetical place. Of course in the nineteenth century there were literary salons – Countess Maffei's if you were revolutionarily inclined, Countess Samoyloff's if you were *bien-pensant* philo-Austrian – and, after the fashion of continental Europe, there were 'movements', a long, fierce critical tussle in the 1800s over the rights and wrongs of romanticism and a kind of anti-bourgeois revolt *à la française* during the 1860s called the Scapigliatura, led by Verdi's librettist Arrigo Boito and that wayward, little-known genius of experimental prose, Carlo Dossi.

But movements don't make a spirit or a voice, and Milan always seems to me to be without either. Naturally there is a Milanese dialect, and novels and plays have been written about the place, but none of them is memorable in bringing the city alive in the way that, say, Goldoni gives flesh and blood to his stage Venetians or Giuseppe Marotta makes us all long to live in the crowded, filthy *bassi* of 'Napoli senza sole'. For all its smartness and grandeur, for all the compelling sense its fabric conveys of layered historical experience, Milan offers nothing to the world in the way of a raw heart.

Ironically this is not how most Italians see it, but then Italians are notorious for not being enthusiastic about those things in their own country which send the rest of us into terminal ecstasies. Thus they are polite about Florence: *'bella, Firenze, eh? molto amata dagli inglesi, anche dagli americani'*. Rome is a city '*dove si mangia sempre bene*'. They do not, for the most part, care for Venice: '*ma è una città sporca, sai, è così triste, è troppo vecchia*', and simply cannot understand why the French and the Germans rave about old palaces and churches whitened with pigeon droppings and bilgy green canals with plastic bottles bobbing up and down on them.

For Milan, however, they have nothing but respect. It is, after all, the true capital of Italy, and the farther north you go, the more often is this statement iterated. Rome, beyond a certain latitude drawn roughly parallel with the old frontier between the Grand Duchy of Tuscany and the Papal States, is envisaged purely as a stew of meridional corruption, a sink of venality and peculation on the grand scale, where the bosses and fatcats of the peninsula's heel and toe, marinated in timeless traditions of cheating Spanish governors and lying to Bourbon monarchs, manipulate their outfits of clients, fixers and parasites, while the Pope, whom most Italians loathe because, in addition to his more obvious shortcomings, he is Polish, smiles benignly upon them from that sanctuary of shady operators, the Vatican.

In the little towns of northern Italy, behind bank counters, in the *birreria* and the *pizzeria*, in the *paninoteca** and, for that matter, the *enoteca*, the *discoteca* and the *biblioteca* if there is one, young men and women dream of Milan. In their dreams it becomes the emblem of a certain kind of seriousness which is not a boring seriousness, not one which will remind them of books and school and study and professors and painfully acquired qualifications, but the sort of seriousness which vouchsafes success and possessions and the opportunity not just to spend money but, most important of all, to be seen to be spending it. They will do something in fashion or banking or interior decoration or magazine publishing or theatre design or in the less energetic reaches of journalism, and find for themselves that ultimate expression of sophisticated urbanism, the perfect centrally located little apartment.

---

* Literally 'the sandwichoteque': who invented this
wonderful word?

The character of the city itself will not impinge more than marginally on this metropolitan idyll. Its essential northernness, the impression it offers to the casual visitor of being a town out of the Rhineland or the Pas de Calais or northern Belgium which has somehow found its way south of the Alps (an impression visually accented by a cathedral which aspires, in its irritated-porcupine fashion, to be more gothic than anything you ever thought was gothic) is a positive hair-shirt to energy and initiative. People work hard in Milan, so much so that you notice it dreadfully when they aren't working. The empty city suddenly assumes the ponderous, moralizing deadness of somewhere like Petra or Fatehpur Sikhri, a place that once knew life but now fairly rattles with the absence of it. In the locked and shuttered and bolted silence you notice the slightly chilly, arm's-length-holding handsomeness of the buildings: La Scala, the Palazzo Reale, the Galleria Vittorio Emanuele, each as formidable in its different way as some nineteenth-century dowager got up *en grande tenue* for an evening party.

There are palaces of dourly classicized refinement and churches dedicated to some of the most recherché saints in the calendar – San Eustorgio, San Siro, San Satiro, San Simpliciano, San Nazaro, San Babila, San Carpoforo – who will recite me their works and deeds from the obscurer pages of the martyrology? But I can't yet touch this city and feel it warm under the hand, with its hair and toenails growing. The streets, with their treelined tramways and gaunt, rusty residential blocks on either side, and the sad, down-at-heel little rectangles of public garden communicate nothing in the way of promise or joy or fulfilment. I never had a Milanese lover who could teach me the town's hidden signs and languages, and of my four friends who live here, one is English, two are emigré Romans and another is a crazy Parmesan.

Yet there's always something contemptible about the blind incomprehension which leaves all this behind to seek the comfortingly artificial solutions for escape offered by the railway station. The fault is mine, not Milan's, and there has got to be something to hold me back, something I sicken to see again because I shall find it nowhere else.

Alas, it is nothing specifically Milanese. Its creator was a Florentine who lived in Rome and Genoa, and it doesn't officially belong to Milan at all, since it was dragged here from a church at Como, where you can still see the space above the altar specially designed to fit it. They have hacked bits off and restored it in ways that have done nothing to arrest the darkness gathering across the surface of the canvas, but it is still the only thing which keeps me in Milan, and if the gallery where it hangs is closed when I pass through the city, then I feel a genuine sense of frustration and loss.

The picture – for it is, after all, just an old picture, of a kind easily ignored in the context of so many masterworks crammed together within a sprawling museum – is in the Brera Gallery, which guidebooks reverently term 'the finest existing collection of north Italian painting'. I am not sure whether it is, but the visual sense, inside its rather gloomy halls, gets swiftly assaulted by the beauty which lurks in the shadows. Raphael's stately, balletic *Sposalizio* is here, filched from an Umbrian church by Bonaparte's soldiers, and so is the authentically ghastly, foreshortened *Dead Christ* by Mantegna. Bellini's most winningly tender *Madonna and Child* hangs together with the cheerfully gaudy fancies of Carlo Crivelli, with the last known work (a Madonna with Saints) by Piero della Francesca, and the dreamlike, shudder-inducing images of that oddest of all painterly oddities, Bartolomeo Suardi, known as Bramantino because he was a pupil of the architect of Saint Peter's.

Because this is an Italian picture gallery you cannot always see all of these things. The traveller in Italy soon grows used to the rhetoric of excuses with which he or she is likely to be fobbed off after having sweated expectantly across town in search of aesthetic uplift. There is *mancanza di personale*, which sounds like the title of a Donizetti opera but which simply means 'staff shortage', and the brutally frank *chiuso per sciopero*, 'closed for a strike', but direst of all is any notice bearing the word *restauro*, 'restoration'. Certain galleries in Italy have been *in restauro* as long as long as anyone can remember. When was the last time you saw the Pinacoteca Civica of Todi, containing, among its other attractions, the radiantly beautiful *Coronation of the Virgin* by Lo Spagna, painted in 1507 for the convent of Montesano? At least I suppose it really is as handsome as the colour illustrations in the guidebooks make out, since for twenty years nobody has clapped eyes on this or on the collection of detached fresco fragments or the sixteenth-century majolica dishes, the mediaeval helmets or the bronze cruicifx attributed to Giambologna, or the various paintings by the seriously undervalued baroque artist Andrea Polinori, all of which the guides patiently list on the assumption that one day before the sound of the Last Trumpet the doors of the little museum will be flung open again.

Does anybody, if it comes to that, recall the Museo delle Berline, which is housed in the north wing of the Pitti Palace at Florence? This is one of those museums formed by accident rather than design from things which just happened to be there at the time: in this case the carriages of the last Grand Duke of Tuscany, that well-intentioned, bushy-whiskered old bumbler Leopold of Hapsburg-Lorraine. When the pressure of political events forced him to abdicate in 1859, he could scarcely manage even this last act with any dignity, hurrying his woebegone family off towards Bologna at such a lick that when they prevailed on him to halt for a moment so that they might have a last look at their beloved Florence, they found they had no handkerchiefs with which to dry their tears. Among the grand-ducal impedimenta they left behind was a whole stableful of incomparably smart carriages, blue and green and scarlet, their doors, wheels and hammercloths gilded with princely badges and symbols which, when the Museo delle Berline was still open, seemed the more appealing and unexpected in their grandiose modern uselessness after a morning of Giotto or Fra Angelico.

The doors have been firmly shut on these for two decades and more. If a visit to an Italian museum is emphatically a matter of potluck, this is as much as anything because of the sheer weight and volume of artefacts which a national instinct for embellishment and décor has caused to be dumped upon Italy over three thousand years. The notion that every gallery is the same as the next, and that if you have seen one *Sacrifice of Isaac*, *Susanna and the Elders* and *Mars and Venus*, you will have seen them all, is simply a philistine sophistication. Sometimes the collection will be one of those dusty omnium-gatherum affairs bringing together for safety the spoils of local churches – doll-like wooden angels with popping eyes and rosy cheeks, silver monstrances with dirty-looking bits of bone and hair inside them, their saintly authenticity guaranteed by scribbled scraps of paper, lavishly braided copes and jewelled mitres, and a score of indifferent Adorations, Presentations, Depositions, Ascensions and Assumptions gathered from parish altars and family chapels. Sometimes you find yourself in a great echoing storehouse of impacted mediocrity, like the frighteningly interminable expressionist nightmare of a Museo Civico at Cremona, which has enough bad canvases to gag the most enthusiastic art historian. Sometimes the museum itself will be more interesting than its exhibits, such as the Pinacoteca Comunale at Spoleto, where the eye is constantly distracted by the irresistibly cheerful tempera designs splashed across the ceilings of the various rooms in 1900 by two artists called Giuseppe Moscatelli and Benigno Peruzzi, or the amazing old glory-hole of a gallery at Padua, whose wormy floors quake as you tiptoe gingerly across their clattering parquet and bits of whose ceiling plaster fall quietly into your hair.

If you are lucky then, you will find the Brera *tutto aperto*, the *personale non mancante* and none but a few works *in restauro*. Among them will almost certainly not be the picture I always come to look at, an altarpiece painted around 1620 by the Florentine artist Orazio Gentileschi. His is a name known for all the wrong reasons by feminists: indeed there can hardly be a campus with a chair of Women's Studies where he is not regularly execrated.

Briefly, what every woman knows about Gentileschi is that in March 1612 his daughter Artemisia revealed that she had been 'violated and carnally known against her will on many occasions' by her perspective teacher and Orazio's trusted partner Agostino Tassi. In a scenario which Browning might have made a poem of, the case came to trial, and Gentileschi's vindictive rage made him perfectly prepared to sacrifice his daughter's reputation by dragging the affair into open court. Tassi was duly flung into prison, but all Orazio seems to have cared about was the effect the whole business would have on his commercial success. Artemisia was shuffled into respectable marriage with a Florentine named Pietro Stiattesi, while her father retreated to the city of Fabriano in the Marche, where he busied himself with decorating one of the cathedral chapels.

Artemisia was a talented painter, whose icons of female suffering and fortitude have since been hailed as agonized essays in autobiography. Eventually she followed her father to England, where he lived and worked from 1626 for thirteen years at the court of King Charles I, who had his family's habit of promising money he could not afford. A document exists among the state papers of the time, drawn up by the dealer-diplomat Balthasar Gerbier, in which we catch the unmistakable tones of the resentful civil servant bewailing government profligacy. Among various entries for 'The Sommes of Money Gentilesco Hath Recaeved' we find 'Item, after his arivall he importunaeted the Duck so long that Mr Indimion Porter was forcett to solicitt for him £500 which was the 500 whaire with his sone with a plott ment to go for Italy.' 'Item, more for to travell, £150. And after the sonne caeme back agayne maide beleeve that he had bin robde at sea and gott an other some wich I cannot tell.' 'In the Ieare he maide one peece for the King got an Yrish Baron for his schaire £1,500,' and so on in plaintive incoherence.

For proof that there was more to Gentileschi than a ruthlessly self-interested wheeler-dealer, we need only turn to his paintings, which are some of the most poetic, sophisticated, exquisitely textured and designed in the whole of seventeenth-century art. To the idiom of Caravaggio, with whom he had worked in Rome, he brought his own free-flowing lyrical imagination, his love of sudden bursts of brilliant colour in the swatches of rich stuffs with which he draped his figures, his astonishing, visionary apprehension of life as something whose transitoriness is not a mournful progress towards death but a sequence, wave upon wave like the sea, of surging ecstasies where saints and madonnas, prophetesses and angels discover a truth beyond truth in the completeness of their joy. Lightness of being, says Gentileschi, is no longer unbearable: it is the only dimension in which we can hope to exist.

His romanticism – for quintessentially he is a romantic – is not of a kind which seeks to ennoble or improve upon reality. What takes hold of him is the legendary, the fabulous, the mythical, on whose absolute, indispensable significance his dazzling strokes insist. When he paints a sibyl, for instance, it is not as some looming, sculpturally-dimensioned demigoddess from an elder world of learned classical exegesis, but as a knowing, experienced young girl, her eyes full of invitation and possibility, a gipsy fortune-teller got up in bright scarves and shimmering brocades, her bohemian curls hanging careless from under her hastily-knotted turban.

This is called realism, though it is scarcely the slavish reproduction of things as they are which we nowadays term realistic. Nor is Gentileschi's spirituality of a sort which, in our nervous modern desperation to hold on to 'spiritual values', we find readily convincing. The greatest of all his works, *The Rest on the Flight into Egypt*, now in the Birmingham City Art Gallery, is also the one which exhibits this quality to the fullest, and it is up to us whether we find the painting purely fraudulent, a mere arch display of painterly poodlefaking, or whether we accept it as one of the most heartfelt and eloquent evocations of the incident ever devised.

The components are of the simplest: on one level, indeed, this is an abstract work created from two horizontals and a vertical. Against a cloudy sky stands a peeling old wall, with a donkey's head poking up at one end of it. Below, sprawled on the ground, totally zonked with fatigue, lies Joseph, head thrown back so far that you can almost hear the rattle of his snores. You wonder if at this rate he will make the journey. Near him under the wall Mary sits, a drably dressed woman with tousled hair, giving suck to a baby. No other detail exists to tell you who these people are, no angels or golden haloes, not the slightest indication that they are anything but a husband and wife of the very poorest, crouching with the thirsty child in the lee of a ruined shed for a doss-down on their southward journey. Yet the painting's elemental plainness renders it a perfect explication of the universal appeal of Christianity, for where better expressed than here can we find the notion of God made Man, of divinity dwelling upon earth?

In my Brera altarpiece the impact is very different. Its subject is a moment in the legend of Saint Cecilia, the Roman martyr who is the traditional patron of music. She had vowed herself to chastity, but her husband Valerianus only agreed to respect the vow if her words were confirmed by the angel. When at length the angel appeared, he was not permitted to see it because he was not yet a Christian. Journeying to Rome, Valerianus was baptized by Pope Urban I, and on his return an angel presented him with a wreath of flowers. Just at that moment his friend Tiburtius entered the room, saw him and Cecilia on their knees, marvelled at the miraculous fragrance which filled the air and was at once converted.

Whether Gentileschi believed all the details of this story is beside the point, though it is arrogant and foolish to suppose he might not have done. What appealed to him was the fancy of it, the dramatic climax of the enchanting narrative which his eager imagination could heighten theatrically through gesture, costume and pose. At a time when the newly-invented forms of opera and oratorio were captivating Italy, Gentileschi created what was in essence a scene from a musical drama, in which, within the mind's ear, we hear the throbbing melismas of recitative and aria borne aloft over a rich continuo and introduced, perhaps, with an airy symphony upon the stringed instruments.

Her back turned towards us, Cecilia kneels upon a tasselled cushion, while Valerianus, on one knee, spreads wide his arms. Both are richly garbed, the saint in a gold brocade dress with a grey-blue cloak flung about her, her husband in breeches striped red and blue. To one side stands a portative organ (the instrument she is credited with inventing), and a martyr's crown of roses lies beside it. Above them hovers an angel. He is not an angel of the dignified Gabriel-Michael-Raphael variety, but an attractively truculent-looking, curly-pated boy, enjoying to the full his gift of flight and satisfying his penchant for taking mortal beings by surprise with apparitions of this kind.

All this might make a handsomely dressed stage group and an altarpiece of which any halfway decent jobbing painter could be proud, but Gentileschi was a genius who saw no reason not to remind us of the fact. The stamp of his inventive brilliance lies not here at the centre of the canvas, where the composition forms a kind of three-pointed star out of the angel's right leg and the extended arms of Cecilia and Valerianus, but in the figure of Tiburtius, deliberately engaged to subvert the initial symmetry of the group so as to make it at once more complex and more dramatically immediate.

He is coming through a door at the left of the picture. We know that door. It is the archetypal door of seventeenth-century painters. Through it come the courtiers of Velazquez, the servant girls of Vermeer, the children of De Hooch, the bravoes of Caravaggio and the rabbis and philosophers of Rembrandt. Through this door Tiburtius leans inwards, a playful, incredulous look on his face, and his hand moves round to try and catch the angel by the last leg. His presence suddenly becomes crucial to the scene. Because he is there, we want to know what happened next.

Gentileschi was a master of the early baroque, and people are leery of the baroque. English people are especially suspicious of its tendency to remind them of qualities in themselves they would much rather not know about. When they dislike it, their dislike is a positive repulsion, as if it had started to unzip its fly and make them an indelicate proposal. They hate its exuberance, its capitulation to the primacy of feeling, its rainbow-hued sumptuousness and above all its erotic physicality. They writhe and gag at its dimpled, milky-papped goddesses, its beefy warriors, its knobbly-jointed evangelists, at the tangible softness and plumpness of shoulders and nipples and buttocks among the dazzling falls of satin and lawn and cloth-of-tissue. If you don't mind awfully, English people would, well you know, honestly they'd much rather not.

For these very reasons my soul cleaves to the baroque. I like the way everybody is so gorgeously got up, I love a bonny sprawl of mythologies tumbled across a ceiling, I'm fond of female warriors in buskins and helmets and panniered skirts, of cheeky yobbo Davids sporting Goliath's head like locker-room bruisers with the ball, of Judith busy hacking at the neck of the dead Holofernes while the provident maid stands ready with the basket, and I revel in the whole scene-swelling retinue of halberdiers, equerries, ladies-in-waiting, children and dwarfs, dogs, horses, camels and monkeys and people who just turned up to have a look. It is the great art of the gregarious, of the crowd and the court and the public occasion. Maybe this explains why it also offers some of the most potent images of absolute solitariness in the history of painting.

Art-historical orthodoxy has instructed us for the last hundred years that Gentileschi was a mere soulless confectioner of fancy sweetmeats to rot the teeth of decadent cardinals and spendthrift monarchs. Let's have no more orthodoxy, shall we? Orthodoxy is only another name for intellectual idleness, the brass plate on the door which opens to let in the commissar, the censor and the Orwellian thought-police. We are told that baroque artists did not mean what they painted and that godliness and true religion died out somewhere around the time of the Council of Trent, in the middle of the sixteenth century. Why believe it? There is as much of genuine spirituality in *The Legend of Saint Cecilia* as in all the simpering Virgins and stick-limbed Christs of the Middle Ages or the Berensonian sublimities of the Renaissance. The very wit of Gentileschi's design – in the furtive, half-doubting intrusion of Tiburtius on the delighted harmony of the kneeling couple flinging wide their arms, in the angel's roguish can't-catch-me smile, and in the compositional zigzags which keep snagging the eye as it wanders the canvas – creates within itself a celebration of an unearthly happiness. I want to be Tiburtius, disturbing that intimate ecstasy. I shan't let the angel get away.

4 Lunch with the Princess

'When you're in Milan,' said my hostess, 'you really must go and call on Principessa Treviglio. I've known her for years. We were at school together outside Paris just before the war. I'll write and tell her when you're coming, and then she can ask you to lunch. These Italians are awfully generous.'

It was the late Sixties, those dear dead days now so fashionably maligned by priggish Thatcherites too old have enjoyed them properly, and, by mistake as it were, I had got on to a list of eligible juveniles kept during the debutante season by Lady Fawcett, the aunt of a girl I had danced with at a ball in

Northamptonshire. I never met Lady Fawcett, but I had reason to bless her name, as a little blizzard of invitations descended on me from all over England. I was invited, 'sight unseen', to the ritual inductions of the daughters of West Country peers, Welsh squires and the Papist *gratin* of north Lancashire. The wives of *arriviste* bankers in the Home Counties, Midland captains of industry and broad-bottomed East Anglian farmers jostled for my attentions alongside the odd marchioness, a viscountess or two, and once – rare delight of the tuft-hunter – even a duchess.

I'd arrive off the train or out of some dusty charabanc, carrying a battered suitcase whose handle was secured by an ingenious arrangement involving Sellotape and string, and feeling distinctly heroic for not having scrunched over the gravel in my Lotus or my E-Type. Only rarely did any of us meet the parents of the girls whose symbolic emergence into marital availability we were there to celebrate. Mostly we were billeted, like the subalterns of an occupying force, in the country houses of the neighbourhood, where the families at dinner had a chance to assess our degrees of appropriateness as potential catches for disposable daughters.

Milan came up over breakfast at a house in the Wiltshire chalk country after a dance at a Queen Anne hunting-lodge where a boy named Alastair had disgraced himself by being sick over the hostess. During most of the evening I had sat on the stairs talking about poetry with a girl in livid white make-up called Zara. She and I had undulated, with some degree of energy and conviction, through 'Hey Mrs Robinson', 'Lady Jane' and 'A Whiter Shade of Pale', but neither of us was of the type to be taken seriously, a fact we both rather relished.

Mrs Waller-Proctor, at whose house I stayed, was mildly arty. She knew something about Leonardo – indeed she knew (and my youthful pedantry thrilled to this) that you should call it 'Monna Lisa' and never 'Mow-na Lisa'* – and over the kedgeree we discussed the famously ravaged *Last Supper* at

* You must be especially careful not to pronounce
it thus in the Veneto, where *mona* is the dialect
word for vagina.

Santa Maria delle Grazie, which I pretended I had seen, though to this day I never have. It was when I told her that I should be passing through Milan in the forthcoming Oxford long vacation that she suggested I should go to lunch with the Principessa.

Rather to my surprise she actually wrote down the dates between which I proposed being in Italy and announced that she would write to her former schoolfriend to introduce me. It was a gesture of spontaneous kindness which I was far too young to appreciate adequately. Now and then I've wondered what became of Mrs Waller-Proctor: her husband, a bored, cynical ex-brigadier, didn't seem calculated to make her happy. Maybe that was why she liked painting so much.

The two friends, Freddy and Tom, with whom I had come abroad, were doubtful, with all the swaggering *mondanité* of twenty-year-olds, as to the prospects of my even entering the Palazzo Treviglio, let alone sitting down to luncheon with its owners. On our southward journey through Bavaria and the Tyrol we had scrimped desperately so as to stay in Italian hotels, because someone had told us that the camp-sites were dangerous and the youth-hostels beyond belief. Armed with these ridiculous caveats, we lurked in a dismal *albergo* near the station, with no hot water, holes in the bathroom lino and the furnace blasts of early June wafting through its mean little windows. I rummaged desperately through my crumpled shirts and trousers and nerved myself to go downstairs and ask reception for an outside line.

When I got back, Freddy was sitting on his bed cutting his toenails as Tom emerged from the bathroom clutching a teeshirt he had been soaking in the washbasin. Formerly black, it had faded to a patchy grey, but he favoured it because he thought it made him look moody and French, 'sort of *Jules et Jim*', and helped to pull the birds.

'Well?' he said. 'Bet you didn't.'

'I did. They want me to go there tomorrow. It's in Via Sant'Orsola, wherever that is.'

Freddy, going on with his hacking and gouging, merely muttered: 'Jammy bugger.'

It had passed off with almost sinister ease. My few words

of Italian had brought the Princess to the telephone, and in humiliatingly precise English she announced that, having heard from Mrs Waller-Proctor, she had indeed been expecting my call. Would I come to lunch the next day? A little family gathering, nothing exceptional, though there were one or two other guests who might interest me. The notion of my interest being consulted was colossally flattering; I was far too young, after all, to know anything of the subtlety with which aristocrats exercise their condescension towards the untitled. The thought of sitting down to table with a princess in a palace was thrilling to me, *et voilà tout*.

English attitudes towards Italy show a remarkably sturdy refusal to accept the almost total reversal of socio-economic realities which has taken place during the half-century since Mussolini's overthrow. Staying recently with some friends who had taken a villa in the Chianti, I was amazed to hear one of them warn the children's nanny not to trust the tap water. In vain I pointed out that Tuscan piped water is a good deal healthier and more efficiently treated than the effluent oozing through the conduits of Hampstead or Islington. I was striking at the roots of an ancestral prejudice, as musty in its antiquity as the notion that Italians smell of garlic and eat 'spaghetti bolognaise' (a dish unknown at Bologna or anywhere else in Italy). The wealthier, more enterprising, more evolved Italy becomes, the more entrenched grow our affectations of superiority. We need to believe that we are somehow better than Italians so as to console ourselves for our increasing material insecurity.

In at least one of our cherished myths about Italian society, however, there lurks an ironic truth. At some stage during the early nineteenth century, English visitors began to wax sceptical about the enormous numbers of aristocrats to be found throughout Italy. Wherever you turned, there was a count or a duchess or a marchesa: a middle rank of society, of the kind for which the 1832 Reform Bill had been designed in England as a political *douceur* to keep the upper classes in being, seemed scarcely to exist. Guidebooks of the period began to warn travellers of the potential dangers. Murray's

Rome and its Environs (1869 edition) devotes four pages in double column to the issue, admonishing its readers that 'the institution of nobles, or what we designate under the general term of *nobility*, is very different in Italy from what it is in our country.' Princes, the anonymous cicerone implies, are all very well – you know where you are with a Colonna or an Odescalchi or a Ludovisi Buoncompagni (which always sounds like a brand of motorbike) – but, 'as to the titles of marquises and counts, it is probable that several who bear them would find it difficult to exhibit their diplomas of creation.'

As an aid to the flustered hostess faced with the problem of precedence, Murray appends a chronological table of creations, from the Caetani, Dukes of Sermoneta (1503) to the johnny-come-lately Lancelotti (1865). You could play safe with the counts and marquises by ranking them according to age, though the guide is unhelpful as to how this was to be determined, short of asking them point blank. 'Dear marchese, do help us settle a little wager: my sister swears you are sixty-four, but I will lay ten to one you are not a day over fifty-nine.' Matters were further complicated by the fact that four marquises – Patrizi, Serlupi, Sacchetti and Theodoli* – belonged to an élite class known as Nobili del Baldacchino, whose privileges included keeping a personal throne with a blue parasol and kneeler.

There really were, as indeed there still are, an awful lot of nobles in Italy. Anything like an Italian Burke or Debrett would probably run to as many volumes and pages as the Britannica. Perhaps the oldest nobility honestly did receive its titles for gallant deeds in defence of feudal masters, with gobstopping Germanic monickers ending in -ulfo and -baldo and -gardo, at some stage in the earliest Middle Ages, but the majority of styles and additions seem to have been handed out for the not altogether contemptible purpose of keeping happy people whose money and clout might sooner or later prove useful. For

* A family which included the inventor of that invaluable aid to surveyors and mapmakers, the theodolite.

example, it is hard to believe that Sixtus V, one of the shrewdest of all popes (his five-year papacy, from 1585 to 1590, wholly altered the face of Rome) did not know what he was doing when he granted every male of noble blood in the March of Ancona the right to bear the title of count.

Every town, large or small, possessed its Libro d'Oro, the golden book in which the names of 'good families' were inscribed, and arrogated to itself the privilege of conferring titles. Visit some little windswept *borgo* in a fold of the Umbrian mountains or a one-street village in the bends of the Po and you will find the doorways of half the old houses keystoned with the *stemmi* (coats of arms) of local lordlings. From time to time the ranks were beefed up artificially. When the Austrians assumed control of Venice under the inglorious Treaty of Campoformio in 1797, they ennobled the heads of all the great patrician families of the extinct Serene Republic. The gesture was the ultimate ironic act of imperial subjugation: the Foscari, Mocenigo, Cicogna and Contarini, whose proud boast had been to lead a state whose only honorific was the elective title of Doge, now found themselves, on payment of the appropriate sum, counts of the Holy Roman Empire. With one or two exceptions, such as the Michiel, who, numbering three doges among their forebears, were far too grand to bother with alien titles, none of the great Venetian clans seems to have been reluctant to forgo the proffered aggrandizement.

Now and then an aristocratic privilege was awarded for purely picturesque reasons. Consider, for instance, the tale of the Duke of Modena's music master. During the latter part of the eighteenth century an English earl, Lord Oxford, was travelling in Italy with his family and chose to stop a week or two at Modena, where he presented himself at court with his wife and daughters. The city had lost much of its attractiveness as the liveliest of the smaller Italian capitals, and Ercole III, last of the Este dukes, was a pennypinching bureaucrat with little interest in renewing the artistic glories of his ancestors. Thus the musical life of the court had been considerably reduced, but there was still a small orchestra which played for dances and ceremonial occasions, under the direction of a youthful and exceedingly handsome fiddler.

In no time at all, Lady Elizabeth, the youngest and most impressionable of Lord Oxford's daughters, had fallen for the dashing concertmaster, and found her passion ardently returned. His motives seem to have been uncommonly pure and lacking in any hint of cynical calculation, but there was no question of such a match being acceptable to the earl and countess, who were preparing to leave for Florence when they made the embarrassing discovery. Eloping into the mountainous region of Massa, which Duke Ercole had recently acquired through marriage to the last of the Cybo Malaspina family, the English miss and her Italian musician were wedded, and settled down to a decidedly humble existence on a little farm in a crook of the Apennines. Though the duke was tactful enough not to interfere, it was made clear to the violinist that he had better stay well away from Modena. From her parents Lady Elizabeth heard not a word.

After a fashion they were happy. The years went by, they had children, took their chickens to market, gave music and dancing lessons to the local gentry, and might have gone on in this sort of cheerful obscurity for ever. One afternoon, as they pottered about the garden, a woman returning from Massa gave them some fascinating news. An English lord had arrived in the town on his way south towards Lucca, and was now having his carriage mended. She had seen the carriage, she said, and was most particular in her description of the coat of arms on its doors and embroidered hammercloth. Elizabeth could hardly believe her ears. She put on her bonnet and set off down the mountain to reclaim the parent she had not seen for nearly a decade.

The earl was not a cruel father. Even if he had scarcely moved heaven and earth to find his daughter, his determination never to forgive her had long since given way to nostalgic regret. To be thus reunited with his beloved child was more than he had dared to hope for, and the mutual delight of the pair may easily be imagined. What, he asked Elizabeth, could he possibly do to make her happy?

Age, experience and penury had made her extremely resource-ful. During her journey into Massa she had pondered this ques-tion carefully and come to a significant conclusion. Assuming that Rome was the earl's final destination on his Italian tour she would urge him to beg a single favour of the Pope. 'And what can that be, my dear?' Unhesitatingly she answered, 'That he grant a title of nobility to my husband, so that he becomes my equal in the eyes of good society.'

Lord Oxford kept his word. So what if he were a Protestant, descended from the gallant Brilliana* Harley, who had held her castle at Brampton Bryan in Herefordshire for the Parliament in the Civil War? This was the eighteenth century, an age when people knew how to stretch a point or two in matters of religion, and Pope Pius VI was a singularly obliging character. So the Duke of Modena's concert master became the Conte di San Giorgio, and husband and wife gave up taking chickens to market, came down off the mountain, and, so far as we are able to ascertain, died in an ambrosial odour of social acceptability.

This tale was told me one hot evening in Siena, during a party following the Palio, that murderous, magnificently rigged race of bony nags round the sloping sides of the great Campo which forms the heart of the city. The teller was a Tuscan count with shaggy eyebrows and a monocle, who, accompanied by his wife, sat on a sofa beside two elderly *marchese* eating rice salad and canapés. One is always supposed to be able to pick out noble men and women from the crowd – it piques their vanity if they suppose you can do so – but it is only fore-knowledge which makes people say that Count and Countess Lucarelli look what they are. They might pass just as easily for a pair of university teachers or a brace of unostentatiously eminent writers as for the holders of ancient estates in the Chianti, a scatter of palaces along the Arno and one of the most distinguished names in Florentine history. Yet catch a

---

* She was named Brilliana after the town of Brill in Holland where she was born. Her sister, for some obscure reason, was christened Helengenwaugh.

glimpse of the count's long-limbed, fine-boned sister scudding down Via Tornabuoni on her bicycle like an elegant giraffe, and the flavour of the patrician in the travel of her glance as she surveys a gaggle of tourists crossing at the traffic lights is unmistakable.

Probably because they are so many, Italian aristocrats have never felt the need to retreat into that kind of embattled stupidity which is the hallmark of their English counterparts. In Great Britain the sons and daughters of the peerage are painstakingly under-educated so as to purge them of any potential suggestion of being middle-class. Lady Bracknell's famous dictum that 'ignorance is like a delicate, exotic fruit: touch it and the bloom is gone' has been taken to heart, and the likelihood of finding an earl or a marchioness in the higher reaches of scholarship, research or artistic endeavour is exceedingly slim.

The absurd and contemptible horror of 'inties', as British nobs apparently call those of us who know how to read and write, is generally unknown in Italy. If only to keep its creditors at bay, her nobility has had to do little more than a spot of tweed-and-leather-elbow-patch farming or keeping a company directorship warm, and the titled turn up in the most unexpected contexts – as composers, couturiers, stage designers, Euro MPs, molecular biologists, classical historians, novelists, journalists, philosophers and architects. This is not to say that the Italian aristocracy is without a more negatively typical aspect. For every maverick or revolutionary in the family, there are a dozen radical reactionaries, perched on wobbling pedestals of tribal honour, venomous old countesses lamenting the decay of 'respect' and 'order', sinister fascist princes linked with unspeakable pan-European brotherhoods dedicated to the extinction of democracy, obtuse monarchists still confident of restoring the frightful House of Savoy, dour Catholic god-botherers wearing out the rosary in hopes that the family saint will vouchsafe a miracle.

It would be wrong, in any case, to lump them all side by side. The scores upon scores of Neapolitan and Sicilian dukes, princes and barons are a galaxy removed from papal counts,

Lombard marquises or the close-knit urban aristocracies of the Emilian plain. I did not, of course, know anything of such anthropological sophistications when I went to call on the princess, nor, probably, would it have availed me much had I done so. Mine was that age so brilliantly encapsulated by the Spanish novelist Benito Pérez Galdós, who in one of his books says of a boy barely out of his teens that he was 'as naked of knowledge as he was clothed in presumption'.

The Palazzo Treviglio was one of those immensely dignified Milanese *case gentilizie* which have no need of 'limbs and outward flourishes' to proclaim the social consequence of those who dwell in them. Apart from a brace of musclebound stone atlanti holding up a little balcony above the main gateway, there was no special decorative elegance in the austere frontage of rust-covered stucco, its lines of windows crowned by the plainest of pediments. I wandered into a drab-looking courtyard, passed through an open doorway at the farther end and found myself plunged into total darkness.

After a while I picked out objects in the gloom, a chest with a large glazed pot on top, a portrait of a woman in seventeenth-century costume, and the beginnings of an enormous flight of marble steps, from whose upper landing I caught the sound of laughter. Rising like a genie from the shadows there appeared a little old woman in a black dress and white apron who, assuming I spoke no Italian, brusquely motioned me to follow her upstairs. As we climbed, the light seemed to change or else my eyes had grown more accustomed to it. Halfway up, where the staircase shifted direction, sat the massive stone figure of an enthroned cardinal, a Treviglio of the Renaissance who had successfully negotiated some advantageous treaty with the Emperor Charles V, and had narrowly missed the papacy by dying of a surfeit of ortolans at the very moment when his election was being gerrymandered.

At the top of the stairs a high, wide-windowed gallery, not unlike that of the Uffizi at Florence, ran the full length of the palace, and down its avenue of mirrors and ormolu tables, tapestries and maimed Roman statuary, were large, roomy sofas on which sat half a dozen smartly-dressed women, all seemingly talking at once in very loud voices. My vanity was not flattered by the fact that most of them, even those closest to me, pointedly failed to acknowledge my presence. The essence of English students abroad is to appear as frowzy and unkempt as possible, and such indeed I was, despite having resorted the night before to the classic ploy of pressing my trousers under the mattress, an operation which rendered them more obviously creased in the wrong places.

The princess (I assumed it was she) rose at last to greet me, with such an evident look of disillusion on her features that I almost turned and fled. Clearly she had expected a tall, willowy *milordino inglese*, in a waistcoat and brogues, with that curious crinkly blond hair which all Etonians in my Oxford generation seemed to possess. The gawkhammer clothes-horse she had fished up instead was obviously not to her taste, but, for Mrs Waller-Proctor's sake if not for mine she must make the best of it. In fairness to her, she possessed the true *physique du rôle*. We had been doing Tennyson with my tutor at Magdalen that summer, and I thought of 'Maud is not seventeen, but she is tall and stately.' Principessa Treviglio, at not quite fifty, looked as if born to lead armies. Her marcel-waved hair was a coarse iron grey like a horse's mane, and both her nose and her jaw had a decidedly equine cast. The expression in her light blue eyes was that of somebody whose version of reality transcends what the rest of us might accept as genuine or true, and who is therefore not accustomed, publicly at least, to being in the wrong.

'You must meet my daughters,' she announced, as though I had wasted my life until that moment by having failed to do so. 'We're all waiting for my wretched husband. He's got stuck at some fearfully boring meeting in Monza.'

Her English had a delicately accented precision, as if she were trying not to squash her words by emphasizing any of them too powerfully. Plainly she had forgotten about the interesting fellow guests she had proposed over the telephone, or else I was too piffling for her now to bother with more than

was absolutely necessary. Leaving me staring at an alabaster
bust of Lucius Verus, the princess marched down the gallery to give orders to an elderly flunkey in a yellow livery
coat.

By the time her daughters appeared I was beginning to feel distinctly uncomfortable, and was thankful for the air of indulgent
bossiness with which the pair of them swept me away through
the palace, under orders, apparently, to keep me amused until
lunch. Their names were Ottavia and Flaminia, and the English
they had acquired from their nanny Miss Membridge had been
perfected at a finishing school kept by a Belgian baroness at
Fiesole. We wandered through a sequence of lofty frescoed
saloons, their walls stacked high with mythologies and battle
scenes, while the two girls quizzed me about Swinging London
and the Rolling Stones, as to whom they were a good deal
better informed that I. They had that relaxed friendliness and
instinctive sociability which makes young Italians seem more
grown-up than other Europeans. By the time we had rambled
over the entire picture collection and looked at a pair of Napoleon's boots, a letter from Stendhal and a fan autographed by
the Empress Charlotte of Mexico, I was decidedly bumptious,
and bounced back into the gallery with a 'how-happy-could-
I-be-with-either-were-tother-dear-charmer-away' air, as though
quite ready to offer myself as husband for Ottavia or Flaminia
should the chance declare itself.

The princess, with all the shrewdness of her countrywomen,
had evidently divined this as well, and her gelid stare pulled
me up sharply. Two newcomers had joined the company, an
American neurosurgeon and his wife, whose presence was creat-
ing something of a stir. The smart sofa-loungers (several of
whom, the girls had told me, were their aunts) had converged
on the pair with a blatant curiosity. Somewhere in Mrs Thrale's
account of her visit to Venice in 1792, she describes catching
sight of a large crowd in a *campo* in front of a church, gathered
around what turned out to be a wholly unexceptional horse, as
fascinating an object to horseless Venetians as the rhinoceros in
Pietro Longhi's enchanting little picture painted earlier during

the same century. The present scene held something of the same quality.

'A doctor!' exclaimed one of the aunts. 'Not rrrreally!'

The American nodded politely, almost compassionately, empathizing, as it were, with the enormous mental leap it must now be necessary for her to make in order to comprehend his arrival in their midst.

'But we never meet doctors, do we?' said another.

'Never,' they agreed in chorus, one or two of them looking askance at the princess, as if inviting a neurosurgeon to lunch were a further indication of some creeping mental illness from which they had long suspected her to be suffering. With a little smirk at them all, she rejoined:

'And he is not the only one who is a doctor.'

The aunts, utterly bamboozled, turned to the American for enlightenment.

'My wife,' he said, 'is also in medicine.'

This was the end. You felt they might have sent the maid to fetch the Empress of Mexico's autographed fan to revive them from their paroxysms of astonishment. Italians have a way of saying '*Noooooh!*' as a testimony of surprise which makes it sound like the operation of a pneumatic drill. A whole volley of '*Nooooohs*' now went off, but the doctor's wife, a wonderfully self-possessed woman, kept her cool.

'Yes, I am,' she said, then added roguishly, 'in paediatrics.' Before any of the aunts had time to enquire exactly what she meant, the princess decided enough was enough and that we should sit down to luncheon. She gave a slight tip of her iron-grey mane to the flunkey, and in a kind of cortège behind him, with me and the girls bringing up the rear, we clattered downstairs to the dining room.

The table was laid for sixteen in a long, barrel-vaulted saloon looking on to a narrow little garden with a fountain weeping out of a wall. To tell the truth, I was rather glad than otherwise that the princess had ceased to take any notice of me, because it meant I could enjoy observing the details of the scene without feeling any compulsion to take part in it. I watched the way in which one of the aunts wiped her mouth, like Chaucer's Lady Prioress, after each slowly-masticated forkful of risotto, the profligacy with which another aunt scattered fragments of bread across the tablecloth and the imperious watchfulness of the princess herself, looking out across her lunch table like a captain on the bridge of a liner.

Soon after we sat down, we were joined by the son and heir, a pasty, cross-looking, bespectacled boy of exactly my age called Roberto but referred to by everyone as Bobby. He made no apologies for lateness, merely threw himself into his chair and gracelessly dished some rice on to his plate from the tureen held out by the old flunkey. Like everybody else, except for a woman in a black velvet bolero who kept calling out with courageous obstinacy, 'But what are you saying? Speak Italian, can't you?' Bobby talked in English, but his temper did not improve throughout the meal, and his two sisters amused themselves by ragging him mercilessly for my benefit.

'Rrrreally, Bobby, you're such a bore,' said Flaminia, 'No, don't you think my brother's boring? He obsessed with – how do you say it? – *i diritti del primogenito*.'

'No, I'm not,' said Bobby. 'My sisters are stupid, *due cretine*, they don't deserve to inherit anything.'

'Why shouldn't we inherit it all?' said Ottavia. 'Probably we'll do better than you at university, and at least we shall appreciate it, which is more than you ever do.'

'What about those old chairs? We have some beautiful old chairs, in *lacca giapponese*, and do you know, Bobby kicked one and it broke. What does one do with such a brother?'

While I sat there simpering desperately, my eye fell upon an object of singular incongruity among the little bowls of artfully arranged rose petals, the silver epergnes and the pyramids of fruit that adorned the centre of the table. It was nothing other than a bottle of Worcester sauce, the more familiar to me since I grew up not ten miles from where they make the stuff, and got used to the smell of it wafting into the train carriages from the Lea & Perrins factory near Worcester Shrub Hill Station. I was fairly mesmerized by that bottle of Worcester sauce. Barely aware of the Italian nobility's ambivalent yet enduring anglophilia (all the Treviglio princelings called the principessa 'mummy') I found this an alien and obtrusive presence. If a bottle of Worcester, what price Daddie's or HP, a jar of Hayward's Pickles or a tomato-shaped ketchup dispenser? It seemed to devalue the genuineness of the occasion, whereas, I now perceive, it was the ultimate guarantor of its authenticity. Nobody else touched or so much as looked at it, but the table, otherwise so impeccably the thing, would have been incomplete without it.

'What are you talking about down there?' barked the princess, a cue for the woman in the black bolero to thump the table and cry: 'What are you saying? Speak Italian, so that we can all understand.'

Not bothering with our answer, the princess declared that she wanted to ask the Americans about her dreams. Again the aunts gave her what used to be called 'an old-fashioned look', and again she directed towards them her withering little smirk.

'Mummy,' said Ottavia, 'has some very funny dreams.'

'Yes,' said Flaminia, 'last week you told us that you dreamed you were chasing after *Gesù Cristo* with a – what is it? – *una rete da farfalla*.'

'A butterfly net,' translated Bobby with gloomy scorn.

'Well, what do you think of that?' said the princess, bursting out laughing. For the first time she appeared almost vulnerably human and attractive.

The air of patient indulgence deepened on the countenances of both the Americans. 'I'm honestly not competent to judge,' said the neurosurgeon, 'I leave that kind of thing to the psychiatrists.'

'Yes, but you're a doctor,' protested the princess.

'And his wife is a doctor,' said the most patently foolish of the aunts, as if to remind herself of the bizarre reality.

'Listen,' said the princess, determined not to abandon the subject too soon, 'my children call me out-of-date, but I really do believe my dreams must be more remarkable than those of my butler. Don't you think so? How can a butler have interesting dreams? My dreams must be more fascinating, I insist.'

For a moment my eye caught that of the neurologist's wife, diagonally opposite me at the upper end of the table, and I realized that we had both come to the same staggering conclusion. For the man the princess spoke of was none other than the wizened, sallow-faced, rachitic old flunkey in the yellow coat who even now was hovering at our backs with a plate of mixed meats, yet the entire spirit of her loud asseveration was one which absolutely refused to acknowledge him as a creature worthy of her tact or delicacy of feeling. What was more, the notion that he might have understood what she was saying had clearly not even occurred to her. She turned again for confirmation to the neurosurgeon, whose expression had altered to something almost like pain.

'I'll ask him tomorrow, I will rrreally,' she cried.

'And will he tell you?' The American's gaze fell pityingly upon the old man, ducking and bobbing among the family.

'Of course he'll tell me,' the princess said impatiently, 'my butler tells me everything, he has no secrets from me. But you still haven't answered my question, *dottore*. Do you seriously believe that my dreams can be the same as his?' That was not the question she had originally asked, but this was beside the point.

Almost wearily, as if responding to the demands of an insistent child, the doctor replied: 'Yes, I must say that I do. For you see, principessa, the subconscious makes no distinctions of rank. It cannot tell that you are a princess and that . . .' he paused and looked up in embarrassment. The butler had proffered the dish to Bobby and was moving round to Ottavia. 'That he is a servant.'

The princess snorted, muttered, 'In any case I don't believe it,' and that, as far as she was concerned, clinched the matter.

After lunch we went into the garden for coffee. I must have looked still shabbier in daylight than I had appeared inside the palace, for the princess began to drop several broad hints that I had better be running along and that my Waller-Proctor credit had now run out. Few things are more devastating than having to say goodbye to those on whom you know you have not made the slightest impression: you would almost rather they ignored you altogether, instead of going through a ghastly parade of insincere valediction. I was glad none of them came farther than the garden door and that I was left to find my own way out.

Beyond the palace gate the existence of anything like Milan seemed incredible. There lay the grey, bald streets, the shuttered shops, black churches and plane trees powdered with yellow dust. It was three o'clock, blindingly hot, and the wine at lunch had given me a headache. I felt crabby and incipiently miserable. The whole occasion appeared stupendously anticlimactic, and I began to wonder what on earth I should make of it once I got back to Freddy and Tom. Then I thought of sulky Bobby kicking a lacquer chair to smithereens, of Napoleon's funny, fat little boots in their glass case, of Prince Treviglio whose empty place had dominated the lunch table like the Siege Perilous, of Mummy dreaming of chasing Jesus Christ with a butterfly net, and of the aunt crumbling bread all over the cloth with her mottled brown fingers, and wondered on what planet I had been spinning.

One detail of the whole occasion hooks relentlessly on to the memory. To get back into the hall I had to pass through the dining room, where the servants had cleared away the remains of lunch. The fruit pyramids had been shifted to a buffet under an eighteenth-century capriccio of ruins, together with the little glass bowls of rose petals, starting to look somewhat forlorn in the rising heat of afternoon. Alone in the middle of the great scagliola dining table, like some holy ampulla or phial of consecrated blood, immovable, untouchable, the very essence of '*procul, o procul este, profani*', a cult object, a shamanistic emblem worthy of a thousand anthropologists, its orange label gleaming in defiance of sacrilegious hands, its brown plastic top eternally rejecting prosaic attempts at unscrewing it, stood, unique, inviolate, Alpha et Omega, the bottle of Worcester sauce.

5 Ways of Escape

Milan, what is more, has a railway station. Actually it is not a railway station, but *the* railway station. There are other stations in Milan – sixteen to be precise, not to speak of an entire underground system – but Milano Centrale is The One, ultimate in the majesty of its affirmations, in its profligate splendour of revealed possibility, in its eternal defiance of all those curmudgeonly, mean-spirited, joyless, inhuman, godforsaken community-haters who tell us that train travel is dead and that our aspirations should soar no higher than the private car.

Milano Centrale sets at nought such banal individualism. Its monstrousness reduces human self-consequence to something quintessentially ephemeral. Its scale is so huge, the terms on which it engages with our experience so apparently limitless, that it does not specially care whether we get to the end of our ticket queues, whether (a frequent dilemma, this, in Italy) we have the correct sprinkling of small coins to please the philosophically glum clerks at the windows, or whether we shall catch the train with whose existence the capricious indicator board at the entrance to the platforms persists in teasing us.

For sheer moral education there are few places like it on earth. It forces an existential crisis on the traveller by the tricks it plays with the rhetoric of architecture. The spaces within its great sequence of booking halls are anarchic in their immensity; whole villages might be crammed into them without squalor or discomfort. Stairs and escalators hurl you up into the realm of an unknown actuality, but even these seem emblematic, ghastly metaphors of ill-judged optimism. For halfway up is a little set of marble terraces, on whose stone benches sit or lie those who, for whatever reason, have abandoned the delusive ascent. The poorest of poor students, with grubby feet and matted hair, their lean bodies burned black, their eyes as visionary with hunger and thirst as those of desert hermits, sprawl beside Calabrian families picnicking off peppery sausage and coarse bread washed down with swigs of wine dark as cuttlefish ink. Pink-shouldered northern girls from a country where the sun is a cheese tied up in a muslin bag scribble their postcards next to snoring nondescripts wrapped in clothes whose true shapes and colours vanished aeons ago. These are the sirens and lotus-eaters and Circean beasts of Milano Centrale, wheedling you to turn back, not to bother with the hopeless business of going on.

They are right, of course, for at the head of the stairs, in the vast grey gallery, with its coffered ceiling and mosaic floor, a man might comfortably pass the remainder of his life. There's a kind of malaise bred in railway stations – and, I grudgingly concede, at airports – which makes you terrified of leaving them for fear of the complexities lying in ambush beyond. Thus, I am convinced, there must be a kind of alternative parasitic community living in Milan station which manages to avoid every attempt by the authorities to dislodge it, perhaps not unlike those peasant families whom Tsar Alexander II discovered existing, complete with their cows, in the attics of the Winter Palace in Saint Petersburg.

Why should anybody want to get out? There are two cafés, five bookstalls, a shop selling designer clothes, a bank and a chemist's and an exceedingly smart lavatory. There are a chapel and waxwork museum and one of those admirable Italian institutions known as *albergo diurno*, in which the traveller, on payment of a modest fee, may take a shower, have a bath, lie down for an hour or two, get his shoes shined and his hair cut and generally be made presentable to the world. And there is the cavernously dismal cafeteria, almost always empty except for an unshaven Sicilian, a baglady in animated conversation with herself, and me, which serves the very worst food in Italy.

Buildings like this induce a kind of insanity. It was erected under fascism, a fact which no sensitive observer can ignore, even without the lictors' axes and gung-ho cracker-mottoes of Mussolinian wisdom which adorned it in the bad old times. Inherent in all political ideologies is a lethal element of fatuity which has much to do with the absence, in most politicians, of any redeeming sense of the ridiculous. Among the many reasons why Italians have not yet managed to come to terms with the experience of fascism must surely be a simple embarrassment of the barking absurdity of it all; considered in this light, Milano Centrale, as an essay in crushing, get-this, look-at-me triumphalism, is devastatingly silly. Its mock-Roman bas-reliefs (including a Rape of the Sabines which expresses everything meant by the Italian word *convincente* – rather more than just 'convincing'), its cliffs of marble and granite and basalt, its great mottled plains of tessellated paving, have the imbecile musclebound grotesqueness of some steroid-popping Mister Universe.

It is this sense of exaggerated contour, of unsustainable weights and unbridgeable gulfs, which must in the end impel the traveller towards escape. The intrinsic romance of the place lies in the drama of release in which it encourages one to take part. To anybody with the merest jot of an associative faculty, the names on the yellow *Partenze* lists are instant spurs to a restless imagination. Suddenly you are Byron's Childe Harold or his musical alter ego Berlioz's Harold in Italy, or you are the wandering Goethe of Tischbein's splendid portrait – 'I slipped out of Carlsbad at three in the morning' – or the President de Brosses or Augustus J. C. Hare or Corot or Claude or anybody else who has imbued themselves memorably in the experience of Italy, and here at once for the taking are the great reverberative toponyms: Venice, Florence, Padua, Vicenza, Genoa, Turin, Rome, Naples, even the promise of distant Sicily.

The anticipation gets still headier once you buy the floppy red-and-green *Orario Generale*, the seasonal Bradshaw of Italy, its cover patchworked with squares of advertising: 'Hotel Cristallo, Udine, tutti i conforts, a 150 metri dalla Stazione Ferroviaria', 'Hotel Mediterraneo, Brindisi, 69 camere tutte con bagno e aria condizionata', 'Pescara è bella con la sua provincia, Mare, Monti, Arte, Terme'. Pescara isn't actually a very interesting town, though Gabriele D'Annunzio* was born there, but the *Orario Generale* has the sort of talismanic potency that makes you prepared to accept such bland assertions at their face value.

I am, for whatever reason, addicted to directories. Almanacs, gazetteers and catalogues induce a strange ecstasy, and their parades of impacted fact, so far from deadening the imagination, open up rainbow clouds of fantasy. Thus it is with the *Orario Generale*. Its introductory rubric of little hieroglyphs – a pair of hammers for trains running only on workdays, a Maltese cross for Sunday services, a bed with pillows for wagons-lits, a bed without pillows for couchettes and so on – and its skeleton maps of the entire Italian railway system are clues to a perpetual romance of movement, chance and destiny.

The very sound of these places, cheek by jowl in the timetable, is enough to drive you mad. From sober-sided Alessandria on its

---

* His real name was Gaetano Rapagnetta, a little-known fact which explains everything else about him.

marshy plain beside the Tanaro in eastern Piedmont, you'll take, maybe, the little second-class-only *locale* to Cavallermaggiore, stopping at Cantalupo, Carentino, Castelnuovo Belbo, Incisa Scapaccino, Calamandrana, Castagnole Lanze and Pocapaglia. From Aulla, at the head of the Garfagnana on the northern frontiers of Tuscany, you will come down among the swift-flowing streams and steep-hung chestnut forests towards Lucca and Pisa via Pallerone, Serricciolo, Villetta San Romano, Pontecosi, Fosciandora, Ghivizzano and Calavorno. And between Bologna and the Adriatic coast, even though you're panting to get to Ancona, you will not greatly mind halting at Mirandola, Forlimpopoli, Gambettola, Montemarciano and Palombina.

It doesn't honestly matter that any of these may be the dumps and armpits of the world, that, even as your fancy toys with their names, Calamandrana, Fosciandora and Forlimpopoli may be the dire provincial instruments of torture and suppression which frustrate or destroy potential genius. 'I might have been a fine poet if I hadn't spent all my life in Pallerone,' 'I wanted to go to university but I stayed in Pocapaglia,' 'There just weren't any nuclear physicists in Gambettola.' Gray's 'Elegy' says it all for such places, but their sound is only the more romantic for that.

At its most practical and gritty and of-the-earth-earthy, the *Orario Generale* is an act of faith. It proclaims a belief in the railway not simply as a rapid and convenient mode of getting from one point to another but as the ultimate means of unifying a traditional fissiparous nation. When trains first arrived in Italy (the earliest ran from Naples southwards to the port of Granatello on the coastal flank of Vesuvius: the line was opened in 1839), they were viewed by certain of the more reactionary rulers as harbingers of revolution. So dire did they seem to Pope Gregory XVI, an ex-monk to whom the least hint of technological progress was anathema, that he forbade the construction of a rail network anywhere in the Papal States. Travellers from the Grand Duchy of Tuscany or the Austrian provinces of Venetia and Lombardy got accustomed to the symbolically retrograde step of bundling into horse-drawn diligences as soon as they crossed the frontier.

So the train, for better or worse, contributed its share to the Risorgimento, and continues to insist on bringing Italians, however reluctantly, together. Railway journeys in Italy are not, as with us in England, a penitential experience designed to make us all travel nose-to-tail in automobiles along endless motorways. Italians love their cars – nobody in Italy walks anywhere if they can possibly avoid doing so – but they will take the train almost as readily, since it is generously subsidized, clean, fast, cheap and, for the most part, punctual.

Yet there is another, deeper, more aboriginally instinctive reason why trains and station platforms in Italy are always crowded. It is because of the Italian horror of solitude, the absolute negation, implicit in the forms and constructs of Italian social life, of the principle of living to oneself. Hardly anyone in this country is without somebody else with whom to share their existence. The unmarried do not, as in northern Europe or America, move away from their families at the earliest opportunity, but remain tied to them in perpetuity, suffering the crotchets and caprices of domineering parents from whose surveillance death alone releases them, as nurses, servants and unpaid companions. The tyranny of family life in small apartments proscribes individualism, annihilates outline and perspective. Without secrets, without worlds apart, without moments of determined solitariness, the grain and colour of personality are rubbed away. Maybe this explains the essentially flavourless and superficial nature of so much Italian conversation.

Much will compensate, however, for such a willing forfeiture of liberty. There is always somebody to talk to, there is a small domestic universe whose incidental problems and vicissitudes are sufficient to beguile your curiosity or engage your sympathy, and above all there is Mamma in the kitchen. Given any number of factors now instigating an insidious but perceptible change in the quality of modern Italian life, it is debatable how long it will be before Mamma and her culinary works are swept clean away, but for the time being she and her cooking are among the most notable determinants of Italian existence. Is it any accident that of the three most significant objects of furniture in the Italian household, the television (perpetually on but rarely attended to), the *letto matrimoniale* or double bed, and the dining table, the last should be the most important? By the way, it is nearly always round or oval, since mealtime chat among Italians must be general rather than one-to-one.

This inbred gregariousness extends into the wider reaches of society. It is by now something of a cliché to remark upon the symbolism of the piazza and the café, those classic *punti d'incontro*, meeting places where hank upon hank of talk is painstakingly unwound. If you sit and watch Italians carefully by the hour, you will notice how seldom they are voluntarily alone. Every Italian boy, for example, has his best mate, his mucker, his chum, with whom he goes about. The warmth and closeness between them is unembarrassed, they touch, embrace and walk arm-in-arm without that pathological awkwardness which compromises such relationships in England. In middle age they will simply turn into the paunchy, dewlapped, prosperous-looking men you see ambling in pairs, very, very slowly, along Italian streets, 'developing' a conversation with the aid of a remarkable lexicon of emphatic gesture. No meaningful segment of their lives will ever be conducted in solitude.

Railway stations encourage this communal feeling. At any decent-sized staging post along the lines criss-crossing the peninsula, you will find people simply mooching about in the station. They may include the usual complement of hustlers, whores and pushers, there will be the odd vagrant or harmless lunatic, and nowadays their number is likely to be leavened by the despised and freely maligned *Gastarbeiter* population of Senegalese, Tunisians and others, known with slighting jocosity as 'Vu cumprà' from a southern dialect expression meaning 'Do you want to buy?' But there will also be those for whom a drink or a sandwich or a paper or a chinwag or just half an hour spent lounging on a bench to take the weight off provides an excuse for sharing the easy camaraderie of the buffet and the booking hall.

It is on the train, however, that this instinctive sociability and companionableness most obviously take over. The English notion of hiding behind a newspaper in the ghastly apprehension that somebody might actually engage you in conversation is shot to pieces as soon as you clamber into the carriage. You have reclaimed your cases from the plug-ugly blue-overalled bruisers in the Left Luggage, and you have providently invested in a *cestino di viaggio*, the little lunch bag sold from the platform refreshment trolleys, with its foil-wrapped wing of chicken, its packet of crackers and cheese, its rather elderly roll and cardboard-textured apple, which is one of the great institutions of Italian rail travel. Two willowy German girls with plaits and sleeveless vests have asked your help in heaving up after them a pair of gigantic rucksacks like Christian's burden in *The Pilgrim's Progress*, and a nun has enlisted your aid in perching her plastic grip on the luggage rack. Perhaps you are honestly not disposed to talk, perhaps your interest in the *Politica interna* pages of *La Repubblica* is genuine, perhaps you sincerely wish to know what Craxi has said to Andreotti or what Cossiga has not said to either of them. But you should never count on being left alone.

You will certainly not be ignored merely because you are foreign. Recent years have somewhat reduced the rampant xenophilia which used to characterize Italians, but the impulse towards courteous interrogation of the stranger (provided he or she is not an African) is still strong. From the initial questions about your destination and why you speak such good Italian (I always fall for that one), it is a short step to a series of variants on standard themes. The British royal family is a favourite topic, especially with readers of gossipy pictorial magazines like *Gente* and *Oggi*, which favour soft-focus pics of the Princess of Wales and double-page spreads on '*Margaret: la vita amara d'una donna sconosciuta*'. The other Margaret, *Margherita di Downing Street*, was a further standby until she got strident and tiresome on the subject of Europe, to which Italians, citizens of a country which spends much of its time infringing or subverting EEC regulations, are ostentatiously proud to belong.

Best loved of all by the compartment conversationalist is the nature of Italy as seen through a stranger's eyes. There are times when it would be nice simply to say '*molto bella*' and leave it at that, but the shrewder of your interlocutors won't let go so easily. At first it always looks as if the Italians possess a rare genius for self-criticism, unlike, say, the insufferably bumptious French or the smug, sanctimonious Germans. The plausible introductory litany of national denigration – 'we're really a disgraceful people', 'part of the Third World', 'lacking in order and discipline', 'absolutely childish' – should deceive nobody however. Underneath all these disclaimers, the Italians like being Italian, relishing the apparently uncomplicated cosiness and tranquil prosperity of their lives, and feeling entirely at home with the most openly corrupt and ineffectual governmental system among those of the seven major economic powers. They envy the Germans because they are more 'serious' (*serio* is an adjective of almost magical ambiguity, variously meaning 'earnest' or 'boring'), the French because they are cultivated, and the Americans for their cultural imperialism. They utterly detest the Swiss because, as they will delphically inform you, 'they're Swiss'. As for the English, they are liked for all the wrong reasons by the crypto-fascists who read *Il Giornale* and the stuffy, *bien-pensant* conservatives who take *La Stampa*, and for all the right ones by that tiny group of literate, cosmopolitan intellectuals who embody rational opinion in the Italian media.

This and much more you will be told on the train and, should it be one of the old-style compartment carriages, others will be tempted to put in their respective oars. These free-for-alls are often so enjoyable that after a while the last thing you want to do is to sink back into a corner with a book. Now and then, however, you may find yourself marooned next to the kind of garrulous autocrat who inspires a hankering for the spiritual comforts of La Trappe. I retain a nightmarish recollection of a journey on a jam-packed train from Florence to Rome (a good three hours by the ordinary express) which was tyrannized over by an old woman with a silent daughter in tow. From Figline to Arezzo, from Terontola to Orvieto, Orte and beyond, she maintained an unbroken flow of chatter so relentless in its vacuousness that the rest of us began perceptibly to falter under its deadening impact. We could not pretend to sleep or look out of the window, though it probably would not have mattered to her had we done so, since her remarks were hardly calculated to elicit any kind of worthwhile coherent response. Now and then one of us would throw a hopeless glance towards the corridor, only to see it pressed tight with schoolkids and soldiers, so that even the ticket inspector with his loud '*Permesso-o-o*' had difficulty in clearing a passage.

On went the dreary recital, engulfing the compartment like the noxious, petrifying mud of Herculaneum. We heard about her recipe for apple tart, the knitting pattern she had started out of *Mani di Fata*,* the friend of hers from Prato who was having problems over naming a dog and the *bonbonnière* she had been given at a smart christening at Calenzano. The heartrending loveliness of Umbria and northern Latium, which makes this one of the most visually stimulating of all Italian train rides, flashed past us with a tantalizing irrelevance, and the silent daughter sat smirking enigmatically, as though she knew a thing or two but was damned if she was going to tell. When at last the express pulled into Roma Termini and we jerked ourselves out of this ignoble paralysis to get our cases off the racks, the old woman crowned her despotic triumph with a wondrous piece of insolence: 'Well,' said she, beaming at us all, 'it's been really interesting listening to you. Other people lead such fascinating lives, don't they?'

What most struck me about this episode, in retrospect, was the extraordinary good manners of everyone concerned. There is rudeness in Italy as anywhere else – Florentine bank clerks, Venetian waiters, nearly all Romans are past masters of it – but the Italians are still the most naturally civil and gentle people on earth. The rhetoric of courtesy is everywhere, in

* Literally 'Fairy Hands', a popular magazine of *tricotage*.

the decorous appeals and injunctions of public notices, in the verb forms and vocabulary of those with whom you deal in shops and offices, a ghostly yet still vivid flourish from the age of Castiglione and Della Casa, when Italy taught politeness to the world.

Such glimpses of Italians being themselves are part of the pleasure of riding the railways, denied to the Cipriani-Harry's Bar-Excelsior-champagne cocktail-private beach tourist, whose sense of real life (which he or she may not want in any case) won't extend far beyond porters, maids and receptionists. From the train, whether it is the souped-up, air-conditioned 'Eurocity' flier, or the trundling rustic *trenino* with slatted wooden benches for seats, you learn to read and interpret a country and its people.

You understand immediately the significance of personal cleanliness in Italy. Those yards upon yards of laundry festooning the streets in small villages and the suburbs of great cities are there not as gala decoration or in order to lend a 'characteristic', 'suggestive' appearance to some photogenic backdrop, but as evidence of the paramount importance of washing in the culture of the nation. Whoever saw a blouse, a teeshirt, a skirt or a pair of trousers on an Italian that was not ironed and pressed to a flawless miracle? Their hair is perfectly cut and brushed and shampooed, their teeth are white and strong, their skins are unblemished, even a pair of spectacles somehow renders them good-looking rather than drawing attention to myopia.

Above all they don't smell, unless it be of detergent, deodorant or scent. They have not yet reached that dubious stage of evolution at which bathing and daily changes of clothes are deemed too bourgeois to be taken seriously. Recall, in contrast, the feculent reek of a crowded English train, with its rancid compound of dried urine, old sweat, beer, tobacco, halitosis and the stale malodorousness of clothes worn many times too often. Brits at large in Italy shame their native country in many ways – by their surly, boozy pugnacity, by their stingy nitpicking over bills and prices, by their arrogant assumption

that they ought not to be expected to know a word of Italian –
but in nothing so much as by their shambling, tawdry, dingy,
unwashed, unbrushed, reachmedown scruffiness.

For by these tokens you are judged in Italy. The grease-spot
on your shirt, the smear on your collar, the crumpled look of
your coat, even a hole in the sole of your shoe, counts far more
gravely against you than the most obvious flaws in your moral
and spiritual constitution. This truth was brought home to me
once in Padua, where I effected what I thought would be the
ideal introduction of two friends to each other. One was an
eminent English writer, versatile, cosmopolitan, intellectually
gifted and notable for the self-advertising sloppiness of his
clothes. The other was a charmingly absentminded, ferociously
brilliant Italian professor of comparative literature. We sat at a
marble-topped table in the Caffè Pedrocchi, one of the monumental cafés of Italy like the Greco at Rome or Florian's at
Venice, lined with empire mirrors and velvet banquettes on
which plots political and operatic had been devised during the
heady days of the Risorgimento, and drank delicious grogs while
the mist gathered in the streets of that peculiarly sombre city.

The pair seemed to get on famously. Perhaps discoursing,
however rustily, in a language not his own made the Englishman
forget to adopt that habitual just-an-ornery bloke pose of the
average British literary man, while the Italian let go altogether
of the awestruck pomposity with which distinguished cultural
figures are usually engaged in Italy, and the two of them rattled
along together as my heart could have wished.

Later I asked each of them independently what impression
they had gained of one another. 'He's nice, isn't he?' said the
writer. 'Not at all the kind of person who judges by appearances.'
It was just as well that I did not repeat this assessment to my
Italian friend, whose response I ought in any case to have
predicted. He was, as it turned out, quite beside himself with
irritation, and, as was his custom when agitated, he insisted
on addressing me in English. 'Your friend, who you say is
a famous writer!' he cried. 'Listen, I ask you this question.
How can a famous writer walk in the street with no strings

to his shoes? But how can he do that? No strings! *Porca miseria*!'

What happens in a country where people get indignant about a writer's shoe-laces is that you begin to worry about such things to a degree you never supposed possible. What also happens is that you start to notice how much is lost by worrying about shoe-laces. In this respect one of the crucially instructive moments in an Italian train journey is the point when the train slows down and enters a station. As the crowd on the platform surges towards the carriages, you are ideally placed to see a lump of compressed Italy in all its unadorned normality, and the sight will tell you a thing or two.

Many of them are beautiful, heart-stoppingly, mouth-wateringly jealous-makingly stunning, with their sun-straightened limbs, long eyelashes, thickly-clustered hair and insouciant grace of posture. Their clothes fit their bodies, and the colours have been selected and matched with that visual awareness which is a birthright with them all. They have looked carefully in a thousand mirrors to ensure a perfect harmony between themselves and the things they wear. They have not had to think about this. And their shoe-laces are impeccably tied.

Yet in essence how boring, how utterly lifeless is this perfection, how lacking in the merest spark of singularity! Look into their soft, coffee-brown eyes or at their generously-curved mouths, and find not a hint of restlessness, animation, violence, bitterness, ecstasy, poetry or desire. They are people about whom nobody could ever write a novel, for the simple reason that their outwardness proclaims no inwardness. There is no difference between them, only an abiding fear of distinction.

Extravagant generalizations of this sort nurture the odd grain of truth. What the sight of such platform crowds most potently discloses is the extraordinary power of convention in Italy, the thoroughgoing, unshakeable conservatism of a people whose favourite delusion is that they are not bound by tradition. Every age, every caste here has its uniform. The smart elderly woman going to the opera in January and February will always wear a fur. The businessman or senior professional employee will don, in early summer, a blue shirt. No young girl is without her fall of Botticelli curls, no boy without his ice-blue jeans and thick-soled docksiders. When the mode alters, everyone moves in step. None of them will ever dress for themselves, indulge a freak or a quirk or a caprice of personality, 'do a number', 'make a statement'. There is bags of fashion, barely a hint of style. So far from being disgusted at the notion of belonging to a crowd, they are frightened in case it should not include them. Protective mimicry ensures survival.

Such are the cohesiveness and universality of Italian railway life that it might be possible to construct a sociology for the nation on the basis of a perpetual train journey. Since all rationalizations are inherently bogus, your ride along the tracks will perhaps guarantee you no more than a specious wisdom and a false security. Outside the station, across the peripheric boulevards, beyond the municipal flowerbeds, the taxi rank and the bus terminus, lies a world immediate, grown-up, resistant to simple answers, from which, once entered, you may never return.

6 Piedmont:
Notes from a Journal

Places become marked with our emotions as if these were indelible stains. What we felt when we were there at the time is enough to damn or bless the city for ever. The ancient seat of kings, the unconquered fortress, the nursery of genius, the haunt of the muses, the admired cynosure of architects and town planners, easily becomes the place where you were sick in a restaurant, had your wallet stolen, got lost, quarrelled with your best friend, parted from your wife never to see her again, went into hospital following an accident, left a pair of shoes in the hotel or simply missed the bus.

So whenever I pass through Novara I think about being in love. The city isn't altogether unattractive. On the early baroque church of San Gaudenzio there is a colossal spire, 121 metres tall, built in 1840 to a design by a local architect named Alessio Antonelli, who constructed another, even more crazily lofty, to grace the top of a synagogue in Turin, much admired, apparently, by Nietzsche. There are tenth-century frescoes in the baptistery of the cathedral, and the theatre is named after the composer Carlo Coccia, who during the 1820s conducted the operas at the King's Theatre in the Haymarket and became the first professor of harmony and composition at the Royal Academy of Music.

This same theatre has a quite spectacular neo-classical colonnade thrown extravagantly along one side of the Piazza Martiri della Liberta, with a pair of tremendously dignified cafés on either flank. Ghastly old King Victor Emmanuel gallops, for the umpteenth time, down the middle of the square, and at the opposite end are the remains of a castle built by the Sforza of Milan in the fifteenth century.

I ought, I know, to find this Piazza Martiri exhilarating, one of the ideal statements of the Italian piazza principle, but I can never divorce it in my mind from an overwhelming wretchedness, associated with a desire for someone who long ago ceased to love me. It was the kind of unhappiness which is made worse by a failure to acknowledge its reality. Only afterwards, when the dreadful cord of mesmeric attraction has snapped, does something jolt you into confronting the depths of misery you affected not to feel at the time.

In this case the spur to embarrassment was an Italian translation of a Danish novel, *Niels Lyhne*, by Jens Peter Jacobsen, which I took down off the shelf with the intention of starting again, since something reminded me that I'd given it only a halfhearted reading on the first occasion. As a market there was a receipt from a bookshop, '*Grazie, arrivederci*, Casa del Libro Lazzarelli, Via Rosselli 145, Novara', dated 31 October. On the blank sheet at the back of the volume I'd jotted 'A bit like a sort of smart Worcester, quiet, sober, retiringly prosperous, quintessentially average, this place. Leaves disengage themselves from the chestnut trees in the avenue behind the square in the manner of people leaving a party who tell you they really must be going but try to do it as unobtrusively as possible. The first leaves to turn are those underneath. Those on top stay green till the last. Squeak of the swings in the park. Heat of the sunlight. Aleatoric bellringing. The calm of bourgeois Europe.'

I must have been in a fair old taking to write anything like this. The recollection of that afternoon in Novara suddenly made me wince at the blatant deception I had practised on myself merely by being in love. For an hour or so I had been left alone in the bland, milk warmth of autumn, in a strangely empty town. The book was a stone to which my hysterical balloon of amatory despair was moored. Perhaps I should have left it on the bench under the chestnut trees, with the jottings inside it like the scribbled message of a doomed explorer. It was three months before I pulled myself together. Now Novara is flawed for ever with memories of my pain and stupidity.

From the city the little train, painted cream and blue and scarlet, with high-backed seats in green plastic upholstery, sets out across the broad plain that marks the frontier between Lombardy and Piedmont. This is rice country, square upon square of paddy fields glistening emerald to the grey fringes of the mountains. They brought the plant from Islamic lands in the Middle Ages, and used the streams that feed the Sesia and the Ticino to flood the plantations between their high clay banks. Some time before the Great War, a local proprietor introduced the oriental method of transplanting the rice which produced a more abundant crop, and brought in armies of women from all over northern Italy to shift the young plants and weed the paddies. They were called *mondine* (*monda* means 'weeding') and in their floppy straw hats, an echo from some Asian rice field, with their skirts hitched up above their knees and jazzy bandannas around their necks, they slopped and shuffled through the mud, singing strange, haunting chants whose pitch and rhythm was given by a leader and answered by the grunting chorus.

All that is left of the *mondine* nowadays is a few recordings of their work-songs and a folk memory of exhaustion and poverty and the squalor of life as a migrant worker. This past is glamorous only to students of working-class history: to most others here on the green, water-dashed plain it simply says 'never ever again', an incubus of misery that haunts their resolve to work harder, save more and get away into the city. Rice is that romantic.

Casaleggio-Castellazzo, Sillavengo, Ghislarengo, Rovasenda, Masserano – the *trenino* whittles them away like a knife off a stick. There is no sense that these places exist as more than stations, so that to each of them belongs a singular impermanence, as if they lived only when the train passed through. People getting off simply disappear into the countryside. Nobody meets them on the platform or takes them away in a car. You find yourself trying, and failing, to imagine a career as the stationmaster, sitting in the office of the little yellow blockhouse at Nibbia or Carpignano, waiting for the chance, twenty times a day, to wave the stick with a red-and-white metal circle at one end, which signals the departure of the trains.

In the fields beyond, a light breeze ruffles the green nap of the paddies, and an egret rises off the dyke, shitting gracefully as it flaps into the distance. There are scores of them here in the rice country, and perhaps this is a sign that something fundamental has changed among the Italians, for a decade ago the hunters would all have bagged them. A hunter in Italy is somebody with a gun. There is little sport involved and a great deal of sophisticated hardware and elegant shooting clobber, but hitting everything that moves, and much that doesn't move, has suddenly become a rather more questionable occupation*

* Unless you live in Calabria, in which case you
can bang away freely from the windows

for those keen to authenticate their maleness. Thus the birds furtively return.

As if to prove this, beside the stream running through a hay-meadow beyond Masserano, there is a stork. I don't believe that until today I ever saw a stork in Italy, and I wonder how long this one is to be allowed to survive before some 'collector' with a rifle picks it off for stuffing and mounting. It has that beautiful spray of black wing plumage offsetting the white curve of its head and pink stilt legs. The essential elegance of this bird, strutting along the watercourse with slow, nervous deliberateness, recalls descriptions of certain modern novelists in the reviews of their books. Watching its long bill probing the weeds, you think at once of critical clichés like 'fine discriminations' and 'painstaking dissection': the stork is the Anita Brookner of the bird kingdom. Perhaps, through some Pythagorean metempsychosis, this one actually *is* Anita Brookner.

I want to tell Vincenzo all about the stork, but I know I'll forget. It is several years since I saw him last – he has been out in Ceylon all this time – and as the train plunges into the tunnel between Chiavazza and Biella and I reach down my case, there's a twinge of apprehension lest something should physically have altered him. On the platform, as he comes towards me, I remember how small he is, and how, unlike most small men, he never tries to make other people guilty for being taller. His face has the same cleanness of line, though the parenthetical curves around his mouth as he smiles have grown deeper, and the East has made his nose and jaws leaner and more weatherbeaten. In thirty years or so, old age will bring him a truly patriarchal handsomeness,

---

of urban tower blocks at the flocks of migrant birds, many of them, theoretically at least, protected species, winging their way annually into Italy from Africa.

when the northern-Italianness of the bony mountaineer starts to declare itself in his features.

We drive up into the hills, among the open pastures and clumps of woodland and shy, orderly farms, and through the village where the square in front of the church, with its fountain and baroque flights of steps, looks as if it is still awaiting the news from some long-forgotten eighteenth-century battle which the diligence will at any second bring in. Slowly, almost warily, our conversation maps out the lost territory of experience embraced by three years. Yet just at present I don't want to say all that much. I'm made inarticulate by the beginnings of a happiness I identify exclusively with this place.

The house stands at the top of a gentle valley, sloping eastwards to the undulating plain and the town of Vercelli on the far horizon, a prospect of meadows and orchards and small, dark coppices in the folds of the hills, with here and there a church tower or the roof of a barn to mark a human presence in the landscape. Fat, butterscotch-coloured cows with chunky forelegs and S-shaped horns graze the slope below the track which winds up to the farm. There is a conical haycock and a plum tree with big, fan-shaped branches, from which a little boy is trying to bring down the fruit by jumping up now and then to give them a tug, then falling after the scattered plums into the feggy tussocks of grass below. A woman in a straw hat and an old flowered overall marches down the hill towards him, a wooden rake over her shoulder.

On the other side of the house, from the balconies overlooking a row of strangely untended back gardens where the hydrangeas appear to have run wild and the docks and nettles stand high in the flowerbeds, the snowy foothills of the Alps rise with the dramatic suddenness of a true frontier. The colours along their screes and ridges shift constantly, together with the texture of the air and the light's intensities. A damp, vapourish grey yields quickly to a hard blackness of outline scored off sharply by the sun, followed by a tumble of dead white cloud which will later roll back to leave everything carefully, deliberately indistinct, as it seems, in the pinks and blues of evening.

So we truly are in Piedmont, Piemonte, the foot of the mountain, the country of plucky, ambitious, clever, smooth-talking soldiers, scholars and courtiers, with as much French as Italian in their speech and culture. Over the other side of this mountain range, beyond the peaks of Mucrone, Mombarone and Monte Mars and into the Val d'Aosta, the place names are suddenly Gallic and the passes are haunted by the ghosts of the Sun King's armies battling with the slippery Dukes of Savoy. Yet from the terraces at the front of the house you can watch Italy beginning to get itself, as it were, into the Italian mode, to arrange and dispose the components of its landscape for the convenience of all the painters who, after the armies have passed, will come down these valleys with easel and sketchbook in search of the picturesque.

Italians cynically call this picture-making tendency on their country's part '*oleografica*', in reference to the kitsch *paysages* popular in middle-class drawing rooms of the last century. If the vistas here are oleographic, the house isn't specially so. Built for half a dozen peasant families in a style which goes back, in one form or another, to the early Middle Ages, it is not one but three dwellings placed cheek by jowl, with the staircases zigzagging up the outside from terrace to terrace, and heated by tall log-burning stoves made of hollow bricks, of a kind more familiar perhaps from German and Austrian castles, where they are fronted with glazed tiles. Setting out for bed in the nipping Piedmontese winter is a dramatically abrupt transference from the cosy fug of stove warmth to the keen, wit-sharpening cold of the mountain night, with the moon fiercely bright over the frosty fields and a vixen's bark giving tongue to the blackness of the woods.

It is not an especially beautiful house in the sense that Tuscan farms or Umbrian cottages, Roman attics or Venetian studios are beautiful. You would not write home ecstatically about the colour of the bricks in the floor, the shape of the door hinges or the carpentry of the lintels. There are no shutters or decorated beams or fireplaces supported by burly *ignudi* or swelling volutes around the windows or patches of fresco across the walls. No photographer, with gushing journalist in tow, will arrive from 'World of Interiors' or 'Town and Country' to do a fancy spread on the colour schemes, the carpets or the wallpaper.

Indeed they had better not, for it is in hardly such a self-consciously photogenic fashion that its rooms invite you to look at them. There is an amusingly ambiguous quality to the way things have been placed and arranged in relationship to one another, to which no amount of painstaking camera angles could ever do justice. Everything seems as if you had come upon it by stealth, as if it knew you were going to be snooping and poking about the house, but is pretending nevertheless to ignore you. The wish that you should observe, admire, learn and enjoy is cloaked in a delightful feigned indifference as to the total effect.

This, I suppose, is Vincenzo's version of modesty, for the house and its interior *mise-en-scène* are, as he knows, his finest creation. Now and then, when he sickens at his friends' attachment to it and accuses us, nearly always implicitly rather than directly, of valuing him less than his possessions, he threatens to sell up altogether, dispose of everything and retreat forthwith to some palm grove by the Indian Ocean, where his essential restlessness will be, for a time at least, assuaged. Though he has no need to be more interesting than he actually is, he knows that his fascination is enhanced for us by these bouts of loudly-voiced dissatisfaction, and that the question that binds us all to one another is whether he and the house will still be there when we return.

There is absolutely nothing of Italy about this exuberant clutter of icons and josses and bibelots and bizarreries which Vincenzo's small, gnarled, brown hands have gathered off the tips and skips and fleamarket stalls of the great world. Perhaps the heavy old Piedmontese farmers' beds, cupboards, *gueridons* and whatnots might be said to form a native base to the occupational layers in the weird archaeology of the rooms, but the sheer dust-trapping huggermugger heterogeneity of everything is of a kind that belongs anywhere but in the ascetic orderliness of domesticity *all'italiana*. There are no plastic-and-tubular-steel sofas, no glass-topped dining tables, black anglepoise lamps or panelled cabinets crowned with lace doilies to hold the best Capodimonte and Richard-Ginori. In fact there is nothing new in the house at all. Everything has some kind of experience to define it, so that the eye is entertained with a continuous riot of jostling perspectives.

There are odd lumps of statuary, conches and corals and fossils, absurd Abyssinian pictures of pith-helmeted soldiers being mown down by the Negus's troops, sepia-tinted Algerian postcards of lubriciously simpering Ouled-Nail goodtime girls, a perfectly hideous lifesize late nineteenth-century portrait of a woman embracing a small, fluffy goat, there are fans and beads and boxes, Amboina-work caskets in curious inlays, ornate Yemeni window frames and Japanese vases in silvery glazes of livid purple and green. There are garish votive pictures, pages from holy almanacs, Buddhas and Chinese goddesses, clusters of old scent bottles, glowering memorial busts, *jardinières* and a glockenspiel high as a tabernacle, with a sort of wooden belfry whose chimes are worked by foot-pedals.

Nothing here is worth anything or likely to tempt the assiduously market-wise burglar who goes about with a van antique-stripping in country houses. Vincenzo is not a collector in the vulgar sense of the term. What he gathers are the *disjecta membra* of his own life, like the geologist piecing together fossilized bones. This is not a text anyone other than he can read intelligibly, but the fun of being momentarily interpolated within it is that you are free to decipher its intimations as you choose. Vincenzo will provide a clue or two: the rest you must make up for yourself.

Spreadeagled on the sitting room carpet, I am reading *Sangue e Petroleo nell'Oriente* by Essad Bey, an Italian translation from the German of an autobiography published in 1931 by an ex-oil baron from Baku who reached Berlin after hairbreadth escapes across Central Asia during the Russian Revolution. This is the kind of book Vincenzo regularly fishes up for me on my infrequent visits, not without a certain triumph at producing something he knows my plodding literary orthodoxy is quite unlikely to have embraced.

The stereo dispenses some obscure American *chanteuse* of whom Vincenzo has unearthed the only recording on this side of the Atlantic. It is early evening, and the last gleam of sunlight slopes into the long, low-ceilinged room. Near me on the floor I have the remains of a cup of tea, a tumbler of whisky and the end of some perfectly execrable Eastern cigar, of the kind I always enjoy. The sudden apprehension of an absolute delight overwhelms me. There is nothing more that I want. It is one of those moments when I fancy I might as well die as go on living, since sooner rather than later gloom and uncertainty will engulf me once more. The genius of the house has embraced me in its passing.

Next morning we drive up through the woods to the sacred mountain of Oropa. There are several of these holy hills in Piedmont, at Varallo, Orta and Varese for instance, survivals, it seems, of the pagan fondness for placing gods and temples upon sky-brushing heights. At Oropa the sanctuary lies at the top of a zigzag sequence of sixteen little chapels running up the hillside, begun in 1617 and carried on throughout the following hundred years. Each has a different design – an octagon, a pilastered cube, a six-sided dovecote shape with a cupola, a simple shed, a tiny porticoed temple, a rotunda or a miniature basilica surrounded by a colonnade – and each bears a separate dedication.

To look at them from without, you would not think they were anything but humble stations for prayer on the way up to the great double-quadrangled convent dedicated to the Christian mother-goddess, which a saint called Eusebius is said to have founded in the reign of Julian the Apostate. The stucco has flaked from their walls, here and there the reddish slates are slipping off the roofs, and on these wild northern hillsides the chapels have the air of mountain refuges or sheds to shelter storm-driven cattle.

The point of it all is hidden within. Each tabernacle contains, depicted in lifesize figures of painted plaster, a scene from the story of the Blessed Virgin, devised theatrically, with an extraordinary poignancy and vividness, by professional statuaries, the D'Enrico brothers of Varallo and the Auregio of Biella, who, with their pupils and assistants, went about the mountains of Piedmont and Lombardy throwing up these astonishing religious tableaux.

To me these chapels, with their deliberate blending of fantasy, realism and humour with something of the peasant life of the villages of this Alta Biellese region, are among the most beautiful things in Italy. Looking at these carefully posed effigies, you are reminded of the operas of the period, in which comedy and pathos were not yet detached; you can hear the plucking and strumming of continuo instruments, the plangent scraping of violins and the melismatic extravaganzas of the vocal line.

Here is Saint Anne in bed 'with the sheet tucked down so bravely oh' over an emerald green coverlet, while a flight of cherubs on fat grey clouds like suet dumplings rises to the ceiling and a maidservant in a becoming green bodice and yellow panniered skirt, spreads her hands in amazement against a background of *trompe-l'oeil* windows and Corinthian columns. The angels, in gorgeous ice blue with gold and silver wings, have come to witness the Virgin's nativity, and the nurse shows off the baby to Saint Joachim while a pair of cherubs rocks the cradle. In the Temple the High Priest and the Levites go into positive 'isn't-she-a-poppet' ecstasies over the infant as she scrambles up the steps: on either side sit the gossips, in their fashionable *fontanges* and ruched sleeves, busy with their spinning and embroidery.

Three grooms carrying riding crops are watching Mary's wedding to Joseph. They have wigs made of something that looks like real hair. One is a redhead, one auburn, the third brunette. Left alone in a spectacularly empty room, with a view across a painted lake to a forest and hills beyond, 'the handmaid of the Lord' kneels in her blue mantle at prayer, as Gabriel, lily in hand, straddles the clouds. At the Wedding at Cana in Galilee, musicians play fit to bust in the gallery, while a curly-headed page in torn scarlet breeches empties his miraculous water-pot.

Most wonderful of all is the Coronation, where Adam and Eve in figleaves the size of tennis-rackets kneel on plump cushions beside the Apostles and the Doctors of the Church, as the celestial consort bursts into the closing chorus, the tromba marina, the theorbo, the violone and the clarini, the shawms and the sprightly hoboys and the soft-complaining flute and the double-double beat of the thundering drum, and all the twenty-four fiddles of the king bash the welkin to smithereens, and the Queen of Heaven is winched up into the flies by a cast of scrambling putti and teetering seraphim.

It would be easy to dismiss all this as mere high camp. People are always saying that sort of thing about seventeenth-century art, as if realism and colour and bright costumes automatically guaranteed insincerity. 'But they couldn't really have meant it, could they?' Couldn't they though? The simple act of making all this, of lugging the brick and stone and timber up the mountain, of carefully siting each chapel within a scheme whose total effect, both decorative and spiritual, could not adequately be grasped for at least a hundred years, by which time many of its original architects and artists would be dead, gave these amazing confections as much truth, beauty and purity as any Cimabue crucifix, Romanesque frieze or Fra Angelico panel, whose holy integrity is beyond the reach of detraction.

Afterwards we go shopping in the market at Biella, a messy jumble of stalls scattered across the featureless yellow piazza dominated by a frowzy-looking old theatre called the Sociale. Vincenzo of course knows all the stallholders by name and has a bantering word or two for each of them. His charm is mesmeric. If they hadn't a living to earn, they would give him everything: fruit, vegetables, designer teeshirts which fell off the back of a lorry, Opinel knives and brass pots, on the spot.

The town loves him, but he has no special fondness for it other than as the place where his family sprang from. It is not preternaturally attractive, and makes no pretence at being so. The *biellesi* are indeed chiefly famous for their parsimony, a fact cynically offered in explanation of the so-called heroic sacrifice of Pietro Micca at the siege of Turin in 1706. When the French were at the gates of the citadel and all seemed lost, the *biellese* sapper Pietro Micca exploded a mine which destroyed the magazine, blew the enemy to kingdom come, and incidentally hurried the courageous engineer into eternity. 'Ah,' say the *biellesi*, 'you don't know the half of it, he was one of us was Pietro. The reason he was killed was because he was too mean to make a long fuse – a true Biella boy, that one.'

Certainly they have never beautified their town with elegant squares, colonnaded streets or florid façades to the churches. Up in Biella Piazzo, the earliest settlement, perched within its city gates on top of a crag with grand vistas into the plain, the palaces are resolutely modest in their affirmations of family grandeur, and the place might easily pass for a fair-sized but unremarkable village – though if you look more carefully at their frescoed courtyard vaults, their arcades and doorways, they are not at all unhandsome.

Down below, the look is even more deliberately draggletail. Either the stinginess is bone-marrow deep, or else there is a determination, unwritten and unstated, not to make the streets and larger buildings too engaging to the eye, lest we suspect what is actually the case, that some of the very richest, seriously well-heeled, copperbottomed megabuck-making industrialists in all Italy are hiding out in these hills. Thus, though after a while it is likely to fool nobody, a rather clever impression is given of Biella as a town in the last stages of collapse, a once great emporium of Piedmontese manufacturing, the paradise of industrial archaeologists and economic historians. There is an awful lot of nobly squalid old factory building, gloomy workshops, tall stack chimneys, sheds with rusting roofs and windows full of broken panes. Anyone arriving at the tatty little station and scrambling up into the grim-looking thoroughfares full of dark, unpromising shops and a resolute determination on being workaday and unadorned to the point of absolute ugliness, might be forgiven for thinking that the place was a nightmare of spiralling unemployment and terminal decay. When eventually you discover the reverse is true, and that the canny *biellesi* have stuffed fat wads under the mattress or into an old sock, the effect is a bit like a practical joke: you feel you ought to laugh, just to show that you're too much of a sport to mind being taken for a ride, but the fun is really a trifle hollow.

Even the churches seem dismally neglected. Vincenzo takes me into one they are belatedly shoring up, with a cloister next to it which is being converted into apartments. The interior is dark and inimical, like some hideous late Victorian godbotherers' barn in Kentish Town, with flakes of blackened plaster and lumps of birdshit littering the floor. In the south transept stands a ghoulish-looking grey effigy, decidedly larger than life, of a woman in a crinoline, her ringleted hair draped with lace 'weepers', kneeling at a prie-dieu. She has a hard granite-jawed profile, and her stone eyes appear signally unforgiving. The inscription records her as an Englishwoman named Margaret Bertie Mathew, the widow of General Alfonso Lamarmora, a local nobleman who became prime minister of Italy in 1864 and signed a treaty with Bismarck two years later which committed the nation to war with Austria. From her surnames I imagine Margaret to have been a tough old recusant battleaxe wearing out her rosary in an English country house full of fawning Jesuits and Oxonian snobs preparing ostentatiously to 'go over'. Probably she was nothing of the kind, but her statue, so unnervingly naturalistic in the half-light from the grimy windows, 'makes a certain impression' as the Italians cryptically say, and I am not slow to hustle Vincenzo out into the sunlight.

There are to be eight of us at dinner tonight, a fact which does not especially please me. Vincenzo is one of those people, of whom I know several, with the distinctly negative gift of making his friends jealous of one another. We become, indeed, perfectly asinine in our quasi-amorous desire to monopolize his attention.

Grumpily I retire with a book to the patch of untended garden in front of the house, where a hammock is slung between two apple trees and an enormous (but in view of Vincenzo's oriental hankerings, not wholly incongruous) date palm towers over all. On mature reflection – and a hammock on a sultry July afternoon concentrates the mind wonderfully – I acknowledge that it is not Vincenzo's friends who most annoy me, or the tiresome obligation to be sociable, so much as the intense envy I feel for his apparently limitless capacity to attract others. Envy is a thoroughly tenth-rate emotion, like guilt or embarrassment: I am the lifelong prisoner of all three.

Some of this power to fascinate is his own, some of it belongs to the house, and not a little derives from the fact that there is almost certainly nobody like him within a radius of a hundred miles. He is the enchanter in his cave, Merlin and Prospero of the *alta biellese*, to whom anyone in the region with the least touch of fancy or originality will gravitate sooner or later. He is to be dropped in on, amid his *magna arcana* of oddities and curiosities, not just for friendship's sake but because of the need he satisfies for something beyond bank balances and creative accounting and conspicuous consumption. There is a certain touching humility about the constancy with which these denizens of a material world climb out of the plain to visit him. He is not arrogant or pompous, offers no advice, gives no warnings. Simply being the thing he is, amid possessions that are not possessions in the sense that other Italians love to possess things, makes him necessary to the equilibrium of these people, vulnerable within their earthbound, acquisitive world precisely because they are sensitive, however unconsciously, to whatever lies outside it.

I observe this at dinner. The conversation is relentlessly trivial, and the round table makes it easy for loud-voiced anecdotalists to dominate, and one-to-one absolutely impossible. There is much talk about food, as always in Italy, which must give a certain pleasure to those of us from nations where eating is carried on merely as a matter of survival, and about hospitals and illnesses, inevitably a good deal more congenial to those with much to say, especially since one of them is a doctor, full of that dreadful medical self-importance and armed with the customary repertoire of hospital shock-horror stories. Nobody will discuss art, literature or politics, none of them will canvass anything in the nature of a theory or an abstract generalization, and since, for whatever reason, my spoken Italian has chosen this moment to catch a severe cramp, I cannot throw in the coruscating epigram or lapidary apophthegm which will imprint a memory of my presence for ever upon the minds of the other guests.

So I sit back and watch them under the lamp, pushing bowls and bottles to and fro and crumbling their bread on the table-cloth. More particularly I watch the three of them whose attachment to Vincenzo is deepest, and speculate, without necessarily reaching any conclusion, as to why each of them should need him so much.

Easiest of all to fathom is Fabio, dour, frowning and silent, who is patently in love with Vincenzo and will probably remain under his spell for ever. We have all of us been through this phase. I spent a year in agonized infatuation with Vincenzo from which I was cured largely by a salving vanity which permitted me to see what an idiot I was becoming. Fabio, it seems, will never arrive at such a perception: hence his murderous resentment towards the rest of us, at whom he sits glowering throughout the meal.

Piero, whom I like immensely, craves the stimulus to his restlessness which this place always gives. He will never be happy, for all sorts of reasons, but his massive solidity of character has prompted him to make the best of things, and while now and then he can escape to this house, for an hour or two in the warmth of its embrace, he will teach himself to endure. I admire Piero, with his drawling Piedmontese accent and his stocky body and ugly dished nose like a bullcalf, because, unlike the rest of us, he asks for nothing.

Carla is the hardest to make out, if only for the way in which she tries more strenuously than the others not to seem as if she needs Vincenzo. With a lover in tow and obedient children somewhere in the background, she is the wielder of unchecked power, the kind of absolute authority which corrupts women because they crave it so intensely. In order to preserve this air of independence, she has always to give the impression of not being struck by anything. Her carefully sustained lack of surprise or curiosity seldom allows her more than a mild amusement or occasional laughter of the Chesterfieldian variety. She never betrays herself through amazement, shock or absorbed fascination of any kind. It is as if, having got everything in her life into exactly the proportion she desires, her effort must now be to impress the rest of us with the irreproachable polish of her sophistication.

As a result, fond though I am of her, easily won by her humour and *mondaine* attractiveness, I find myself longing for something terrible to happen to her, something calculated to jolt her into emotional responses over which she has no control. A sudden bust-up with her lover, an accident or a serious illness for one of the kids, a burglary or an assault, anything to shake her out of the awful pose of serene control she has assumed as the safest mode of affronting life.

Smiling sardonically in her world-weary, seen-it-all-done-it-all-darling fashion, she watches Vincenzo playing patience. He plays it every night, game after game, an inflexible therapeutic ritual and an ideal image, what is more, of that solitude with which he challenges us all. Carla hangs over him, muttering occasional encouragement as a row looks like coming out, and laughing her warm throaty laugh when Vincenzo curses the cards' perversity. From the pool of lamplight he looks up, catching my gaze surveying her, and I turn quickly back to my book. The games go on, the shuffle and snap of the pack, as I again glance furtively towards them. Seen thus huddled in collusion over the table, they might almost be husband and wife.

In the night a curious dream: it is some thirty years ago, and I am in the stables at school with a dandy-brush and curry-comb, preparing to groom the pony Gingerbread I always used to ride. As I enter his stall, with its high wooden manger and ornately carved newels under which his name has been chalked, a sinister darkness descends and I cannot find him. I call his name and a voice comes from the shadow. 'You were cruel to me,' it says, 'and gave me nothing to eat. So now I am going to eat you.' All of a sudden he is there, hideously starved and mangy, so that I can see his ribs and the sharp apex-point of his withers. His head swivels round towards me, and I can see his eyes full of anger and his teeth bared to attack.

At which juncture I wake up, thoroughly conscious, as one invariably is on being aroused from such a dream, of the absurdly Freudian transparency of it all. One might as well have dreamed of the sea or a railway train or a pile of excrement as anything so symbolically banal as a horse. Switching on the lamp, I find it is five to five. The weak light of earliest morning shows through a crack in the shutters. I get out of bed and move stealthily, so as not to wake the sleepers in the adjacent rooms (there are no corridors in this house) to the window, open it as quietly as I can, and go out on to the balcony.

Thin whorls of mist cover the mountain slopes, but the faint brightness of dawn has already begun to show the colours in the trees and roofs and stretches of pasture. The cocks crow, and then, with their customary matter-of-fact abruptness, the chimes of the two village churches strike the metallic hour. A car moves on the road and a dog barks. Slowly the shape of the mountains starts to unveil. The dank green scent of everything before the sun has got at it hangs in the clear air, still tingling and chilly from the night.

Standing on the balcony, my bare feet not unpleasantly numbed by the cold stone, and peering at the dawn as it steals into the upland meadows to wake the farms, I feel once again that barely sustainable joy which is the gift of this house, but also the reward of Italy. I may as well not drop dead just yet, while an Italian day remains to enjoy. Getting back into bed, I fall asleep again. This time the dream surpasses all expectations.

Vincenzo will drive me to the station. Before leaving, I sit on the bed in my room, according to the old Russian custom, and count to ten. There are innumerable questions I have not got round to asking him, whole fields of recent vicissitude untraversed by either of us, so much destined to remain, like prayer in the poem, 'something understood'. Thus it will always be between us, a link that binds me to him through his ability to make me feel guiltily insufficient as a friend. In some way I acknowledge, as we kiss in farewell, that I shall always have failed him, yet perhaps this was how I wished it to be from the outset. When the train reaches Masserano, I remember too late how much he would have enjoyed hearing about the stork.

7 Reading the Campo, Reading the Church

One of these days somebody – me for preference – will be allowed to make an original television documentary about Venice. There will be no more aerial views of Saint Mark's Square, out will go the shots of tourists feeding the pigeons or eating ices outside Quadri, moody views of San Giorgio through a forest of mooring poles or arty-farty close-ups of gondola ripples on a canal. The Vivaldi mandolin and double trumpet concertos will be put to silence, and the commentator will be forbidden to perpetuate the gross historical untruth that Venice went into terminal economic decline in the eighteenth century.

The abuse which the city suffers derives not simply from criminal neglect by successive Italian governments or from the grandiose money-spinning schemes of local politicians, or even from its own citizens whose insensate greed has despoiled and brutalized it, but from its own fatal gift for manufacturing endlessly seductive cliché. The truth is that all of us, from the day-tripper buying glass gondolas and straw hats as souvenirs to the rich aesthete in his *palazzetto* on the Dorsoduro, imagine that we own Venice and feel inclined to place territorial keep-out notices on our blessed city. Venice is the great masseuse of our hankerings and illusions: she discovers us not for what we are, but for what each of us would like to be, and in her sly, insinuating fashion, sets about shaping the conditions in which we become the creatures our fancy has devised. She solicits our possessiveness so as herself to take possession of us with her comfortable twaddling myths of decadence and sadness and the wearying infinitude of her décor.

The weather assists this process of enslavement. In most other parts of Italy climate appears a simple matter of hot and cold, fog, rain or sunshine, a series of wonderfully obvious absolutes. In Venice the air and the light are continuously protean, and the fluctuation of your moods is attuned to this capricious changeableness. One afternoon at the end of May, a notoriously unreliable month anywhere in the world, I decided on a whim to go out to the dunes of the Alberoni at the southern end of the Lido. The sky had a curious coppery tinge to it, and a keen breeze corrugated the surface of the lagoon. By the time I reached the path leading through the pinewood on to the beach, a furious wind was whipping great curtains of sand off the top of the dunes and curling the sea into breakers. I spent the afternoon under the trees, not altogether alone, then wandered up towards the road leading along the western shore, from which the city, with its towers and domes, is generally visible.

What the wind had done in my two or three hours of trifling in the forest was to clean, as it were, the picture of Venice, scaling away the metallic haze and the bands of dark purplish thundercloud, like the markings on a cow's belly or the underside of a fish, which earlier hung so ominously over everything. In its place there was set a superbly vivid, acute, eye-straining prospect of the city, in which every roof, every cupola and campanile sounded the accents of an excited voice. Up beyond them, in the manner of some nineteenth-century diorama, swept the grey Dolomites under little sprinklings of cloud, their folds and outlines so sharply defined that the mountains seemed ready to fall upon Venice and crush it to powder. The sight was in the nature of an epiphany, but I knew that the slightest trick of wind or sunlight could blur or smudge it into nothing.

This is why we need the *terra ferma*, the plain prose of mainland places like Mestre and Dolo, Campodarsego and Portogruaro. The dry land corrects the senses, boxes our ears and pulls us by the hair, convincing us of the folly and vanity of those emotions we left behind among the *calli* and *campielli*. There are times, amid the earthbound stolidity of the dull little towns of the Veneto plain, when you long for Venice to realize the prophecies made about it by Byron and others and to fall into the sea and disappear, so that it becomes one of those submerged cities favoured by legend, where they say you can hear the church bells clanging under the swell of the waves. Let corals encrust the Pala d'Oro of Saint Mark, let the Café Florian become a shell grotto for mermaids and the Ca' Rezzonico a dark unfathomed cave for fish to dive in and out of.

Because Venice is such an extraordinary palimpsest on which everyone delights to scribble, the place is constantly inviting your eye to read and annotate it like some fascinatingly garbled text, an exercise made easier by the fact that there is no wheeled traffic to prevent your standing exactly where you want so as to examine, to ponder and revolve for as long as you choose. This is why, among other reasons, I prefer it to Florence, because it makes no pretence at integrity, but flings its experience of art and historical vicissitude blatantly and untidily together, so that there is always something to amaze and mislead your concentration. You stare at a Veronese ceiling and find yourself admiring the gilt carving of its beams; you glance at the wall-mounted sarcophagus of a mediaeval doge and get sidetracked by the clever use of coloured marbles on the baroque tomb next to it; or, dropping your 200-lire coin in the box to illuminate a Renaissance altarpiece, you find yourself mesmerized by the silver casket underneath that holds the remains of some Byzantine martyr pilfered during the memorably inglorious (but to Venice most happily profitable) Second Crusade.

All this flatters that most un-Italian of virtues, curiosity. Perhaps for so emphatically not being like the rest of Italy, Venice, as I have noted elsewhere, is not greatly loved by most Italians, and practically everything of value written about it since the sixteenth century has been the work of foreigners, responsible to a large extent for preserving its singular character by remaining alert to the city's thoroughgoing heterogeneousness, its uncompromising scramble of contradictory detail.

Everything in Venice acts as a spur to the inquisitive imagination, every bricked-up gothic arch, every high garden wall, every half-demolished *scuola*, every shuttered house and cat-whiffing lane, even (or maybe especially) the names of the streets themselves, painted in tall black letters on white rectangles high up the wall. The Venetian-ness of Venice, the sound of its unmistakable vernacular, the sweetness and sense, fun and vulnerable, bantering immediacy which Carlo Goldoni caught for us in his dialect comedies, is in these names, preserving, by means of an admirable law passed by the civic authorities in 1949, the authentic contractions and mutations of the Venetian idiom.

Each sort of thoroughfare has its generic. A paved canal bank is a *fondamenta*, and a lane which gives off a large *calle* is a *ramo* or branch. A row of shops becomes a *ruga* (French *rue*) and the grander sort of street is either a *salizada* (meaning 'paved'), or a *lista*.* A canal which has been earthed in and paved over

* In Kerkyra, capital of Venice's former possession
Corfu, the long colonnaded walk in the central
square is still called the Liston. Contrary

is a *rio terà*. Many of these places bear the dialect names of trades formerly carried on there. Campiello del Pestrin, for example, is 'the little square of the dairy', and 'Salizada del Pistor' is 'Baker Street'. Others, like Fondamenta del Osmarin, 'Rosemary Bank', near San Lorenzo, who is shown flourishing his gridiron in a little relief panel on the wall of a mediaeval palace by the canal, or Calle dei Nomboli, 'Entrails Street', close to the Frari, preserve a memory of whatever used to be sold there, even if it was only on some humble stall kept one day a week by an old woman coming in from the country with her wares.

The loveliest names are the most eccentric, 'the Bridge of the Honest Woman', 'the Street of the Proverbs', 'the Rio Terà of the Assassins', 'the Bridge of Slaughtered Men', 'the Street of the Love of Friends'. There are no names, or hardly any, of famous battles, rulers, influential politicians or great men and women, and for this reason you feel, in a fashion almost inexplicable, entirely at home within the city, as if it were dealing honestly with you by telling you what you were about to discover through turning down a certain way, as if there really were still spice merchants in the Calle de lo Spezier, makers of wooden chests in the Casseleria or Armenians from the Persian city of Julfa in the Ruga Giufa.

This is Venice's device, this homely naming, to make it impossible that you should ever lose your way. Nobody who is really interested in looking at things or who possesses any decent visual memory ever gets lost in this maze of three thousand *calli*, one hundred and seventy-seven canals, four hundred bridges and one hundred churches, and even if they do, they will invariably stumble upon some disclosure of the marvellous which validates a brief bamboozlement. After a while, in any case, once Venice

---

to what is stated in every English guidebook, the name has nothing whatever to do with a supposed 'list' of the nobility who were allowed to walk along it, but is simply the Venetian *lista* with an augmentative ending tacked on. Of such taradiddles is tradition made.

has clutched you to her, you learn the secret twitchens, snickels and ginnels which make the short cuts, and remember the dead-ends which land you by a pile of plastic sacks beside a moored barge on a silent canal with mineral water bottles and Coke tins floating in it.

The *campi* are the places in which to read the quartos and folios, cancelled sheets, foul papers and learned footnotes of the Venetian text. They are not squares in the sense of cleared spaces, as in the mainland towns, but pieces of paved ground which preserve the recollection of those open fields suggested by the very word *campo*. They are the spots most readily brought to life in my Venetian imagination because each preserves such an extraordinary distinctness of identity.

There is the Campo Santa Maria Formosa – broad, airy and populous – where the *Cazze* or bull-baitings used to take place, and where nowadays they hold a little daily market with stalls run by children purveying old comics, *fumetti* (photo-romances), pirate videos and cassettes, and a fat old man sells mousetraps, dusters, corkscrews and those enormously useful vices for turning stubborn bottle caps. There is the relentlessly gloomy Campo San Maurizio, where grass grows between the stones, and where in one of the tall, sad palaces dwelt the libertine poet Giorgio Baffo who wrote cock-and-cunt verses in Venetian dialect. After him, by an amusing irony, there dwelt the stupendously unattractive figure of Alessandro Manzoni, illustrious author of *I promessi sposi*, who, even if he knew the meaning of Baffo's smutty vocabulary, would never publicly have admitted to using it.

I love these, as I love the Campo Santa Margherita, a massive, sprawling affair, with a weekly fishmarket, a Chinese restaurant, a couple of junk shops, several cafés and in the middle the old Scuola dei Varotari (*Varotaro* is the Venetian for tanner) with a marble relief of the Virgin with attendant worshippers. I am fond, too, of the lopsided square surrounding the church of San Giacomo dell'Orio, which marks the site of an island once called 'Del Lupio' since it was roamed by wolves, and of the quiet, slightly melancholy space in front of San Giovanni in

Bragora, where Vivaldi was baptized, and whence the hapless Bandiera brothers Attilio and Emilio set out on their quixotic and ultimately fatal expedition in 1844 to free the Kingdom of Naples from Bourbon tyranny.

In one particular *campo*, however, it might be possible to encapsulate the entire Venetian experience – always excepting, of course, the canals, which in this instance are merely peripheral. The Campo Santo Stefano, largest in Venice after Saint Mark's, is crossed and crossed again each day by scores of people who perhaps never give a thought to looking at it for what it has to tell them about the city, yet here, more than anywhere else when I return to Venice, I feel that sense of continuing life which assures me that the Most Serene isn't yet quite ready to give herself up to the Adriatic.

At the western end stands the most beautiful gothic church in Venice, lovelier than the great basilicas of the Frari and San Zanipolo simply because it is smaller, and because the entrance of more light than is allowed by the windows of either of those two churches allows you to appreciate its design more thoroughly. Santo Stefano was founded in the thirteenth century by the Augustinian hermits who had formerly dwelt at Sant'Anna on the very edge of the Castello district, at the northernmost end of the main island of Venice. The original church was enlarged during the fifteenth century, and the handsome cloister, built in 1532, was adorned with frescoes (long since faded alas!) by the painter Pordenone.

The façade, topped with little crocketed aedicules of white marble, is of plain dark brick which lends a greater impact to the splendid tabernacle above the doorway framing the figure of God the Father; above Him is an angel on a plinth, between two polygonal pillars with ballflower mouldings. Around the central arch runs an exquisitely chiselled, tremulously vivid pattern of gently curved and swelling leaves like those of some underwater plant: the work, maybe, of the great Bartolomeo Bon who fashioned the Porta della Carta at the entrance to the Doge's Palace.

It is the perfect herald to the church's interior, this late gothic portal with its alternating bands of foliage, ropework and barley-sugar in the marble pilasters on either side of the door. Everything about Santo Stefano is a touch poetic and fantastical, as though whoever had anything to do with the building was immediately inspired by its dreamlike quality to emulate the inherent romance in Bon's garland of submarine fronds. For a start, the nave is no ordinary gothic nave, though it has its just complement of ogival arches and decorated capitals painted and gilded. Look up, and there above you, the wildest thing, above the great flower-patterned crossbeams and the twelve saints of the Augustinian Order over the cusps of the arcade, each holding their attributes and symbols, is a long coffered ceiling deliberately made to simulate the upturned hull of a boat, *la carena di nave* as it is called in Italian, and decorated all over its barrel vaults with a chequerboard of little rosettes.

All along each aisle runs a sequence of rococo altars, the work of the architects Carlo Gaspari and Giorgio Massari, their columns of variegated marble – *giallo di Siena, bardiglio, broccatello, rosso di Verona* – framing gorgeous altarpieces by deft imitators of Tiepolo and Piazzetta, and a statue of the Virgin crowned with a silver diadem and wearing panniered skirts as though just returned from a ball, her hands raised in a perpetual 'oh-but-you-really-shouldn't-have' gesture. Behind the tall Palladian stage-set arches of the high altar, the branching vaults of the apse gather over what remains of the marble choir screen and the almost crazed ornateness of the stalls, making a final concession to gothic in their topmost layer of decorative moulding.

What I like best about Santo Stefano, perhaps because it is the cause of that intrinsic sense of imaginative vitality which the church conveys even to the weariest tourist, is the fact that it scrambles together fine examples of every single style in Venetian art from the Middle Ages to the nineteenth century. For instance, I am insanely addicted to baroque funerary art, and in Venice I shiver with delight at such gems of the lapidary confectioner's skill as that colossal mausoleum to the Valier Doges in San Zanipolo, designed in 1708 by Andrea Tirali, complete with massive swatches of fake brocade in coloured marble, and a riot of statuary so good of its kind that you want to break bits off and eat them. In Santo Stefano I am not disappointed, for here, on the way into the sacristy, slewed across one corner so that you can hardly miss it, is a consequential yellow medallion monument to the jurist and diplomat Lazaro Ferri, who died in 1692 after representing Venice at Vienna, which perhaps explains why his shield is supported by the Hapsburg double eagle – actually more like a vulture, so long-necked and fierce it looks. Ferri's portrait bust, in a great periwig, leers from above.

The age of the periwig enraptures me. I love its art and music and the learned communion, across frontiers and seas, of its philosophers and scientists. Venice, by then, had lost its economic lead in Europe and was becoming a second-class power, but it could still mount two wars against the Turks and recapture, however briefly and unpopularly, its hold over part of Greece. Whatever else it might slowly be letting go, the city would never lose its power to attract and nourish great painters, as well as fostering those content merely with being extremely good.

Probably nobody except his mother thought that Gaspare Diziani was a great artist, yet the four canvases with which he embellished the entrance wall of the sacristy in 1733 remain for me some of the most enchantingly conceived in all Venice. Diziani came from Belluno, up in the passes of the Dolomites, and like his fellow mountaineer painters Titian, Cima di Conegliano and Sebastiano Ricci (himself a *bellunese*) he seems to have possessed that visionary gift of those who dwell among the high peaks for descrying some curious species of unearthly reality whose cloudborne romance and lurid illumination is made to seem more substantial than anything we have hitherto taught ourselves to consider real.

This tetralogy of paintings showing scenes from the Childhood of Christ has been imagined without the slightest concession to the idea that such events are actually supposed to have happened. Diziani, with all his scene-painter's talent for décor, with his flair for dramatic lighting effects and his delight in arresting us with his figures' recherché poses, wants us to accept the validity of these things not as fact but as myth. Thus the incandescent pinks and reds and blues of his palette and the deliberately surreal jumble of architectural motifs – a flying balustrade, a half-finished arch, a broken column – invite us to discard the viewpoint which prosaically asserts 'it must be true because it says so' in favour of 'it happened because that was how I imagined it'. The beauty of Diziani's *Flight into Egypt*, with an angel dressed as a gondolier in sash and breeches, ready to row the Virgin and Child to safety, is the beauty of that legendary, fabulous element with which we oppose the finite plainness of our lives. If ever blockheaded Christian fundamentalism needed a stout riposte, it is here in Diziani's captivating fancies. There are other things in the sacristy you would probably rather admire, the miraculous silver icon of the Virgin of Artocosta, brought from Nauplion* in Greece in 1541, two exquisite Vivarini gold-ground paintings of Saint Nicholas and Saint Lawrence, and an outstanding Tintoretto of the Agony in the Garden, in which dramatic effect is achieved by sinister little wisps and flickers of light on the branches and leaves and the gathered folds of the apostles' robes. But do not ignore Diziani just because he is not Tintoretto or has more craft than a Byzantine primitive. He too has something to tell you.

There is an even stronger, more portentous Greek connection with Santo Stefano than a Peloponnesiac *odegetria* rescued from the Turks. This was the family church of one of the most illustrious Venetian clans, the Morosini, whose palace is at the northeastern corner of the *campo*. It is possible that the Morosini were themselves of Greek origin: their name renders into Latin as Maurocenus, but I was not surprised to find it on a memorial on the island of Paros to a local heroine of the independence struggle against the Ottomans, named Manto Mavrogenos. Or more likely, since so many Hellenized Venetian names – Foskaros, Kontarinos, Kornaros – turn up across the Cyclades, Manto was a descendant of some branch of this great house, which gave four doges to Venice and held fourteen palaces in the city alone. If she genuinely was a Morosini,

* The topographically confusing Italian name for
which is Napoli di Romania.

did she remember an ancestor of hers who, a century or more back, had revived, however briefly, the glory of Venetian arms by driving back the Turks with such success that they were forced to make an unworthy peace and yield the whole of the Morea to the Serene Republic?

The tomb of Francesco Morosini called Il Peloponnesiaco is marked by the curious bronze roundel let into the floor within a frame of military trophies and warlike instruments at the south end of the church. For the memorial to one of the most justly admired of all Venetian doges it is remarkably humble, more especially when contrasted with the hamfistedly opulent monument over the main doorway to General Domenico Contarini, who died at the famous battle of Marignano between Francis I of France and Emperor Charles V in 1515.

Morosini, who became Doge of Venice in 1688, was among the greatest military personalities of his martial age. He began his career as a naval officer in the long and ultimately hopeless struggle with the Sultan for mastery of Crete, culminating in the nine-year siege of Candia (modern Heraklion). To him fell the responsibility for deciding to render up the city, after the French force which had been fighting at Venice's side decided that enough was enough and finally slipped anchor. On 30 August 1669, Morosini, as 'Captain General of the Sea' began peace negotiations, and a month later four hundred years of Venetian rule in the island came to an end with the inglorious embarkation of almost the entire population of Candia, with their icons, sacred vessels and holy relics.

When Morosini returned to Venice he was, as is invariably the custom with defeated commanders, impeached (unsuccessfully) and the feasting and celebration which would ordinarily have attended his election to the high office of Procurator of Saint Mark were ostentatiously boycotted by the citizens, smarting from the international humiliation occasioned by the Republic's loss of Crete. He must have savoured the irony which, fourteen years later, decreed his appointment as *generalissimo* of the Venetian forces in a new and dramatic strike into Ottoman territory.

With his fellow commander, the Swedish adventurer Count Koenigsmark, he pursued a relentless conquest from fortress to fortress in the Peloponnese. Navarino, Argos, Nauplion, Patras, Corinth and Lepanto fell within two years, and the seizure of the half-ruined city of Mistra spurred the victorious army northwards towards the bombardment of Athens, where one of Koenigsmark's cannon balls struck the roof of the Parthenon, touching off the Turkish powder magazine inside and bringing Phidias's magnificent frieze crashing to the ground, thereby giving the Elgin Marbles that battered look they retain to this day.

Venice's colonization of the Peloponnese was not an especially happy undertaking. The Greeks, particularly the wild, untameable Maniots of the south, resented the Republic's attempt to impose its political structures on the region and detested still more the decree, suicidal in its greed and unworkableness, which ordained that all locally produced goods must be sent to Venice for sale. The sole remnant of that thirty years of Venetian imperial presence in the Morea is a handful of massive fortresses, raised with the funds of a state which, however strapped for cash, built for eternity.

With Morosini finally elected Doge, the war against the Turks was vigorously pursued, a foothold being established in Albania and the island of Lesbos threatened, and even the recapture of Crete a sudden possibility. When the Doge was persuaded in 1689 to accept supreme military command for the fourth time, age and ill health were starting to tell, but his loyalty, that unshakeable Venetian sense of duty to the Republic, whose spirit flares up even today, made a refusal out of the question. Six months later, after taking the islands of the Saronic Gulf, Morosini died of exhaustion at Nauplion. His successor as commander, Antonio Zen, having failed to follow up a naval conquest of Chios, was arrested and died in prison.

Old Francesco was not forgotten. His surrender of Candia came to seem a noble act, designed to save the Cretans from Turkish massacres, and his moustachioed figure, wearing the curious round barber's-basin headpiece of a Venetian general, is seen all over Venice. They show you his robes and the flags he captured in the Correr Museum at Saint Mark's, and the people had cause, in later wars when the Senate adopted a contemptible bet-hedging neutrality regularly ignored by belligerent powers, to recall their Morosini the Peloponnesiac, the last champion of La Serenissima.

The Palazzo Morosini, with its appropriately severe façade, is set back from the main body of the Campo Santo Stefano, with one side of it facing on to the canal of San Maurizio. They have given the Doge's name to the square, but nobody uses it except presumably in official documents. The place belongs, without dispute, to the stoned Protomartyr, the long, russet-hued body of whose church so handsomely closes the prospect.

People say admiringly of James Joyce that one of his party tricks, after he had gone blind, was to identify and describe in order the shops on either side of O'Connell Street, Dublin. So what is remarkable about that? I am writing this chapter in a house in Clapham, but in my memory the palaces and colours and adornments of Campo Santo Stefano are as intimately detailed as if I were standing at this moment in the middle of the square, beneath the shadow of the Caccalibri.

The what? The Caccalibri of course, 'the book-shitter', the cheeky appellation given by Venetians to the indifferent statue by Franco Bazzaghi (1882) of the writer Nicolo Tommaseo, because the pile of books against which he rests looks as if it had been defecated from under the skirts of his frock coat. Tommaseo was even more of a Venetian hero for having been born at Sebenico (modern Šibenik) in Dalmatia, which had been part of the Republic's Adriatic territory and traditionally devoted to Venice.* It was he who, together with the Jewish

---

* The troops who showed most readiness to defend
Venice when Napoleon threatened it in 1797 were
Croats from Dalmatia. Ironical it was a respectfully
fired salute from their guns which frightened the
Grand Council into voting the Doge out of office
and proclaiming the demise of the Republic.

lawyer Daniele Manin, led the phenomenally tough, against-all-odds opposition to the Austrians that sustained the great siege of 1848–9, for the sake of which the Venetians deserve forgiveness for their manifold sins and wickednesses elsewhere in Italian history.

Staggeringly wide-ranging in his interests and achievements, Tommaseo, when not on the run from the police or urging the heroic defenders towards suffering yet more privations to keep the Emperor's troops at bay, edited magazines, wrote a classic commentary on Dante, translated the Psalms and the Gospels, compiled a huge Italian dictionary, studied the origins of folksong, poured out a stream of learned articles and produced a remarkably original novel, composed during his exile in Corsica in 1840, entitled *Fede e Bellezza* ('Faith and Beauty'). He may not be among those very few Italian poets of the past who are read and admired nowadays, but his shining integrity and conviction make him worth lingering over when you turn him up in the anthologies. He deserves a better monument than this from the city he tried to save, yet however mediocre Bazzaghi's sculptured image, there is always something reassuring about the old boy's presence here, with a pigeon or two on his head for company.

It is no doubt appropriate that the Caccalibri has turned his back on the Renaissance palace of the Loredan family, on the south side of the square, rebuilt from the remains of a Gothic original in 1536, for this long, low-pitched building, decked with marble facings and once covered in allegorical fresco, was commandeered by the Austrians when they took over the city in 1810, and turned into a garrison.

Their rule in Venice, lasting some fifty years, was fair, competent and beneficial. The trouble was simply that nobody really liked them enough. They ate potatoes, drank beer and spoke German, and you could hear the officers' sabres clanking on the stones of the *calli* like tin cans. The smarter sort went into society, and John Ruskin's young wife Effie got tremendously chummy with several of them, who beguiled her time with harmless gallantry while her husband was taking casts of ogival cusps and drawing Byzantine reliefs. After the failure of the 1848 revolution, when Manin and Tommaseo went into exile, the Austrians tried again with the Venetians, this time with even less success. When Emperor Franz Josef and Empress Elisabeth arrived on an official visit in the autumn of 1861, the response was a series of laborious snubs which the imperial couple had to take on the chin. At a gala at Teatro La Fenice for example, the patrician families who might normally have filled the boxes ostentatiously hired them out to government functionaries and their wives and stayed away for the evening. When one of the Emperor's retinue obtusely enquired, on their arrival, why Saint Mark's Square had been specially illuminated, a perfectly audible Italian voice answered, 'So that His Majesty may see that there is nobody here.'

In fact, as the Venetians now rather grudgingly admit, much of what saved the city from becoming a ghost town, a sort of Italian Baalbek or Palmyra, was the work of benevolent, if not always terribly inspired Hapsburg administrators. They brought the railway across the lagoon, they built the Accademia Bridge,* they rescued the Doge's Palace from irreparable damage through its use as municipal offices, they introduced the first public steam launches, the famous *vaporetti* by which most of us get up and down the city, and gave Venice its earliest adequate street lighting. Doubtless it is easy to be blasé and derogatory about these achievements and say that Venice would have been better off without them. This is a foolish sophistry. Venice not only did well out of the Austrians but (it may be said) could make use of them now that her own citizens, bent on making a quick buck out of the city at whatever cost, are choking the poor old thing to death.

Every trace of their presence as imperial overlords was wiped away – or almost every trace. For over the main doorway of the Palazzo Loredan in Campo Santo Stefano you will see, if you

---

* In 1854, of cast iron. The present wooden structure replaced it in 1938, preparatory to a stone
bridge, yet to be constructed.

look carefully, the very faint outlines of the German inscription 'K.u.K. Festung' and something else now illegible. I hope no intemperately purist restorer or conservator of buildings is permitted to rub this out, for it is part of the palimpsest of the Campo, an image in itself of Venice's habit of not absorbing its past too thoroughly, so that stray passages and fragments are always tempting you to recover them.

The power of Venetian *campi* and *campielli* over the visual memory derives in large part from their total absence of plan. Even Saint Mark's, which looks harmonious enough today, was flung together piecemeal. The Procuratie Vecchie on the western side were finished in 1532, the Procuratie Nuove opposite (sheltering Florian's café) were completed in 1640, and the so-called Ala Napoleonica, which has its critics even now, was begun on Bonaparte's orders in 1810, after the church of San Geminiano had been torn down to accommodate it. Elsewhere it was mostly a matter of who built their palace in the space available, yet the resulting omnium gatherum invariably creates the impression, if not of harmony, then of a subtle concord, in which differing heights and widths and styles attain such a fellowship that only a maniac would try to impose homogeneity on them.

So it is with Santo Stefano. Doubtless Antonio Gaspari and Andrea Tirali, who rebuilt the church of San Vitale in 1700 to fulfil the terms of a bequest made fifty years before by the Doge Carlo Contarini, did not specifically intend its fine, chastely Vitruvian façade to create the effect both of an eyecatcher at the end of the square when entered from the direction of the Rialto, and of a grandiose prelude to it when reached across the Accademia Bridge, yet such is the result of its presence on the edge of the *campo*. Nobody has consciously worked at any of this: it has simply happened upon its beauty; the sombre green chemist's shop on the northern corner, the hotel over the way that has grown somewhat smarter of late (a pity – there must always be one or two seedy hotels in central Venice), the blistered stucco of the houses by the church, the little *fondamenta* going down to the back of Palazzo Barbaro where Henry James used to stay, the blackened and bleached hulk of the Pisani Palace and the glimpse of red pantiled roofs, attic windows and *altane*, the wooden railed platforms on the rooftops where, on the night of the Festa del Redentore, the third Saturday in July, you sit eating slices of watermelon and watching the false dawn of a thousand fireworks, with the *campanili* black and recalcitrant against the blaze of light.

I have left Paolin till the last, because even to write its name induces unassuageable longings. There are other cafés in the Campo Santo Stefano, an ugly little pizzeria for trippers and a frowzy bar where junkies shoot up in the loo, but Paolin is the real thing, the essence, the nonsuch, the transcendent, the *sans-pareil*, the absolute ultimate biz. Why, you might ask? It is only a small, unremarkable bar on the corner of the *calle* going down to San Samuele, with a rather dingy interior and battered chrome tables and metal chairs outside, yet it acts as the *clou* of the Santo Stefano experience, as indispensable to a total apprehension of the square as the chunks of granite with which it is paved.

Paolin is, what's more, distinctively Venetian in a way that certain other well-frequented cafés in the city alas are not. Because it has made no compromises with tourism, has not, to use the charming Americanism, 'gussied itself up', the establishment has hung on to its ethnic clientele, with the result that, for whatever reason, it always feels more sophisticated, more grown-up than many of the grander, glitzier bars elsewhere on the lagoon. When you look at the drinkers at Paolin, those standing at the bar or the punters at the tables, they look as if they have been there for decades. Even the tourists tend to be those whose affection for Venice takes the form of an independent curiosity and who have transcended the glass gondola and straw hat phase of evolution, if they ever went through it in the first place.

Venice is one of those places where you find regular drinkers in the sense that these exist in English pubs and American bars. I don't say that you will not find *habitués* in all Italian cafés, but Venice is a city that takes drinking seriously. It isn't the unspeakably dull, swinish, aggressive, sorrow-anaesthetizing tank-up which the British make such a dire religion of; however, it is something you notice as soon as you arrive off the *terra ferma*, part of an invariable social rhythm. The tipple is the small glass of red or white wine known as *un'ombra*, 'a shadow', so called because it used to be served in Saint Mark's Square under shady awnings, as you can see by looking carefully at the details of the magnificent *vedute* of the Piazza by Guardi and Canaletto. Every bar has its complement of gravel-voiced, stubble-chinned men knocking back an *ombra* or two, and barking at the barman or woman who keeps the till, before sloping off into the thick of the city.

Paolin nurtures its faithful topers, who do not mix, as a rule, with the café society at the tables but stay firmly on their feet inside. Out in the square the waiters, who – excellent sign! – have been there for years, shuffle to and fro, insisting with weary politeness on the observance of the somewhat eccentric hours of service, which seem to alter from day to day. Nobody greatly minds about such technicalities. It is far nicer, in the end, than sitting in Saint Mark's and paying 'the wrath of God', as Italians say, for your chocolate or your ices. You are not made sad by the awful physical inappositeness of tourists, and because there is no music you can overhear the conversation at the neighbouring tables, which is, after all, one of the chief joys of sitting in a café.

Several of those around you will have that agreeable air of understated seriousness and left-leaning cultivation which the Italians humorously term *intellettualoide*. They buy *La Repubblica* and *L'Espresso* and *L'Indice* from the green kiosk beside the church, and punctuate their long, parenthetical sentences with stabbing motions of their cigarettes. There will always be a brace or two of insouciantly *soignée* women, whose hair looks as though it has been carefully tousled into fashionable negligence that morning by at least three maids, but who scorn to parade their elegance too brassily and whose make-up seems deliberately toned down to accord with the general no-fuss-no-nonsense character of Paolin. There is perhaps, sitting at one of the tables, the smart American with an art historical curatorship in some New York museum who is waiting, with a look of slightly peevish apprehension, for the tardy lunch guest he will sweep off to Da Arturo, a tiny restaurant with enormous *réclame* among smart Americans. There is a French couple who sit in absolute silence with their heads at ninety degrees over the Livres de Poche they have providentially brought with them for those moments of speechlessness which extreme intimacy guarantees.

Another table is thronged with a jovial crew of what might be termed 'mature students' who periodically go off into wild salvoes of laughter, for it is the birthday of one of them, and even if the *spumante* and the *festa* are being kept until this evening, she is still to get the Italian version of 'Happy Birthday to You', *'Tanti auguri a te'*, which colours her face with embarrassed delight. Near them, the solitary German boy writing his postcards, the Longhis and Bellinis he picked from the stands after a morning's emoting and enthusing in the Accademia, looks a trifle cross and envious. He would like to make friends with these people, but will probably never manage it. Instead he stares out at the Campo, and its migrant life brings something almost like contentment to his expression.

The most threadbare of clichés about cafés is that they enable you, guaranteed the possibility of sitting still in a commanding position, to watch the world pass by. But how many people, sitting on a terrace in the Boulevard Saint Germain or the Kurfürstendamm, ever consciously indulge in this exercise or even want to? Apart from anything else, the world of the pavements in most modern cities is not one which tends to dawdle for contemplation by the would-be *boulevardier* engaged in the business of 'seeing life'. The *flaneur*, as once we knew him, has more or less disappeared.

Paolin, however, is among the few cafés left where this legendary form of study is still feasible, being, indeed, one of those places of which it is fatuously asserted that if you sit there long enough, your entire acquaintance will walk by. Certainly most of those whom you might care to see in Venice will turn up sooner or later, Santo Stefano being sited on one of

the principal axes of the city, in the direct line from the Rialto
to the Accademia, but the pleasure derives more from watching
those you don't know than expecting the arrival of those you
do. Something about the sudden, lavish openness of the Campo
encourages people to make gestures of happy liberation as they
walk across it. Emerging from the narrow *calli*, they seem to
laugh more loudly, they stagger about and clap their hands and
skip and run as if the great paved space were a playground over
which old Caccalibri were watching like a benevolent giant,
ready to get down off his plinth, overturning his posterior pile
of books in the process, were any of us to commit a nuisance,
and gently but firmly tap us on the shoulder.

A playground indeed it sometimes becomes. One morning,
around midday when the coming and going was especially busy,
I watched five youngish men in business suits and carrying
briefcases enter the square. They were clearly very pleased
about something – a deal clinched, a contract signed – and they
paused a little way beyond the café to chat, before presumably
going in various directions to lunch. After a while, they began
looking furtively around, though furtiveness is hardly in order in
so public a place as the Campo Santo Stefano. Then, one by one,
they advanced towards a pile of café chairs which, for one reason
or another, had not been set out, unstacked them, draped their
jackets over the backs and rested their briefcases on the seats.
By now giggling helplessly, they proceeded, in full view of us
all, to play at leapfrog, taking it in turns to be the vaulting-horse
and doing it, in view of sartorial constraints, really very well.
So well, indeed, that one of them rushed to open his case, got
out a small camera and took a snapshot of his chums at their
sport. Later that afternoon they would be back at their desks
and their telephones and their screens making the macho grunts
of international finance to Paris, Frankfurt and Milan. For now,
they were five jolly boys playing leapfrog in the frank, strong
light of a Venetian day.

8 Ridiculous Gundilows: A Venetian Notebook

This morning at the hotel there is grapefruit juice for breakfast. Yesterday it was pineapple, tomorrow it will surely be orange, but today they offer '*pompelmo*', which in any event must always sound so much better than the eternally prosaic and inexact 'grapefruit'. English ears are perpetually playing irreverent games with Italian words, because the Latinate homogeneity of the language has such a peculiar effect, romanticizing and ennobling the humblest of objects and transforming them into works of art or pieces of music or characters in a lyric drama. We have all at some stage or another made our silly little quip about the types of food that sound like painters or composers – The Mad Scene from Tortellini's 'Pastina in Brodo', an early work ascribed to Ravioli, and so on; nobody with the slightest associative power is beyond cranking the pump-handle of such primitive humour.

Only once has this childish sport ever had potentially serious consequences for me. While still an undergraduate, I found myself at a grand Anglo-American expatriate dinner in a villa outside Florence, accompanied by a mischievous fellow student, the pair of us being placed either side of an attractive young newspaper correspondent who had come out to cover a sale taking place that week in the palace of a recently defunct noblewoman. The journalist, besides being pretty, was sharp and resourceful, and had busied herself, while drinks were being served, with gleaning the necessary detail to give body to her article by making a careful conversational tour of the *salotto*. She wasn't, however, proof against the simplest kind of practical joke, as we realized when she asked us about the paintings we had been looking at that morning, mostly, as it turned out, of that gold-ground Madonna type of which the unsophisticated eye soon grows weary.

There had been a good many unspeakable cracks about Gaddi and Daddi, and my friend had in any case devised an all-purpose mediaeval master to whom the umpteenth doughy-faced Virgin and scowling, dropsical Christ Child might be attributed in an emergency, by the name of Bimbo della Maremma. We invented an entire Vasarian biography for Bimbo, a star pupil of Giotto, who had got about and had affairs with nuns and written Dantesque verses, before dying, in the flower of his middle age, of an apoplexy brought on by too much *vino sfuso*. He had followers, had Bimbo: there was Bimbuccio, there were Bimbotto, Bimbone and Bimbino, and Bernard Berenson had even postulated an Amico di Bimbo, let alone a *scuola* and a *bottega* for the benefit of those dealers' catalogues in which every stray artistic mongrel gets a dog-collar.

So this evening, 'flown with insolence and wine', we gave hapless journo the full Bimbo treatment, which she absorbed with patient credulity. The temptation to go one better and add other rogues to the bogus gallery was irresistible; we launched forthwith into the on-the-spot creation of Uscita della Galleria,* a woman painter contemporary with Sofonisba Anguisciola and Artemisia Gentileschi, who had somehow not found her way into Germaine Greer's pioneering book, but whose buccaneering exploits were made by us to sound like Jeannette Winterson *avant la lettre*.

Years passed, grey hairs and a sprinkling of wisdom arrived, and at a party in London I met a picture restorer who had done her professional training in the bowels of the Uffizi. For whatever reason, the name of our erstwhile victim surfaced in the conversation.

'God! Her!' cried the picture restorer, hooting with reminiscent laughter, 'she, my dear, was notorious for going round Italy asking people in all seriousness where she might find the paintings of Bimbo della Maremma and Uscita della Galleria.' Whereupon I disclosed my part-authorship of the hoax. Yet my conscience was genuinely wrung, as it would probably not have been at the time, by the realization that I had helped the poor woman to make a perfect ass of herself.

It was, in a sense, the language's fault. To a people so neurotically, obsessively verbal as the English, Italian will always end up sounding like something in excess of what it actually means. Thus the word *pompelmo* cannot simply be allowed to mean a humble yellow pomelo, 'a synonym of the POMPLEMOOSE or SHADDOCK' as the dictionary has it. For me Pompelmo will always be a character in an eighteenth-century *opera seria*, the villain whose last-minute repentance allows him to join in the final concerted number. Pompelmo is of course a bass – with a name like that, how could he be anything else? – and in the manner of *opera seria* basses, is not permitted an independent vocal line in his arias, but has to have the instrumental bass galumphing along at

* This was a lousily uninventive name, simply
meaning 'exit from the gallery'. Still, it was
believed; that was the thing.

his side like a tame hippopotamus as he sings. Incidentally, this opera, a little-known work to a libretto by Pietro Metastasio, is called 'Termosifone, Re d'Egitto': Termosifone* himself is a castrato soprano, the princess is called Anagrafe,† her rival is named Palestra,‡ and the plot is further complicated by the presence of the warlike prince Ecatostilo.§ You see the kind of thing. Need I go on?

The morning is spent in the company of R–, a highly intelligent Frenchwoman (did you ever know a Frenchwoman who allowed herself to appear stupid?) with decided views on everything, according to which you are either endorsed as culturally sound or else hurled into outer darkness. I am too much of a practised hypocrite not to have lied occasionally to R– in order to save my skin, but my suspicion that she knows this anyway lends a certain spice to our relationship.

Together we amble pleasantly among the churches to the north of Saint Mark's, as she chucks about the superlatives and pejoratives. San Giovanni in Bragora gets a gold star, and its beautiful Cima da Conegliano of the Baptism of Christ renders her ecstatic as, predictably, does the great Carpaccio sequence adorning the lower hall of the Scuola di San Giorgio. The little church of San Martino, however, close by the Arsenal, she finds utterly '*affreuse*' and professes herself unable to comprehend why I am so fond of it, let alone why I should also like the admittedly rather gloomy San Francesco della Vigna, where she is unmoved by Antonio da Negroponte's Virgin Enthroned, and starts ominously complaining, though it is an extremely hot day, that the church will give her a *grippe*.

The genuine bone of contention arrives somewhat later, when we have worked our way back towards the Piazza and fetch up

* Central heating boiler
† Register of births, marriages and deaths
‡ Gymnasium
§ Having a hundred columns

outside Santa Maria del Giglio, one of those Venetian churches I am ready to defend to the last ditch against all the Gallic intellectual scorn in the world. Whether the heat has made her vapourish, or because it is time for lunch, or because that element of décor on which she has harped all morning as one of the essentials of the Venetian experience is somehow lacking here, R— pitches in good and proper. She is utterly scathing about the high altar, which features a marble tableau of the Annunciation, Gabriel on one side, Mary on the other, by a seventeenth-century German sculptor named Heinrich Meyring, and thinks the exquisite small Stations of the Cross, the work of various eighteenth-century artists, merely silly. Nobody ever believed the Rubens in the sacristy was genuine, but the notion that she is looking at a fake Rubens is the ultimate affront to R—'s intelligence. On either side of the picture are glass cases containing a gallimaufry of holy relics in silver-mounted monstrances, various bits of arm, shank, knuckle and cranium with accompanying labels of authentication: a display not unlike one of those medical museums you find in the older London teaching hospitals. The virulent anticlericalism of those reared in Catholic cultures is always a source of rich amusement to me, and when R— gets going on '*ces horribles bondieuseries*' I realize it is time to leave.

Actually it is the décor in Santa Maria del Giglio, to which these bones are intrinsic, that makes it so attractive, but nothing here quite beats, for me, the church's stupendous northern façade. In a few years from now it will probably all have fallen to pieces, black as it already is with layers of pollution and sprinkled as its various protrusions are with deposits of pigeon guano like icing sugar dredged over a pudding. The Venice in Peril Fund is unlikely to have put it high on the list of priorities for artistic salvaging, possibly, I suspect, because the aesthetic of this admirable enterprise is too distinctively Ruskinian.

Hats off to Ruskin, but let's not be entirely uncritical: in certain respects his influence on the way we look at art has been disastrously limiting. There was a time, only a few years ago, when if you showed any sign of taking baroque and rococo art seriously, people thought your name was Sitwell and started giving you what used to be called 'old-fashioned looks'. At least one popular and much-commended guidebook to Venice airily assures its readers that the only names they need bother about when exploring the city are Ruskin and Canaletto, and to hell, by implication, with the rest. So the heretical traveller has rather an uphill job of it at Saint Mary of the Lily (also called Santa Maria Zobenigo after an extinct patrician family), given that Canaletto never painted the church and Ruskin abominated its façade.

His maidenly horror was inspired by what is effectively a morsel of baroque theatre, devised, to designs by Giuseppe Sardi, as a colossal snook cocked by members of the Barbaro family at the Morosini, whose distinguished scion Francesco the Peloponnesiac had dismissed Antonio Barbaro from his staff during the Cretan campaign against the Turks, and whose palace stands not far away. There they all strut like figures in a masque, the senators and procurators and admirals and proveditors, robed and wigged, their gestures frozen in perpetual terpsichorean elegance, as if the ritornelli of their arias had just begun and they were ready to launch into death-defying acrobatic melismas, while underneath runs a frieze of little relief maps showing the fortresses they defended – or not, as the case might be – Zara, Corfu, Split.

The effect of all this on R– is devastating. Apparently unaware of any inconsistency with her earlier position, she is shocked by what she deems the irreligiousness of the whole wondrous confection. She finds it, besides, 'tout à fait vulgaire et banale', a monument to the decadence of Venetian sculpture, and is disgusted at my wish to see it all – staring, bleached Istrian marble – once more. As if my enthusiasm for these birdshit-covered periwigs and grimy attitudinizings were indicative of a tendency she had long ago suspected, she gives a final snort of contempt and we pass towards a stormy luncheon at Bacareto.

I'll say this for her though, she has got modern Venice just about right, and this is what, over a glass of Fernet Branca, finally reconciles us. Fernet is the best of all those alcoholic cough mixtures, known as *amaro*, with which a meal in Italy is so agreeably rounded off. Averna, with its dark Sicilian asperity of flavouring, will do, and Petrus is not too sweet to be intolerable, but Fernet, which is reputed to contain laudanum and looks like a solution of Indian ink and motorcycle grease, sets you up a treat, makes you feel a real cracker, especially with a little espresso as a chaser.

R–, emboldened by her *amaro*, gets tough with Venice. She says the end must come soon, not in the form of floods or the pollution which chokes the lagoon with algae and breeds swarms of *chironomidi*, harmless little midges which do nothing but feed and fornicate, but as the result of short-term greed which aims at turning the city into a bijou theme-park, with fast food restaurants, enclaves for the rich among the choicest bits of the Dorsoduro, spaces cleared for pop concerts and trade fairs, and every grocer and baker and chemist transmogrified into shops selling carnival masks in the form of pierrot faces weeping golden tears. I have, alas, to admit that the vision is all too credible. For once, a swig of Fernet does little to cheer me up.

Talking with R– underlines for me the fragility of Venice's existence as a cultural construct. Each nation has made its own Serenissima, like something cut out with scissors and glued together. R–'s French *Venise* is the city of Musset and George Sand notoriously not getting their act together, of Proust and Fauré and Monet. There is a German Venedig, replete with *Sehnsucht*, *Schwärmerei* and *Weltschmerz*; the American Venice of Henry James and William Dean Howells, whose *Venetian Life* is, when all is said and done, the best book written on the city; and – endlessly, like now for example – the Venice of the English, who, taken together in a lump over five centuries, have understood and cherished the place better than anybody else (certainly more than the Italians, very few of whom properly appreciate it) and probably better than it has at times deserved.

Nevertheless, it's a consolation to me to see so few Brits here this year. I'd rather not find them among the vulgar touristical mobility thronging Saint Mark's, about whom I'm a disgraceful snob. Foolish optimism, following the line recommended by

Our Saviour in the parable of the lost sheep, suggests that together with the ninety and nine shambling grossly through the colonnade of the Procuratie Nuove behind a guide waving an umbrella, there may be one redeemable soul whom Venice will clutch to her for life. Well, *magari*, if only, as the Italians say, but I don't believe it. This kind of scepticism is called 'elitist' in England, but the reality which it postulates, a reality shamelessly underpinned by the diseased enterprise culture of modern commercial Venice, is perceptibly poisoning the city.

What, beyond a glass gondola, an ice-cream and a straw hat, do these vast cattle droves of trippers carry away with them? The question is scarcely new. One of the most gifted of nineteenth-century Venetian writers, the novelist and poet Ippolito Nievo,* wrote some witty verses entitled *Il Touriste*, whose translation runs more or less as follows:

> Hotfoot from Marseilles, with guidebook in his pocket, comes the illustrious ultramontane gentleman, and tumbles straight into the Piazzetta. He takes a sniff at Saint Mark's, throws a glance in the direction of the Scala dei Giganti in the Doge's Palace, buys a pair of gloves and then sprawls at a table in Florian's. He strokes his new copy of the *Revue des Deux Mondes*, looks at the newspaper to see how his shares are doing, pays for his cigar and a cup of tea, gets back on board ship and sails away while demolishing a beefsteak. Venice might as well be Mecca, for all he knows or cares.

Plus ça change, as the tourist himself might have said.

*

---

* He was actually born in Padua (in 1831) and related on his mother's side to the Colloredo family, notorious for having produced Mozart's tiresome employer Hieronymus, Archbishop of Salzburg. Nievo's best-known work is *Le Confessioni d'un Italiano*, a large-scale historical novel. He was killed in a shipwreck on his way to join Garibaldi in Sicily, when he was only thirty-one.

I bought the book with Nievo's poem in it from a remainder shop on the Fondamenta della Toleta near the Campo San Barnaba. Italian bookshops are something of a conundrum. In a country where so few people actually read for pleasure and interest, how do so many such establishments survive? Evidently there is no thought, as in Britain or America, of publishing as an exclusively commercial venture, publishing as conceived in the pages of *The Bookseller*, with displays and hype and sales conferences and marketing managers. The fortunate result, for those of us who like reading, is that we can find things in Italy which no Anglophone printing house would dream of putting out, designed, what is more, with an impressive insistence on the chastity of cold print as opposed to ritzy, glitzy dust-wrappers.

The difference between English and Italian publishers is that the former must always proceed from the assumption that the reader is illiterate. In Italy a hundred super-elegant little series (all in soft covers – hardbacks are for downmarket bestsellers) with tiny print-runs offer translations of works which most of us might be happy to discover in the remoter reaches of the London or New York Public Libraries. Where else but here could I have purchased the Augustan Deist philosopher John Toland's *Letters to Serena*, or a version of Achim von Arnim's *Isabella von Ägypten, Kaiser Karls des Fünften ersten Jugendliebe*, or *The Tale of the Seven Princesses* by the mediaeval Azerbaijani poet Nezami of Ganje?

Such is the otherworldly nature of Italian book production and distribution that many of these obscurities and *introuvables* end up in the last places one might expect to discover them, on the newsstands in the streets and railway stations. Thus I was not surprised to find recently, inside the vast booking hall of Santa Maria Novella station at Florence, the newly-issued translation of Milton's *Areopagitica*, lying among the yellowback thrillers and Mills & Boon romances of the *Collezione Armony*, nor should I have been astonished (though indeed I was) at seeing displayed for sale at a Milanese *edicola* a two-volume edition of *De Nugis Curialium*, the most celebrated work of the twelfth-century English Cistercian monk Walter Map.

Yet can you imagine such a thing among us? 'I'll have twenty Benson & Hedges, *Autocar, The Independent* and, oh yes, sorry, the new version of William of Malmesbury that's just come out. Oh, and I see you've got Herder's *Auch ein andere Philosophie des Geschichtes* – great, I'll take that as well. And a packet of Fisherman's Friend, the mint-flavoured ones, while we're at it.' I fancy not, somehow. It is touches like these which at least create the illusion that Italy is a highly civilized country, and while you can sustain the illusion there is no reason to doubt the likelihood of a certain reality.

There is much talk of this at tea time in the flat of some friends who live down a smelly alley in what has to be the most squalid area of Venice bar none: the knot of excessively narrow streets surrounding the Rialto market. Some may find the big postwar tenement houses on the north end of Cannaregio pretty forbidding, and the quarter to the west of San Nicolo dei Mendicoli is as down-at-heel as it always was, but at least the sun shines in these places, there is room for children to play and dogs and cats to roam, and the washing flaps cheerfully in the breezes off the lagoon.

On the Rialto, around the Ruga Vecchia, the former street of the goldsmiths with its jutting penthouses, there is barely a glimmer, and the lanes running down towards the Canal fester with shit and cockroaches. If Venice were altogether less law-abiding, murders might be done here and benighted wanderers waylaid by the modern equivalent of those stiletto-waving bravoes with whom the Romantic imagination peopled the city. As it is, the zone, emptied at nightfall of its traders and their wares, simply fills me with a claustrophobic desperation to get out into the great amphitheatric space surrounding the church of San Polo, or up towards San Cassiano where the light suddenly creeps in again between the houses and the windows brighten with flowerpots once more.

My friends are not especially worried by their Cimmerian existence in a small apartment looking on to a grey courtyard,

above which a patch of sky is dimly visible. I've never successfully discovered on what terms they live in the flat, since there's
always a faint air of here-today-gone-tomorrow about everything
they do. In essence, the place is a sort of post-Sixties hippy
commune where people drop in and out with carefully practised
insouciance. Last night somebody was sleeping underneath the
grand piano jammed awkwardly into one end of the sitting room,
and a pair of blankets and a pillow were scattered at one end of
the corridor. This afternoon four of us are sprawled on the divans
ranged *alla turca* round the walls, and the two women – Oriana,
who like her husband Cesare teaches at Padua, and Tamara, who
is half-Russian and tells fortunes – have scarves wound about
their heads, which completes the odalisque illusion.

Tea has been brewed in their particular fashion, to which I
fancy they adhere only when I am present because they know
it will annoy me. With much ostentation, Oriana throws a
large number of teabags into a saucepan as if they were giant
ravioli, and boils them up together. The resulting black liquid,
unbearably strong even with milk, is decanted into an enormous
breakfast cup bought in the Portobello Road (on whose pavements you will hear Italian spoken every day of the week) and
I am set to drinking it as a kind of performance which they
observe with imperturbable good humour.

They enjoy winding me up about being English, and the
conversation on our infrequent meetings nearly always takes a
little turn along the path marked 'national differences'. Like
most Italians, they think of the English as more than slightly
crackbrained, crippled psychologically by obsessions with class
and social background, tainted by hypocrisy and mean with
money. It is not difficult to agree with this assessment, but
when I add to this my belief that Italians are generally better
behaved than the English, that good nature, generosity and
politeness are instinctive among most of them in ways that
would be impossible among us, there is a general outcry, and
I diplomatically return to sipping my Darjeeling soup.

'*Ma che tipo di cretino sei*, Jonathan?' cries Cesare, shaking
his mop of curls and spreading his hands in amazement. 'This

is a nation in terminal decline, don't you realize? Nothing can save the Italians except what has always saved them, which is a certain genius for survival, like the Jews. Except that, unlike the Jews, we haven't earned the right to survive.'

'Who can talk of a right to survive?' asks Tamara, grandly rhetorical. 'The fact is that we're barbarians. My mother says one day she'll go back to Russia, as long as there's something to eat.'

'That shows she has become a true Italian,' Oriana says, 'because in those words lies the national philosophy, "As long as there's something to eat". They used to have a rhyme where my family come from, "*O Francia, o Spagna, pur che si magna*", France or Spain so long as we can eat, they didn't care about laws or governments or independence. Maybe that's why history in our schools is so boring. God, when I think of it!'

The three of them look at me with expressions of pained sympathy. At first I imagine it is the tea, but then Tamara says patiently, as if talking to an invalid:

'You know, *tesoro*, you really must give up the notion that when you come to Italy, you are coming to some sort of elysian field, in which it is always summer even in winter. This is a terrible place.' She takes my hand across the table. Her voice is tremulous with sincerity, more Russian, I suspect, than Italian.

'"A country that's upset people from the beginning of the world"', I answer, 'as E. M. Forster said. But I know that.'

'And you come to see us because we're terrible,' says Cesare, sardonically twisting his moustache.

'Precisely. You don't think those of us who really care about trying to know what you are, who carry you within us, just come for the bloody art, do you? And even if we didn't care, we still wouldn't cross the Alps only for a fresco or two.'

'Or three, or three thousand,' Cesare laughs. 'God, it's hot today, isn't it? They say fish are dying all over the lagoon because they can't breathe any more.'

He gets up, kicks away his shoes, crosses to the window and pulls down the slatted blind. Then, without more ado, he strips off his shirt and trousers, seats himself at the piano and starts to play. Of course, I've almost forgotten, it is one of his gifts, of which he has so many that he has never bothered to exploit any of them seriously.

'What is this?' Tamara asks.

'Debussy, *Estampes*.' He smiles at me over the music desk. '*Ehi, cretino inglese italofilo*, come and turn pages, *subito!*'

Oriana has taken a jar from a shelf in the kitchen and is studiously rolling a joint. Tamara, flopped back on the divan, has pulled her scarf over her eyes. A delightful atmosphere of companionable indolence, as though we were students again and not superannuated ravers in our forties, has descended upon the room. Cesare, in his underpants, serenely fudges on through 'Jardins sous la pluie'. He has exceptionally beautiful legs, long and elegantly muscled like a dancer's.

'You've got the best legs in the business, Cesare,' I say, whereupon he stops playing, turns round with a radiant grin, and asks: 'Which would you prefer, *piccolo imbecile*, my talent or my legs?'

'No question. Any fool can have talent. In my next life I'll settle for your legs.'

Dinner that night at Da Ignazio, practically never open but a rival to the ever-glorious Montin as one of the few restaurants in Venice where the menu is not either riotously overpriced or else, as more generally happens, insulting in its savourless banality. The waiters at Da Ignazio always seem to have contributed, in some vague fashion, towards the preparation of the food. A large, dewlapped, motherly woman presides like a sibyl over the establishment, and the staff become the hierophants of the kitchen sanctum, whose rites are conducted under her direction. They adumbrate the contents of the various dishes with an air of family pride, so that you are persuaded to take the john dory or the bass, the cuttlefish with polenta, the nettle pie, almost because you feel that to refuse it would be a violation of their hospitality.

Tonight everything is as rewarding as ever, and I set off well recruited for a quiet digestive saunter alone though the silent streets of the Dorsoduro. There are certain pleasures I am grateful for having lived long enough to enjoy, and one of them is that elemental delight of walking in Venice after dark. No theatrical designer created the illumination of the *calli* and *campi*, but stage lighting was seldom more effective than that alternation of muted brilliance, shadow and absolute murk which clothes walls and pavements and slick-surfaced canals. In winter the fogs roll in across the Piazza, bundling in long whorls through the arcades, and now and then there arrives a miraculous fall of snow, having seen which – lodging in the hollows and flutings of statues, windows and columns, feathering the cupolas of churches and powdering the tops of the striped mooring poles on the Canal – you feel you might as well finish with life, since there is surely nothing more beautiful to be seen anywhere else.

Since the air is thick and humid this evening, I shall walk, maybe, to the Ponte della Frescada, between San Tomà and the university, where, according to a Venetian tradition which has some truth in it, you may always, no matter how stifling the atmosphere, catch a wisp or two of a breeze, hence the name, 'the bridge of the freshening'. Then down, perhaps, to San Pantalon, where there's a fountain I like to drink and splash my face at, into Campo Santa Margherita, deliberately losing myself at last in the unpeopled stillness of the streets around the twin-towered church of Angelo Raffaele, where grass grows between the paving stones. If there is a sound of any kind, it is the plop of a rat into a canal or the chirping of a cricket, and at midnight, far off at Saint Mark's, the tolling of La Marangona, the great bell of the campanile, deep, fitful, solitary. Perhaps by then I shall not be alone.

Wandering back towards my hotel, I feel a spot of rain, a little gust of wind, and a flurry of heavier drops. I am in Campo Sant'Angelo, in whose voluminous emptiness, like that of a wilderness to be crossed, there is something almost fearful. I lope towards the newsstand, where the projecting roof offers me shelter, and stand watching the shower turn quickly enough into an apologetic drizzle and inhaling the bilgy smell blown off the nearby canals.

While I'm deciding whether or not to make a run for it, I hear voices through the swirl of rain, and two boys, Venetians by their accent and build, come into the square. Beneath the lamp on the water-dashed wall they pause, and without the least self-consciousness fall into an embrace and kiss each other with lingering ardour. Then the taller of them, in his booming, confident voice, says, 'Tomorrow at six, the door by the grocer's, the top bell. And if you're late I'll kill you, you know?'

They hug once more, swinging each other about and laughing under the rain. The tall boy, after watching his chum into the distance, begins to walk slowly and reflectively towards the newsstand. Catching sight of me lurking under it, he turns and cries, 'What the fuck do you think you're doing standing there? Rain does you good, it washes your face, it brings life. Enjoy it, can't you?' and swaggers off across the glistening pavement into the night.

Things in Venice *da archiviare*, to archive, as the Italians say. Drinking a hot grog at Florian's in winter, with the café windows steaming, and a certain huddled intimacy with those around me, before walking to the Fenice to see – probably the only time I shall ever see it – Verdi's *Stiffelio*, an absolute Cinderella among his operas but one of the most arresting, a steely little nugget of brilliance about a Protestant minister who forgives his wife for her involvement in a love affair. Hearing even the worst performance at the Fenice is still a kind of luxury, given the theatre's singularly successful mixture of handsomeness with cosiness, flattering and coddling you simultaneously, but the Fenice *and* Verdi *and* *Stiffelio* – this is the very knickerbocker-glory of voluptuousness.

Not riding in a gondola. Samuel Pepys, who saw them given

as presents to Charles II by the Venetian ambassador, labelled them 'ridiculous gundilows'. Though I don't share his contempt, I have still, in twenty years of getting to know this city, not embraced the experience by which ultimately we distinguish it from other places. The nearest I ever come to a ridiculous gundilow is taking the *traghetto*, the ferry poled by a pair of oarsmen from one side of the Grand Canal to the other. To be bounced to and fro, for how brief a spell soever, on the backwash of motor-launches or the swell created by a passing *vaporetto* gives you a curious little charge of excitement at having taken part in a rite so ordinarily Venetian as this. Yet what a sin of omission to have to confess!

Three night pieces. The first, at the Rialto, in the small hours of the morning. Nothing moves on the Canal, then through the arch of the bridge comes a small *sandolo*, a twin-oared rowing boat, with a lamp at the prow. In the triangular shadow which, for some reason, the curved semicircle of the bridge throws on to the water, there appears a contrary triangle made out of light, with the oarsman's rhythmic strainings picked out in profile against the blackness of the houses behind. Through pictures of this kind Venice nonchalantly seduces you.

The second, on top of the Accademia Bridge, looking at the moon riding over the dome of the Salute, and a sudden sensation of enormous power communicated to you by the prospect, as though you had climbed here to draw upon this reserve of strength before beginning again, as though the city, whatever the odds, would never allow you to fail.

The last is lying awake in a lover's arms in the darkness behind closed shutters and hearing disembodied voices drift past you outside the window. As if you had whispered to one another, 'Be quiet, they're coming,' and were lying doggo in ambush until they were gone, you feel the embrace tighten around you.

9 A Venetian Episode

I remember reading a French novel, written around the turn of
the century, in which the bedridden narrator spends the entire
book listening through the walls of his cheap apartment to the
conversations between a man and a woman plotting a murder.
The possibilities of such a vicarious existence, in which real life
is reduced to the overheard, never fail to seem enthralling, but
only once has the opportunity to savour the experience seriously
been granted to me.

Whenever I go to Venice I always stay in an hotel. The
notion of friends with smart little flats on the Dorsoduro or

the Giudecca remains one of those fantasies which arrive at moments of nocturnal self-pity when I pass some lighted *piano nobile* on a canal or hear the brittle laughter wafting through half-opened shutters as I maunder down the *calli*. So hotels it is, and none of your Danielis, Bauer-Grunwalds or Gritti Palaces, with their Mister Fixit desk clerks, satin-striped waiters and private gondolas putting off from among the embanked geraniums.

No, these are the unassuming dosses of the poor-but-honest. The beds are invariably hard, the towels are little cotton squares with the rasping hardness of ice-cream wafers, and the soap is always Palmolive. For a solitary Englishman with his shabby green suitcase there is seldom, if ever, a view: shutters rattle open on to the peeling back wall of the next-door house on the other side of the narrowest of *calli*, loud at night with copulating cats. At breakfast, in a dining room which inevitably suggests that something far more exciting once went on there which you just arrived too late to enjoy, there are always the plaster-of-Paris rolls, the tiny rectangles of butter and jam and (if you are me, which of course you aren't) the teabag, its label hanging mournfully out of the steel pot and inscribed 'Thé Liptons'. Printed in capitals, without the acute accent, it looks oddly like the name of some huge suburban house in Tooting or Acton where a murder took place in the 1930s: 'Death At The Liptons' by Dennis Wheatley, 'The Liptons Affair' by Edgar Wallace. One's mind easily toys with such fancies as the breakfast maid trots to and fro with the desiccated croissants.

As for the staff, they are only marginally friendly. Why should they be anything else? We who stay at these hotels are not of the complaining sort, and if we don't like the noise in the corridors or the failure to clear the floor of the sand we brought in yesterday off the Lido or the fact that the maid has barricaded the stairs with dirty laundry, there are a hundred other benighted innocents jostling to take our place. Sometimes the rudeness is spectacular. Once, at a hotel off the Campo Manin, a part of the city I rather like for its frowzy, churchless emptiness, I failed to tip the snuffy old fellow who did duty as hall porter and receptionist – I had only a 50,000 lire note and bugger me if he was getting that – but for the rest of the week I was repaid with churlishness on the majestic scale to which only a nation as courteous as the Italians can rise.

It was a long time before I discovered the real function of the night porter in such establishments. Rollicking home in the small hours, I would adopt my habitual posture of cringing apology as the bolts were shot back and some sleepy fellow in vest and pyjamas offered me the only key left on the rack, accompanied by a yawning '*Buona notte*'. However gamey the savour of that night's adventure, there was always a lingering guilt at being the naughty boy who didn't keep regular hours and go to bed at half-past ten to read up the relevant bits of J.G. Links or Hugh Honour on that morning's trot round San Zanipolo or the Ca D'Oro. Only recently was my obtuseness purged by the realization that night porters are there not so much to let guests in as to stop them flitting with the bill unpaid.

One hotel was notorious for having no night porter, and indeed practically no staff of any description. Guests were issued by the manager with their own latchkeys, while a single silent maid, gaunt and sergeant-majorish behind her mops and brooms, made the beds and swept the floors. For reasons which will become obvious I'm not going to tell you exactly where it is. Apart from anything else I'm not altogether sure if it still exists, but in its wonderfully clever combination of shabby splendour (the first-floor bedrooms were all frescoed in mauve and white with the most charming *capriccio* landscapes in a sort of Biedermeyer style) and unabashed loucheness, it encapsulated something imperishably Venetian.

The patrons were all what is called, less for the sake of euphemism than convenience, 'artistic', of a kind that emphatically doesn't tuck itself up in bed at half-past ten and is correspondingly grateful for the use of a latchkey. Since the hotel offered nothing in the way of breakfast, we used to congregate at the café on the *campo* outside, appropriately named *Bar ai Artisti*, and dawdle over the *brioches* as morning made itself alive. Over various years I recall an exiled Cuban poet, an intense young doctor from Grenoble whom we mischievously nicknamed 'The Profile' and his Greek girlfriend who always wore black; a Norwegian woman called Agi who had abandoned what she contemptuously referred to as 'real life' for cut-price nomadism with an inexhaustible parade of lovers thrown in, and a pair of Brazilian boys with one of whom we idled away a morning discussing his ambition to become a transsexual. None of us was ever Italian: an Italian wouldn't have been seen dead in that hotel.

If anything bound us together more than the fact that we stumbled up the same dark pair of stairs and used the same mephitic bathrooms, it was an intense, knowing affection for Venice. Like children who have evolved a secret language, we swapped enthusiasms, for the mad sacristan at Angelo Raffaele who mutters '*Godi, godi, divertiti, divertiti!*' as you peer up at Guardi's 'Story Of Tobias' on the panels of the organ loft, the smell of incense and flames from ochre-coloured tapers in the Greek church, a plate of *bigoli in salsa*, the house where Cimarosa died, the sound of someone calling 'Beeeepiiiii!' down an empty street, or the metallic chill of water sucked from the tap at a conduit on a hot midnight. Wandering into the remotest reaches of Castello, under the flapping tablecloths, socks and underpants hung from the washing lines like gala decorations, or among the dismal, barrack-like houses beyond San Nicolò dei Mendicoli, you'd find one of us sitting on a step or leaning on a bridge, held in sensory alertness to Venice, thus ordinary, thus palpable, thus dowdy, thus beautiful.

The incident I was going to recount took place during a sultry late August when the nights were so hot that sleep became impossible and the latchkeys worked apace till dawn. Among the artistic clientele at the Pensione S– that year, and in the room next to mine, was a bald, bespectacled Frenchman of a certain age, who kept himself very much to himself. He spent his mornings and afternoons at the beach and went out cruising at night attired as a *matelot*, the complete outfit, white bellbottoms, blue collar, red pompom, Jean Genet crossed with Pierre Loti. Far from its being decorative, there was something woefully ridiculous in such a costume which made the rest of us rather glad of his unclubbableness than otherwise. The crucial mistake made by so many visitors to Venice is to be either conspicuously underclad, like the huge frankfurter-pink German *Burschen* who lurch through the streets wearing only exiguous bathing trunks as if the place were a seaside resort, or to overdress wildly, an excess of décor intended to proclaim good taste but usually looking like fatuous exhibitionism.

Monsieur Lunette (let us call him that, since he sported a pair of them) went to the latter extreme, and in our stand-offish we-got-here-before-you way, we gave a collective shudder whenever we saw him cross the *campo*, a dumpy, myopic Querelle peering anxiously after each strapping Marco or Angelo who passed by. Jean-Luc the Profile voted him, not without a certain self-gratulatory relief, '*un désastre*', while Agi muttered mysteriously 'he looks like the ghost of my second husband.' The Brazilian boys giggled about what they would do if they happened to meet him on the hotel's impenetrably dark, tortuous staircase, but I don't recall the opportunity ever having presented itself.

On the night in question I'd been out to dinner with some friends at a crazy jazz restaurant in Cannaregio, full of alternative, right-on Italians being bravely bohemian. There was a not unpleasant dampness in the evening's warmth, and the notion of simply hopping aboard the *vaporetto*, and pottering up to bed was intolerable. After we'd said our '*ciaos*' and '*buona nottes*' in that infinitely prolonged ritual of leavetaking which operates in Italy, I wandered off alone through the humid darkness, half resolved on a walk to Saint Mark's and a late ice-cream, but then deciding it might be nicer, in my present mood of benign contentment, to cross the Rialto bridge and find some secluded *campiello* to sit in and listen to the water in the canal, the scrapping cats and the oddly comforting sound of some cretinous television game show gurgling out of a first-floor window.

It was half-past midnight when I let myself in at the *pensione*, and I thought it was pretty certain that nobody else was back when I heard voices on the little terrace that opened off the corridor next to the bathroom. Jean-Luc Profile and his girlfriend, the sombre, hollow-eyed Margarita, together with another woman, were talking in quietly measured tones about the recently-published work of a contemporary philosopher. Pointless as it seemed to break in upon them, I stood for a while listening on the darkened landing, until I realized that the discussion would be audible to me from my own room.

In bed I opened my copy of *Peter Wilkins And The Flying Indians*, a faded red Everyman with 'T. Bussell, Angmering, 1946' on the endpaper, and started to read. The gentle French voices in the darkness and the chirping crickets were extraordinarily soothing, but I was still reluctant to switch off the light. Then, as if in answer to my demand for a pretext, there came the noise of somebody coming up the stairs. It could only be Monsieur Lunette, and evidently he was not alone.

There was an unwritten, unspoken rule at the *pensione* that you never brought anyone back for sex. Philosophy in the small hours was all very well, and some of us might now and then slip along the corridors for a little more than Althusser and Derrida, but the comfort of strangers was not what the latchkeys were for. Fancy, as they say, my surprise when I realized that Lunette had fished up not one but a brace of gentlemen callers.

I should explain at this point that the walls were of the very thinnest. The top floor of the little *palazzo* had simply been divided by primitive partitions, and we might have been in Japan for all the privacy they afforded. It was one of the occupational hazards of sleeping in the *soffitto* that you could hear every snore, every grunt, every twanging spring from the next room, so that you soon acquired a mousy discretion in getting in and out of bed or in making sure that your shoes didn't fall with too loud a thud when you took them off.

What now ensued was a demonstration of this principle of audibility to an operatically exaggerated degree. *Peter Wilkins* was consigned to the bedside table, and I sat bolt upright, mesmerized by an episode all the more vividly realized for being invisible. Lunette's two guests were – well, somehow they would be – sailors. More specifically, country boys from a village somewhere down south, doing their military service on the lagoon. They had that thick, slurred meridional speech and that vocal timbre impossible to isolate in words except by saying that it strikes resonances you never hear north of Rome. When they spoke, I could almost smell their singular southern smell – pungent, lingering, never wholly attributable but compounded of artichokes, tomatoes, rancid oil, sweat, tobacco, coffee and cheap soap.

Their voices, as they answered their host's questions, were full of a comradely innocence. It was clear that with a creditable yet wholly professional solicitude he was putting them at their ease before getting down to business. Did they miss their families? Yes, they did, but look, there were lots of southerners, really good kids, up here, so it didn't matter much. Had they ever been to France? No, they'd never been to France, it was too expensive, but one of them had an uncle who worked in a bar in Lille, so maybe one day. . . . Were they always together? Always, Mimmo and Ciccio, since the *prima media*, before that even, ask anyone back home.

This last detail obviously appealed to Lunette. There was a perceptible thickening in the intensity of the atmosphere, registered by the silence that followed. One of them offered a cigarette. 'Yes,' said Lunette, 'let's relax a bit,' and together they started to undress.

I have to admit that at this point I felt slightly annoyed. It is presumably a not unusual experience for concealed listeners or watchers to want to intervene so as to direct the occasion theatrically to make it go as they wish. Thus it seemed quite out of character that these two peasant lads from the Abruzzi, reared to due proletarian modesty, should suddenly choose to strip, however sultry the evening. A quick embarrassed jerk-off and goodnight would have been the appropriate scenario. But of course it wasn't like that at all. There was the noise of belt-buckles undoing, the thump-thump of shoes, the clumsy shucking-off of trousers and vests and then an eternity of silence, in which, above the occasional soft indrawing and expulsion of breath, I could hear a subdued *ostinato* of French conversation from the terrace – 'c'est la vérité elle-même qui fait la démarche', 'on demande pourquoi un tel système exige . . .', 'c'est à dire . . .' – the metallic scratching of the crickets and now and then a plash of water in the canal beneath.

Transmitted thus, the noises in the next room assumed a strange hieratic eloquence, like the sounds made by hidden worshippers. In my prurient curiosity I felt like Clodius spying on the rites of the Bona Dea or the ridiculous poet blundering in upon the celebrants in the *Thesmophoriazusae* of Aristophanes. A gentle yet insistent chorus of alternating gasps and moans signalled imminent orgasm, breaking at last in what sounded more like surprise than outright excitement as both boys came simultaneously. There was another silence, then a little embarrassed laugh or two.

'God, we've made right pigs of ourselves, haven't we?'

'Yeah, we're a couple of dirty pigs, we are. Aren't you coming too?'

The question had a good-humoured ring to it, as if they were anxious their friend shouldn't miss out on the fun.

'Er, no,' answered Lunette softly, 'no, I can't. Not just now.'

'Never mind. Maybe later.'

I heard one of them sit down on the bed and light a cigarette. 'Well,' he said, 'that was my first time with a man, I don't mind admitting it. With a woman it's different.'

'Was it your first time too?' Lunette asked the other boy. It was exactly what I would have asked, though there was something positively anthropological in its detached tone, as if Mimmo or Ciccio, whichever, were merely a unit in a field study, to be written up in a notebook afterwards.

'Yes . . . I mean no, not really.'

The ensuing pause was made significant when his friend, sounding suddenly very hurt and angry, exclaimed: 'What do you mean, not really? Have you done it before?'

Another pause.

'Yes. Once or twice.'

'Shit, you never told me!'

The charm of the moment (and in garrulous Italy the talk which follows sex is worth everything else for pleasure) evaporated under a shadow of guilt and betrayal. I imagined that inseparable comradeship as it might now fragment, Mimmo's mother, with grey bun and black shawl, saying anxiously that he didn't see much of Ciccio these days, they used to be such friends, the frosty salutation in the bar at evening as the old men in hats silently downed their drinks, and the perpetual twinge of ambiguous pain caused by a single revelation.

Without saying anything, the three got dressed. While they rustled and scraped into their clothes, I caught again snatches of the terrace symposium, which had now turned into a discussion of the affinity between the concept of beauty and the idea of mortality. 'En effet nous nous trouvons dans le pays du néo-platonisme', 'la beauté va toujours à la recherche de la mort', 'oui, elle veut mourir'. It was two o'clock and they had been at it since before midnight. There something comfortable in this relentless looping and unwinding of articulated ideas, highflown Gallic poppycock though most of them were, a conceptual hot-air balloon floating serenely over a terrain of bruised illusions and shattered friendship. I longed suddenly not to have heard anything through the bedroom wall.

'Well, we'd better be off then,' one of the lads was saying.

'I'll come a bit of the way with you,' said Lunette.

'There's no need.'

'It isn't any trouble, really.' His tone was pleading, submissive. For a moment nobody moved or spoke. Then he said: 'Can I see you again? Perhaps a drink or something?'

There was an embarrassed cough. 'Yeah, well . . . like, well, it's a bit difficult. We don't get much free time. And then there's . . . well, you know.'

'But don't worry, if we see you in the street and we're with our mates, we'll still say hello. It's not as if we wouldn't. Don't want to be rude or anything, but . . . like I say, it's difficult. You being . . .'

The implications of this were all the more devastating for

their ingenuous charm and sincerity. Lunette said nothing in response, and the three of them went tumbling downstairs again. It occurred to me afterwards, in a moment of cynical reflection on the episode, that at no stage had there been any suggestion of money changing hands or of the boys intending to roll their trick.

My sleeplessness had passed into that sinister phase of bogus vitality which precedes total exhaustion. *Peter Wilkins* was worse than useless under the circumstances. I lay there staring at the gap in the shutters as the mosquitoes gathered on the ceiling to descend as soon as the light was switched off. What consumed me, I realized, was a dubious mixture of amusement and envy with a sense of the occasion's emotional nuances, heightened, as I felt, by my having been an auditor rather than a spectator. The French had by now suspended their *causerie* and sloped off to bed. A real loneliness of the hard hours was starting to grip when I heard Lunette rattle his key in the lock and let himself back into his room.

He gave a little sigh as he got undressed, and said very distinctly, as if he knew somebody could hear: 'Oui, c'est ça. Vraiment c'est ça'. Then, with great energy and despatch, he brought himself off, and lay there a while groaning softly. And after that he burst into tears.

The sound of him weeping softly into his pillow made me feel gross and stupid. I wanted to tell him it didn't matter, they were only ignorant clodhopping boys who couldn't have known they were wounding his dignity, that it was just a night's entertainment of the sort Venice throws up everywhere, and that next morning he'd savour the anecdotal possibilities of the experience. Only that wasn't the point. These muffled sobs were perhaps the witness of a bleak interval of self-acknowledgment, when, amid all his dwindling resources of vanity, he knew momentarily what he was. Tomorrow night he'd be bravely out again, bumfreezer, flyflap and all, desperately getting the show on the road. For now he weltered in the gloom of his apparent failure.

I didn't say anything to the others when we met at the bar in the morning, because there was no way in which my relationship with them enabled me to address the subject seriously. As for Lunette, whom we watched scuttling down the lane towards the *vaporetto*, I suppose I might have wanted to be a little more friendly when we passed each other on the stairs, but I never bothered.

10 Dancing the Bergamask

Sitting in the café at Bergamo, I began to develop my Shakespeare theory. Everyone has their mad idea about Shakespeare, but some are a mite less crazy than others. Scholars act in the capacity of mental nurses, straitjacketing the fractious, taking the whip to one or two, and applying more emollient restraints to the rest. Not, of course, that it does the slightest good. Shakespeare, if the lunatic theorists are to be credited, was a lawyer with an expert knowledge of medicine, botany and entomology, who went to sea, served for a time in the army, was sent on diplomatic missions and trained for the priesthood.

A life, as Lady Bracknell says, crowded with incident, to which I may as well add that at some stage as a young man he travelled extensively in northern Italy.

The notion is scarcely original. People have been arguing the toss over it since the middle of the nineteenth century, though unfortunately the adverse party currently has the upper hand, and the Italian plays are made out to be a tissue of ludicrous inaccuracies on the part of someone who had probably never got farther than those cliffs of Dover halfway down which Edgar pretended to see 'one that gathers samphire, dreadful trade'.

According to this Shakespearean orthodoxy, the dramatist, when not imagining that it was possible to get from Verona to Milan by water, or that Venetians had names like Salerio and Solanio (not to speak of Salarino, who turns up in some editions of *The Merchant of Venice*), got his Italy all from books and, because he happened to be William Shakespeare, made a fuller use of his material than even Ben Jonson in *Volpone* or John Webster in *The Duchess of Malfi*, both of them highly convincing essays in what might be called armchair Italian tourism.

I'm not convinced by this and never will be. The enchantment of *Twelfth Night* – 'enchantment' is clichéd as stale cakes, but no other word will do – derives precisely from its fusion of two worlds, the country house Elizabethan of box trees and cakes-and-ale, beating Puritans and baiting bears, and the Adriatic of *La Bella Dominante*, with grappling pirates off 'Candy' and sightseeing from The Elephant and salt waves casting venturesome girls on to the Illyrian shore. He knew, believe me, the Mediterranean. Nobody who reads *Pericles* or *Antony and Cleopatra* or that uncannily meridional play *The Comedy of Errors*, let alone *The Tempest*, can possibly doubt it. The sound of its waters and the thrilling incalculableness of its port cities are there in the poetry and the stories. So too, it may be, is a knowledge that he would probably never see such places again.

As for Italy itself, there is something just a shade too coincidental in the fact that all Shakespeare's Italian plays are set in the same carefully demarcated area, stretching from Milan to Venice, bounded on the south by Mantua and on the north by Bergamo. Why no Naples, no Florence, no papal Rome? All of them offered colourful enough backgrounds to other dramatists. How is it that Portia in *The Merchant of Venice* is a Titian-haired blonde marooned in a villa on the *terra ferma* or that the quintessential *contadino* Old Gobbo (his name, meaning 'hunchback', was popularly used to refer to a statue on the Rialto) brings to Bassanio the traditional gift of a basket of pigeons? Whatever their Elizabethan Englishness, are not the Nurse and Friar Laurence and the Capulets in *Romeo and Juliet* still unmistakably Italian?

In at least one play, *The Taming of the Shrew*, Shakespeare actually made his source, an anonymous comedy called 'The Taming of a Shrew', more rather than less Italian in transmogrifying it. For me at any rate the whole work has the smell of late Renaissance Italy upon it like no other English work of the period. Of course he *might* have mugged it up, he *might* have got his details from expatriate Italian friends, he just *might* have read so many neo-Terentian, post-Ariostine comedies in the original that the atmosphere rubbed off on him like a second skin. Nah, I don't buy that. These people – Tranio, Hortensio, Vincentio, Lucentio, Bianca – were all painted by Moretto and Savoldo and Paris Bordone, they sang the madrigals of Luzzaschi and Marenzio and had Bembo's sonnets by heart. Their very names belong to that north-Italian merchant world of slashed black velvet doublets and pearl-embroidered stomachers, of Paduan university students and cunning lutenists and nonchalant allusion to the classics. Biondello, the pert serving lad who 'knew a wench married in an afternoon as she went to the garden for parsley to stuff a rabbit', is 'the little blond' one of those fair-haired Veneto boys hanging about on the edge of some great biblical wedding or supper of Veronese's. To Baptista, the harassed father of Kate the Shrew, Shakespeare gave the surname Minola, which you will find in the Padua telephone directory. Why bother with an authenticity like that unless you actually know the place itself?

Bergamo made me think of all this because it picks up two sidelong mentions from Shakespeare. In *The Taming of the Shrew*, Vincentio, exposing Tranio for the servant he really is, tells us that 'his father was a sailmaker in Bergamo', something scholarly orthodoxy always drags in as proof that the Bard didn't know his *culo* from his *gomito* where Italy was concerned, since Bergamo is not on the sea. Nothing suggests he ever thought it was: canvas was made in Bergamo and sent to Venice for the great galleys of the Republic, another little local touch which, at the risk of sounding like a certain self-styled 'expert', settles the argument conclusively in favour of my theory.

Well maybe it doesn't, but I like to think that Shakespeare knew Bergamo and had seen the peasants of its hilly, rocky *contado* dancing the rustic dance known as the *bergamasco*, that 'bergamask' with which Bottom and his rude mechanical mates wind up the play of 'Pyramus and Thisbe' in *A Midsummer Night's Dream*. After all, Shakespeare is the only Elizabethan writer to mention it, which again rather goes to show . . .

The sophisticates of Venice, Verona and Padua thought the bergamask a wonderfully comic example of the irrepressible, rough-hewn individuality of these north Lombard mountaineers, and laughed at them as freely as Londoners laughed at the Sawney Scots who came south with King Jamie. *Bergamaschi* were the porters and handymen of Venetian noble households and turn up in the plays of the period, speaking their astonishingly mangled and lopped dialect, which looks odd enough even on the page. In the anonymous comedy *La Venexiana*, for instance, written around 1550, the story of a young traveller locked in an amorous triangle with a widow and a married woman, the only other male character is the old Bergamasc serving man Bernardus, whose speeches go like this: 'A' no so do' vegni mi. Basta mo, ch'a so' tornat alò per quel cant.'

'I don't know where I'm coming from. It's enough that I've returned because of that song.'

'Olà a bass, che diavol spetef? Non m'hef sentut zufolà plú de ses fiadi?'

'Hola, down there, what the devil are you waiting for? Haven't you heard me whistle six times?'

Even today the *bergamaschi* are notorious, once launched into their patois, for being utterly incomprehensible to the rest of Italy. You feel, in any case, that they are a different race, among the Lombards but not of them, mountain Celts who called their city 'bergheim', 'the hill town', and still speak of that mysterious quality known as 'bergheimidad' which has set them everlastingly apart. For this uncompromising singularity they intrigue me, and everyone from Bergamo I have ever met has been memorably attractive in their fearless strength and directness of personality. If I chose to return to earth as an Italian, it would be either as a Bolognese or a Bergamasc, and I fancy in the end the Bergamasc would win.

You'd have something to be tenaciously proud of in your town. The place is a sort of urban overstatement, a double helping, a civic supererogation in which, at the first encounter, you cannot quite believe. Maybe, having come up across the plain from Brescia or Cremona, you expected it was going to be just such another grand city as those, with a Romanesque cathedral, a street or two of noble palaces and a liberal use of white marble on the churches. There would likely be a gallery with three or four masterpieces among a discreet throng of local daubers, and an old theatre with much velvet and gilt, swirling deities across the auditorium ceiling and a painted drop curtain 'by the esteemed nineteenth-century master' showing 'Frederick Barbarossa receiving the defiant answer of the Lombard League'. Whatever you were prepared for, it certainly wasn't this.

For a start there are two towns of Bergamo instead of the customary one, and each is so different from the other that it is difficult at first to establish any sort of connection between them. Bergamo Bassa, the lower of the two, looks and feels like somewhere in Middle Europe, with sedately smart cafés along tree-lined, wide-pavemented boulevards and a score of those austerely grandiose municipal buildings with which the Italy of the Risorgimento and the Savoy Monarchy self-consciously sought to raise the tone of provincial capitals. The opera house is here, and the museum and the prefecture, and the neo-classical town hall in ochre stucco which used to belong to a Swiss merchant family, and the colonnaded propylaea of the Porta Nuova which once housed the Austrian customs offices, and the surprisingly harmonious and restrained fascist clock tower, while up and down the avenues laid out in the 1920s by Marcello Piacentini and Luigi Angelini, *Bergamo bene*, not to speak, now and then, of *Bergamo poco bene* of which there is some, swans and pomps it under the suffocating sweetness of the lime trees.

This would be enough, you might think, what with a scatter of Renaissance churches and a whole street, Via Pignolo, made up of palaces built in the early sixteenth century for the town's rich cloth merchants. In essence, Bergamo Bassa is perfect north Italy, the small, accessible metropolis, with enough air to breathe and a sufficient veneer of worldliness, in which you might live without annoyance.

What you have not reckoned with, however, is the settlement piled, more than a trifle haphazardly, within its wildly zigzagging ramparts and bastions on top of the hill. The Lion of Saint Mark, clutching his open book with 'Pax tibi Marce Evangelista' over the main gateway, proclaims the presence of the Venetians, who took Bergamo from the Visconti in 1428 and kept it with the help of the great *condottiero* Bartolomeo Colleoni, whose statue by Verrocchio stands outside the church of San Giovanni e Paolo in Venice (the canting heraldry of his coat of arms features what look at first like figs but are in fact testicles – rampant? passant? regardant? – *coglioni* for Colleoni).

It is this commanding position on the hilltop which gives Bergamo Alta its enormously strong profile, like one of those unforgettably craggy, deeply-lined, heavy-boned faces whose big noses and jutting chins are as powerful as the fierce, lambent gaze within the eyes. Bergamo isn't a hill town like Assisi or San Gimignano or Asolo, or any of the myriad other examples by which we remember Italy because their very essence characterizes the landscape of recollection. Places like those are beautiful because of the way in which they seem to grow from their hillsides like the olive groves or the avenues of cypress along the zigzagging roads winding up towards their ramparts. Bergamo is magnificent for precisely the opposite reason, that it integrates with nothing in the ragged, shaggy outcrops which herald the mountains of the Brembana and the Orobian Alps. There's a blatancy, almost an arrogance in its arresting stance against the skyline, with its cock'scomb of towers and cupolas which entranced the makers of the old topographical engravings of the city, who contrived to make it look far more majestic than it actually was, as if in deference to its indwelling, unconfounded spirit.

There's a Duomo – of course, what did you expect? – but since this is Bergamo, you should not be surprised to find that it is part of what in the Far East the guidebooks call a temple complex, with a memorial chapel to one side of it and a Romanesque basilica beyond, either of which might be mistaken for the cathedral proper. Originally designed by the Florentine humanist Filarete in 1459, the Duomo was remodelled two centuries later by Carlo Fontana, an architect from Mendrisio on Lake Como, who worked principally in Rome. On to the front a local talent named Angelo Bonicelli stuck a grandiose but by no means unpleasing triple portico, with little domes and allegorical statuary. The date is 1886, yet the illusion of late baroque, with balustrades and a fall of gently curving steps, is flawless.

More absorbing by far than the cathedral is the basilica of Santa Maria Maggiore, begun in 1157, whose south porch is wonderfully deceptive, since it looks Romanesque – spindly Corinthian capitals on the backs of roaring lions in white marble, and alternating bands of green and white above the arch – but was actually finished off in the late Middle Ages, a proof that mediaeval architects' aesthetic sympathy easily overcame their subservience to changing styles. Inside, everything is so immoderately handsome that the cumulative effect is of some palace presence chamber in which courtiers are getting ready to doff their bonnets and duck low on the imminent arrival of majesty. The walls of the nave and the choir aisles, of the choir

lofts themselves, are hung with extravagantly billowing tapestries from the workshops of late sixteenth-century Flanders and
Tuscany, nine of them on the Life of the Virgin by the Florentine
painter Alessandro Allori, but most of the rest distinctly secular
in theme, with the Triumphs of the Emperor Vespasian, a deer
hunt and a Flemish landscape among them.

Odder still than these great arras hangings are Gianfrancesco
Capoferri's choir stalls of 1525, featuring a sequence of inlaid
wooden panels created from cartoons by Lorenzo Lotto. The
painter had spent nearly thirteen years in Bergamo before returning to his native Venice, painting, among other things, the set
of lively little frescoes on the life of Saint Barbara which adorn
the oratory of the Suardi family at Trescore Balneario, east of
the city, and invite us to respond to the story as if it were some
folk legend which Lotto could scarcely resist telling.

From Venice he sent his meticulously detailed designs to
Capoferri with instructions that the craftsmen were to follow
them to the last stroke. He was not concerned with payment, he
said, but his drawings were to be returned without fail. Lotto's
anxiety was understandable, since the whole scheme embodies
that obsession with the language of emblem and allegory which
is so typical of the early sixteenth century, mad as the age was
for shows and pageants and the world of personified abstracts.
None of Lotto's meanings is directly comprehensible, but even
as riddles these images hold a hauntingly surreal fascination.

Look, for instance, at the so-called *Crossing of the Red Sea*.
Any other painter of the period would have summoned up
Pharaoh's horsemen and chariots and the waves parting to let
the fleeting Israelites across with their pillars of fire and cloud
that so bemused the wretched Egyptians. What does Lotto give
us? A mysterious swag from which hang a mask, a feathered
helmet, a pair of eyes and a cardinal's hat, framing a nude male
in a swirling cloak, his head inside a birdcage, carrying a pair of
compasses and a looking-glass and riding on a strange creature
which might be a donkey if it were not so like a rabbit, from
the end of whose tail issue smoke and flames. And you thought
only Bosch and Breughel did this sort of thing? Lotto got his

cartoons back and took them with him to Ancona whence, having failed to sell them in an auction of his works, he carried them off to Loreto, where he died in 1557, a poor, worn-out, but still unquenchably original artist.* The cartoons have gone missing, for ever it seems.

Next to Santa Maria Maggiore is the super-ornate Cappella Colleoni, built as a memorial chapel to Bartolomeo Colleoni in 1472 to designs by Giovanni Antonio Amadeo. To get it made according to his wishes, Colleoni characteristically ordered the destruction of the old sacristy of the basilica. I can't help wondering whether it would not have been better if he had been killed in battle, this dour, dull war-machine, before a stone of the sacristy was harmed. As it was, he died in his bed, praised for his piety and benevolence, at the splendid castle of Malpaga, to the south of Bergamo, which he purchased and rebuilt as a home for his honourable retirement.

People rave about the Cappella Colleoni because, I suppose, it is remarkable within the context of that fifteenth-century Lombard architecture which fuses gothic trefoils, ogees and crockets together with Renaissance pilasters, niches, pediments and medallions. Actually it is rather disgusting, a tasteless clutter of bits by an architect who, in terms of what was on offer, clearly resolved on having his cake and eating it. So there is a perfect encrustation of little plaques and garlands, bijou mini-busts, pizza-shaped marble roundels, ghastly little ridges of diamond-patterned relief, lines of fussy balustrading surmounted by mullioned gothic windows, a row of fancy merlons, a set of niches like decorative knuckle-marks round a piecrust, and goodness knows what fripperies in the spaces that are left.

Military men are seldom noted for their taste (unless you count Charles V, Napoleon and Wellington, who was a baffled violinist and fond of Correggio), and the atmosphere at Malpaga was probably a bit like that of some retired colonel's draughty villa

---

* Berenson calls his *Presentation in the Temple* at Loreto 'the most modern painting by an old Italian master', comparing it with Manet and Degas.

at Camberley or Cheltenham. Colleoni's tomb, which Amadeo decorated with bas-reliefs, is topped by a small gilt statue of him by a German called Master Sixtus of Nuremberg, silly enough to make you long to hear the sound of Verrocchio's great warhorse coming clopping across the piazza and into the church, its sides streaked with sweat after the ride from Venice, and on its back the frowning, helmeted *condottiero*.

Some felicitous meddling with the interior of the chapel took place during the eighteenth century, resulting in a potent disharmony enduring to our own day. In England some imbecile Victorian, his head full of 'the last enchantments of the Middle Age', would have stripped out these rococo embellishments in the interests of taste and integrity. Sometimes this has happened in Italy as well, but since looking at handsome things is more important to Italians than factitious considerations of authenticity and what goes where, they generally know when to let matters alone.

So it is a more than agreeable surprise to find, in the gilded stucco of the vault spandrels and framed along the walls, a whole series of richly-toned panels by some of the most agile hands in eighteenth-century art. Angelica Kauffmann is here with a Holy Family, and Giuseppe Maria Crespi with Joshua Halting the Sun, and Giovanni Battista Pittoni with a chubby David kneeling exultantly on an enormous blue Goliath. Best of all is a sequence of early Tiepolo, painted in 1733, Charity in a pink robe upon sunlit clouds, the Beheading – or as Italian has it, the Decollation – of Saint John the Baptist, where a harridan Herodias waits to give the blood-boltered head on a silver charger to Salome, whose spaniel is worrying her brocade skirts, and a Flaying of Saint Bartholomew, in which the old apostle is lying lashed to a tree in a typical Tiepolo landscape, surrounded by a malign crew of louche-looking bravoes, one of them paring away at his skin with a knife, others pausing for a chat.

You would know they were Tiepolo's people by their very odd and wholly unmistakable eyes, which seem never to be looking at anything the rest of us might see in the picture.

These are the eyes of no recognizable sector of the human race, though there is often a weirdly mongoloid touch to their deeply incised slits, a trick of style even more marked in the work of his son Giandomenico, which makes you wonder whether Tiepolo himself had some kind of Oriental ancestry.

Behind the basilica, silent, brick-paved streets are stacked with the grandest palaces in Bergamo, including one tremendous essay in a sort of proto-Palladian idiom by a native architect, Pietro Isabello, whose work seems to have been confined almost exclusively to his own city. Built in 1520, its grey marble façade adorned with three tiers of pilasters framing pairs of round-arched doors and windows, it was built for the archpriest of the cathedral, but in these altered times, when priests or archpriests are not especially anxious to be found living in splendour in Renaissance palaces, they have turned it over to the Diocesan Museum – which, in the grand old tradition of such establishments, is permanently closed.

The Palazzo Scotti next door is a smart seventeenth-century affair, with one of those swooningly graceful wrought-iron balconies curving over a stone scallop above the gateway. Stuck thus elegantly on to Italian palaces of this sort, these always remind me of the little turreted headdresses worn by court ladies of the period and known as *fontanges* after one of Louis XIV's mistresses, the Marquise de Fontanges. In this soberly beautiful palace, at five o'clock in the afternoon of 8 April, 1848, died the composer Gaetano Donizetti.

Since he is one of those masters – like Handel, Purcell, Berlioz, Verdi, Schumann and Marc Antoine Charpentier – whose music offers me a reason for existing, I can never read of the circumstances surrounding his final illness and death without feeling close to tears. For if ever an artist should have died happy, it was surely Donizetti. Among the larger talents of nineteenth-century Italian opera, he is the only one I should have wanted as a dinner companion. Rossini would have been too fussy about the food; Verdi, cross old curmudgeon, having refused to talk about music, would probably have kept silent throughout the meal; Bellini, that slithering asp, that slimy toad, that cold-blooded worm, would slag me off to the other guests as soon as I left the room.

Donizetti, on the other hand, would make sure I was comfortable and had all I needed, would laugh and joke with me, would want to feel that I was enjoying myself. Through the music of his operas sounds the voice of a good man. There are sixty-five of them, counting the little one-acters, a fact for which he has been ridiculously censured by those who decree that a composer ought to spend ten years agonizing over every bar of an opera before committing the work to paper. Donizetti could no more have prevented himself from writing sixty-five operas than he could have stopped breathing.

On the 'life writes lousy scripts' principle, his reward for augmenting the sum of human happiness was one of the most tragic of all those miserable endings with which his century so cynically extinguished the fires of art. At some time before his marriage in 1828, Donizetti had contracted syphilis, whose fatal tertiary phase was not to manifest itself for another fifteen years. During that time, shattered though his personal life was by the death of his wife Virginia in childbirth, he became the most popular operatic master of his generation, his success crowned by an appointment to the imperial court of Venni as Hofkapellmeister and by acceptance on the Parisian stage to which every composer of the period aspired.

During rehearsals for the epic five-act *Dom Sébastien* at the Opera in 1843, Donizetti started to show alarming signs of mental and physical breakdown, bursting into ungovernal rages, losing his memory and oscillating violently between excitement and gloom. His friends and family watched in horror as his hold weakened on even the simplest kind of articulate expression and the various letters he wrote degenerated into hopeless incoherence, '*Pazienza*! The grave! It is finished!' 'Save me . . . save me, for I lose my honour and the carriage. May there be good will. *Le pauvre Donizetti*.'

At length, after nearly a year in a sanatorium for the insane at Ivry outside Paris, the wretched Gaetano was taken home to Bergamo. A daguerrotype made during this time shows him slumped in an armchair, the creator of *Anna Bolena* and *L'elisir d'amore* reduced to a pathetic vegetable, one of the saddest photographic images of an artist ever recorded. For several months during the winter of 1847 he clung to life, while those around him in the Palazzo Scotti tried desperately to locate some remaining flicker of intelligence. They played his music on the piano for hours at a stretch, they chatted to him in *bergamasco*, they even summoned the star tenor Rubini to sing him pieces from *Lucia di Lammermoor*. There was nobody at home. In a last sweating convulsion he died, as the distant rumble of cannon was heard from the plains below, where Austrian and Piedmontese armies slogged it out in the abortive revolutionary conflict of 1848.

Peace to your spirit, my Gaetano! You deserved better than this, God knows. In the palace they keep the buttonbacked armchair in which you sat during those last days, along with your bed and your desk, your little piano and your smart dressing-case with its bottles, combs and hairbrushes. Your portraits did the best they could with that face, whose big nose and chin you caricatured with typical self-deprecating humour, but nothing in them could smooth out the lines of that choppy, rawboned Bergamasc phiz, whose owner was the son of a poor doorkeeper in the town pawnshop.

The palace where all these relics are preserved is now a conservatoire of music, and the old convent opposite has been turned over to practice-rooms where from the street you can hear the students thrashing away at the piano, blasting off on horns and trombones and scraping the plaster off the walls with passagework exercises on the violin. There is something exhilarating about the resultant cacophony to anyone who loves music, and the listener may amuse himself by trying to pick out the familiar melodic strands thus bundled together. Among these invisible soloists there may be no geniuses, their technique may be execrable, their future – even as indifferent orchestral players in some tenth-rate opera festival – may be doubtful indeed, but in Italy it is remarkable to find anything like this going on at all.

A lot of nonsense is talked and believed about Italian musical life. It is supposed that the nation which brought us Palestrina and Vivaldi, Verdi and Monteverdi, which articulated the technical language of music, which devised and evolved the traditional forms – sonata, symphony, concerto, opera, oratorio, cantata – in which we still cast our musical inspirations, must somehow be alive with orchestras, chamber ensembles, choirs and concerts. A great many Italians themselves imagine this to be the case, so too, even more strangely, do several of the expatriates living in Italy.

The sad fact is that this land is a musical wilderness, in which the occasional arrival of a concert or opera season is like the apparition of an oasis to a thirsty traveller. In a country which mushrooms with music schools (every small town must now have its *conservatorio*) there is not a single world-class orchestra. The one Italian string quartet anybody remembers, the Quartetto Italiano, also happened to be the finest in the world, and we still prize its recordings beyond any other, but this has found no adequate successors. There is no tradition whatever of choral singing. Cathedral music in Italy is so excruciatingly bad, with droning chants, toneless organs and no conception, as in Anglican churches, of a properly directed musical service as a valid and dignified medium of divine worship, that one had rather the entire liturgy were said instead of sung.

There are three obvious reasons for the apparently irredeemable state of musical life in contemporary Italy. One of these, and perhaps the most obvious, is the total enslavement of the nation by the lyric stage during the eighteenth and nineteenth centuries. Opera was what everybody wanted and got, and the creative energies of most composers, competent or otherwise, were dedicated to providing operatic entertainment for the stage, the church and the salon. Up and down the provinces of northern Italy every pelting one-horse township has its Teatro Sociale or Teatro Comunale or Teatro named-after-long-forgotten-minor-early-nineteenth-century-operatic-master, often in a dreadful condition of disrepair, but still recognizably the white, gold and plush horseshoe of boxes, pit and pillared gallery, where once the notables and commonalty of the little place crowded together in winter to keep themselves warm and listen to the warbling diva and *primo uomo* and *basso cantante* of some travelling company going through their paces in one of those innumerable operas whose titles are Whatyoumaycallem di Thingummybob (Donizetti himself wrote twenty-four such pieces, including of course *Lucia di Lammermoor* and the one which every English opera queen likes to snigger at, *Emilia di Liverpool**).

As soon as I catch sight of one of these theatres, even if its blistered old doors are firmly locked and the glass in its rusty lamps is broken, I feel a certain lifting of the spirits, if only because it denotes a dimension of life neither commercial nor religious but devoted entirely to the pleasures of the senses and the imagination. Yet it also reminds me that between 1750 and 1900 there was no serious attempt to continue or to renew the great traditions of Italian instrumental music which had produced the concertos of Vivaldi and Corelli, the violin sonatas of Tartini and Veracini or the keyboard compositions of Frescobaldi, Pasquini and Scarlatti. The voice dominated all, and instrumental agility was by the way.

Such exceptions as there might have been – Niccolo Paganini is an obvious example – were all virtuoso soloists, and this fatal obsession with dazzling technical brilliance has knocked another nail into the coffin of Italian music. The dream of most young pupils at the provincial *conservatorio* is to end up on the concert platform absolutely alone, wowing the all too impressionable audience with their circus tricks on the fiddle or the piano. The notion of playing together, of making chamber groups or even small orchestras, is quite foreign to them. They will do it, yes, but their hearts are not honestly in it. The noise of an Italian brass band is not without ethnic charm – in its context, at some local *festa* with the clergy and the *sindaco* in full fig, it is honestly rather sweet – but Lord, how it makes you long for Lancashire!

* Donizetti wrote a second version of it called 'The Hermitage of Liverpool'. In the play on which the libretto was based, the place was apparently called Laverpaut.

The ultimate bang of the mallet on the coffin lid is sounded by the Italians' utter abhorrence of amateurism. They simply do not understand about having a go. In northern Europe, hundreds and thousands of us play musical instruments and sing because we enjoy it. We don't do it well, we make an atrocious racket, we are indeed engaged in that business so memorably encapsulated by Conrad in the phrase 'murdering silence', but we do it and it brings us socially together, in choral societies and madrigal groups and ad hoc chamber music, piano duets, scratch orchestras and bands. In Italy even the schools are without choirs or orchestras, and you are lucky to find anyone within fifty miles who actually plays an instrument for fun – and this will probably turn out to be an American, a German or a Swiss rather than an Italian.

It is not, after all, as though this nation were by nature unmusical. Perhaps there is more instinctive musicality among the Italians than in any other race on earth. Perhaps, yet the musically inclined Italian child will receive no stimulus to his impulses; should he or she venture to learn an instrument, there is nobody else with whom to perform or compete, and by degrees the child will sink beneath the prevailing tide of ignorance and vulgarity. *Le pauvre Donizetti* makes several revolutions in his grave.

He lies buried beside his teacher, a marvellously intelligent old friend of Beethoven and Mozart named Johann Simon Mayr, at the west end of the basilica of Santa Maria Maggiore. The square beyond the church, the Piazza Vecchia, where they keep the autograph score of *Lucia* in the civic library, is one of the most winning in Italy for not being all of a piece. There is a fountain guarded by white marble lions, given by one of the Venetian Contarini in 1780, and a mediaeval palace whose arches were opened in the fifteenth century to allow a vista of the Colleoni Chapel, and an ineptly carved statue of the poet Tasso crowned with a laurel wreath. Opposite these, and the houses with red and green shutters and the cafés and restaurants on either side, stands the Library itself, a modern completion in impeccable taste of a design begun as long ago as 1604 by Vincenzo Scamozzi, whose bands of balustrading, ample decorated cornices and arcaded loggia will remind you at once of those buildings he created in Venice as lofty stone expressions of the Most Serene Republic's inalienable dignity.

The evening comes down, and you are maybe sitting at one of the piazza restaurants dining off *riso alla pilota* or *stufato* and listening to the scream of the swifts divebombing the midges in the clear upland airs of Bergamo Alta. Something similarly avian is happening down here in the colonnade of the Biblioteca Civica, something not unlike that celebrated moment in Hitchcock's *The Birds* when those sinister winged eponyms begin gathering in ones and twos on the telegraph wires. A brace of girls comes and sits down under one of the arches. A young man arrives and leans against a column. A boy with his arm around his girlfriend leads her into the shadow of the arcade, and they stand, hands clasped, intent in conversation.

By slow degrees others perch themselves comfortably on the smooth marble ledge that runs along the row of tall pilasters. They are quite clearly waiting for something or someone, but without any particular anxiety, as if they can take the fulfilments of their expectations entirely for granted. By now it is dark, that burnished darkness of nights south of the Alps, and the bats have taken over from the swifts, and the waiter has lit a candle on your table. There is pudding, not something you ought ever to expect in Italy, but which, as a northerner from a land of cake and sweetmeat-eaters, you are pleased enough to find. Tonight it is *sottobosco*, which smart Italian restaurants rather pique themselves on serving, a glass full of berries of various kinds in an alcoholic syrup, and afterwards there will come a little espresso, slick and viscous as molasses, with a packet of sugar to shake into it.

You don't really bother to taste these things, for what is happening in front of Scamozzi's loggia is far more absorbing than red currants and black coffee. The people under the arcade have moved on, others have taken their place, and the whole thoroughfare leading in and out of the square has been suddenly turned over to the immemorial rhythms and ceremonies of that oldest of Italian customs, the *passeggiata*. The habit of taking a walk in the street in the cool of the evening is not unique to Italy. You will find it anywhere in the Mediterranean where there is a settled habitation. Neither is it a seasonal affair. In Milan or Turin, during those foul Italian winters when the cold mist clamming the pavements and tramlines cuts into the bones, you will see old ladies in mothball-smelling furs and serious, jowly-faced men in loden overcoats perambulating to and fro through the galleries and under the arcades, instinctively maintaining the tradition.

If we assume that the principle of physical exercise is to sustain wellbeing, then the *passeggiata*, though it has nothing whatever to do with exercise is nevertheless a deliberate affirmation of life. It underwrites the reality of the town as a commonwealth in the truest sense of the term, whose continuing existence is guaranteed by this nightly ritual of reassurance on the part of its citizens. 'Here we are again,' says the *passeggiata*, 'we have survived the Goths and the Longobards, the Guelphs and the Ghibellines, the *lanzichenecchi* and the Wehrmacht, plague, cholera and famine. Now when you watch us saunter and laugh and reason and gesticulate, you see what endures beyond the Duomo's marble steps, the travertine palace of the Cardinal, the Doric loggia of the grainmarket or the brick pavement of the nuns' cloister.'

The most potent footnote to this message of continuance is afforded by the *necrologie*, the funeral notices stuck on the walls of the buildings between which the *passeggiata* flows. Death too is published here, in these oblong black-bordered squares of paper that speak of 'the profound emotion', 'the unspeakable sadness', 'the universal grief' of a row of little names under one looming and ineluctable. She was here yesterday, that widow, not walking with the others maybe along Via Garibaldi or Corso Matteotti, but game enough to watch from her balcony. He, the *commendatore*, tottered out on his stick for a quarter of an hour. The accountant is in mourning for his son, tipped off his *motorino* by a careless HGV on that dangerous bend at the bottom of the hill, who only last week swaggered down

Via Larga with Paolo, Andrea and the rest in their Timberland moccasins and Armani jeans with little eagles on the back pockets. As for Daniela, we thought she looked a bit pale that evening outside the Gelateria Armony. You see, we didn't realize . . .

Yet this mortality somehow doesn't triumph. Death picks off the ranks of the evening walkers and papers the walls with their names, but it never thins them out. Especially not here in the upper town of Bergamo, which has the noisiest, most furious *passeggiata* of them all, because, I suppose, it is Bergamo, which has never made a habit of doing anything surreptitiously. You walk, what's more, not down a broad, straight boulevard, but along a winding lane that leads you right through the walls of the ruined citadel and out on to the terrace looking across the deep valley behind the town. And in this zigzagging narrowness you are flung, deliberately it must seem, into a direct engagement with the Bergamascs, with their verve and quirkishness and shameless down-facing, out-staring, who-gives-a-toss? manner which sweeps you with it like the undertow of a wave.

They keep it up all night in Bergamo. Waking at three in the morning in my room in the Agnello D'Oro, I hear, above the steady plash of the fountain outside, a boy singing down the alley, in one of those ball-squeezing Italian voices, fit to bust. Maybe his father was a sailmaker in Bergamo. Or perhaps just the porter in a pawnshop.

11 Breaking Down at Motta Baluffi

The trouble with writing books about Italy is that you can never stop sounding like somebody else. Hundreds of people have got there before you, and as you cast about for something fresh to say and a new way of saying it, you become conscious of the dreadful avenues of other people's experience stretching out behind you and making your efforts at being smart and original in your perceptions look very puny indeed.

Sooner or later most of us end up sounding like Edward Hutton. I am not at all sure that any of his books is still in print, but in what appears to have been an exceedingly long life, he managed, between the end of the nineteenth century and the early 1950s, to tidy most of Italy into a set of neat volumes, *Siena and Southern Tuscany, Cities of Umbria, Naples and Southern Tuscany, Cities of Sicily* and so on, all more or less following the same pattern and employing a similar prose style.

Once you start reading old Edward H., it is very easy to fall into the trick of him. Very easy is it, ought I to say, for indeed syntactical inversion is crucial to the patter. Actually it is more a case of Pater than patter, since the Hutton manner is basically that High Art drawing-room mode so beloved of our great-grandparents, in which the loftier flights of Ruskin and Doughty are called in to add 'body' to artistic and topographical descriptions and elevate the discourse appropriately.

Bless thee, Edward, thou wert a chuckleheaded old nincompoop maybe, but oh, how thou didst love Italy! Thy tastes were painfully limited, and thou thoughtest everything painted or sculpted or built after about 1550 utterly beyond the pale of civilized discussion, and thou drooledst quite insufferably over some twopenny-halfpenny mediaeval crucifix in a village church and unscrupulously inventedst encounters with local children who miraculously materialized for the purpose of recounting to thee the legend of the local saint, thou rabbitedst on incessantly about the miles thou coveredst on foot between one *borgo* and the next, and leftest out everything one would really like to have heard about the history of the towns thou fetchedst up in – and yet, and yet, oh Edward, if we all catch thy style like a disease, it is because, in a weird, haunting fashion, Italy gets us writing like this.

There's a famous sonnet by the poet Vincenzo Filicaja, a Tuscan who wrote at the end of the seventeenth century, in which he represents Italy's fatal gift of beauty as the source of her misery at the hands of successive invaders (Byron paraphrased this in two stanzas of *Childe Harold*, Canto III). In some way he seems almost to be implying that it was her fault that all these armies hurled themselves upon her. He was a nice old man in a wig who addressed character-building odes to members of princely families, so perhaps the poem doesn't really mean more than it says, but there are times when we feel that Italy's onslaught on the senses may be having a distinctly deleterious effect upon our critical judgement. The inner eye mists over, the vision blurs and we end up writing sub-Edward Huttonishly about things and places that anywhere else we might have treated with more circumspection and detachment.

So, with a respectful not to say grateful nod to the old man, but trying not to sound too much like him, I came down off the hills into the plains of Lombardy. Things have been going on lately in Lombardy about which I am none too happy. The region used to be famous for the openness and generosity of its people. That landscape of great flat fields, criss-crossed with stands of poplars, spreading out unreservedly beneath the bare, absolute sky, was held to mirror the sincerity of plain, hardworking folk whose frankness and integrity compared so favourably with the false-fronted charm of the Piedmontese or the high-living bumptiousness of the Emilians.

The Lombards have decided to shut up shop on this image, supposing it ever had any substance, and project another entirely, in the form of a political movement known as the Lega Lombarda which will effectively sanctify some of the worst aspects of the north-Italian bourgeois character at the close of the twentieth century. Ostensibly this Lombard League, which has had runaway success in local government elections, is designed to counter the creeping corruption of centralized authority imposed from Rome, and, as most people freely admit, a vast pie from which every little Jack Horner with an ounce of skill as a fixer and manipulator can stick in his thumb and pull out a plum or two.

So far so good. Greater regional autonomy will liberate Lombardy from the dead hand of bureaucracy, and public funds will at last be used to answer pressing local needs. In fact, of course, it is not this simple. The real animating impulse of the League isn't a mere cutting loose from the corporate state to give more power to the people, so much as a fetid resentment of southerners and all their ways and works by self-righteous northerners. Behind the political triumphs of Lega

Lombarda as the party of Joe Soap the honest little businessman, Mister Average from Lodi or Brescia or Monza, the Man on the Metanopoli Omnibus, standing up for his independence from administrative stranglehold, is the spectre of an age-old, narrow-minded, small-town shopkeeper's priggishness challenged by the sleazy, reach-me-down, hand-in-glove racketeering of the Mezzogiorno.

Racism, it need hardly be said, is a powerful card in the League's pack. Among its fistful of simple answers is an implied pledge to act against the northern operations of southern criminal organizations – Mafia, Camorra, 'Ndrangheta* – and the arm of African migrant workers and street traders they control. The golden scenario is a vision of Lombard industry and agriculture humming prosperously away without interference from greasy little meridionals with slurred accidents called Don This and Don That, and, more significantly, without a black face in sight.

Essential to this idea is a truly Italian brand of hypocrisy which refuses to acknowledge that, with one or two significant modifications, there is as much lying, venality, peculation and clientelism in the north as in the south. Those thousands of us who lost our hearts to Italy years ago, seduced indeed by the Filicaja Factor, spend a great deal of time inventing excuses for it. 'Ah, bless their hearts,' we say of the Italians, 'they've simply had to be dishonest to survive. Those little lies and subterfuges and exaggerations are merely ways of struggling through the appalling mesh of tax laws and official bamboozlements which threaten otherwise to stifle them.' And we pat them on the head for these dear little mendacities and sideways wrigglings and economies with the truth, for who are we, pompous hyperborean Protestants 'with our terrible notions of duty' to condemn them for such stratagems?

* The Camorra is, roughly speaking, the Neapolitan version of the Mafia and 'Ndrangheta – God knows where that word came from – is the Calabrian variety.

Up to a point such patronizing indulgence is justifiable. Like a naughty child Italy goes on violating and abusing EEC directives while flamboyantly proclaiming its allegiance to rococo ceiling fresco visions of a Greater Europe mounted upon roseate clouds and attended doubtless by half-dressed females representing Integration, Common Currency and Political Unity. Community cash meanwhile goes on disappearing into capacious individual pockets while smoothiechops politicians do the rounds of Paris and Brussels and Strasbourg selling dreamticket notions of A Wider European Tomorrow.

Thus the increasing political clout of the Lombard League will change nothing. It will merely confer a certain smug respectability upon the element of dishonesty fundamental to Italian life by containing it within the provincial power structure. There will be the same hierarchies, the same backscratching and favours done, the same lorries off which things conveniently fall in the middle of the night. All that will be absent is the southern smell of garlic and tomatoes, a touch of Sicilian *omertà* and a few corpses in the street, and a writer or two to tell us how Timelessly Mediterranean everything is.

Like much else in Italy, this new regionalism has a long historical shadow. In the very name Lega Lombarda is couched an appeal to the spirit of that older Lombard League which at the end of the twelfth century united the cities of the plain against the imperial thug Frederick Barbarossa and about which in 1848 Verdi wrote a riproaring opera, *La Battaglia di Legnano*, to celebrate the hard-fought encounter near Como where the hideous German was trounced.

There is the ghost of an elder world even than this, a world of which Italians do not always like to be reminded, especially when they require you to think of them exclusively as a 'Latin' race, a world whose significance for the life and culture of modern Italy has still not fully been taken on board. It is that of the people who gave their name to this fair, fat, rich plain between the Alps and the Po, the Lombards, the Longobards, the men with the long beards. Somewhere around the middle of the sixth century they had worked their way down from

Scandinavia across the Hungarian reaches of the Danube and over the mountains into Italy. If they were more successful than earlier barbarian invaders, even than the Goths, it was because they integrated with much greater ease into whatever was left of disintegrated Roman imperial culture. Between themselves and their Byzantine emperors they parcelled out Italy, and we can trace their presence from Friuli in the far north to the very tip of Italy's Calabrian toe.

Superficially they look, these Lombards, like just another wave of Teutonic hordes, part of that warrior infrastructure stretching from Scotland to Gibraltar which created the traditions and lifestyles of early mediaeval Europe, but which nowadays seems so repugnant to us in its crude, sword-brandishing, mead-quaffing shagginess. They left artefacts in their graves, finely wrought brooches and clasps in gilt bronze and coloured enamels, necklaces of variegated pebbles chased with intricate carving, and, already half Christianized, they built beautiful brick churches like the Tempietto of Cividale and the monastery of San Salvatore at Brescia. Yet even the loveliest thing of their making, the resplendent Cross of Saint Helen which Desiderius, last of the Lombard kings, together with Ansa his queen, gave to the Brescian monks, has a curious air of makeshift vulgarity about it, spangled all over as it is with a loot of antique gemstones, pagan Roman camoes, and even two or three little Fayyum portraits of dead Greek-speaking Egyptians.

Nevertheless their presence in Italy, among the shattered, traumatized remnants of the classical world, exerts a strange fascination. When, a year or so ago, a modern paperback edition of Paul The Deacon's great *Historia Langobardorum* appeared with a parellel Italian text, I snapped it up at once and stayed enthralled till three in the morning. Paul, a contemporary of the Venerable Bede, writing during the eighth century, was enormously proud of the Longobard pedigree of his Friulan father Warnefrid, but remained freely critical of the kings and dukes of his nation and their deeds. What held me, I suppose, on that summer night on a Tuscan terrace, with the crickets chirping and the nightingales improvising their operatic melismata out of the darkness, was the untrammelled brutality of these people towards one another, their utter lack of faith or truth, the sheer spontaneity of their beastliness. While they piously founded abbeys and endowed cathedrals, they were turning each other's skulls into drinking vessels, dragging one another at the tails of wild stallions and nonchalantly cutting off hands, breasts and testicles. They seem to stand as a metaphor for all those aspects of the Italian character of which Italophiles, and not a few Italians themselves, would prefer not to know.

The Italians use Lombard words every day of their lives. As well as obviously heroic, saga-singing, Germanic-tribal terms like *faida*, feud, *elmo*, helmet, *staffa*, stirrup, there are less obvious links in words such as *orgoglio*, pride, *schiaffo*, slap, *abbandonare*, to abandon. The word for 'back' or 'spine', *schiena*, is Longobard, so too are *fiasco*, flask, *fresco*, fresh, and *bugia*, a lie. A dog-lead, *guinzaglio*, a cheek, *guancia*, and a swarm, *stormo*, have all stayed Longobard, as has that wonderful Italian word *grinta*, which basically means the guts to get on with the job and see it through.

And what names they had, what super-indigestible, jaw-crackingly ugly yet ineffably haughty-sounding monickers! Adelprando, Ardefusa, Aridruda, Austricunda, Bruniperto, Ermesindo, Giselbaldo, Guadelberga, Guarneprando, Iselmondo, Lubomperto, Malchenolfo, Rachiberga, Scauniperga, Trasamondo, Truderico – you can see them plain in the very resonances, their women's blonde, coarse hair gathered into plaits, their menfolk sporting whiskers and the pointed beards from which the original Scandinavian tribe had taken its name.

More importantly, you can feel them still about you in the very making of the Lombard landscape. Their place-names litter the plain: Camairago, Vidolasco, Oscasale, Farfengo, Berlingo and, north of Manerbio on the Cremona-Brescia road, the ultimate Germanic toponym Offlaga, meaning 'the village that *lies off* the highway'. Their way of making fortified encampments was adopted by the local farmers, who evolved over successive centuries a specific type of grange-cum-fortress-cum-hamlet in which barns and cottages, cowsheds and stables are tacked together in a sequence of colonnaded courtyards, a dwelling known as a *cascina*, of which scores are still scattered across the countryside.

It is difficult to get Edward Huttonish about the little towns of the Lombard plain. You can't imagine, as you bowl down the open roads between the maize fields and little squares of pasture and hay meadow, writing something like 'And so, in the smiling eventide, I came to Martinengo/Orzinuovi/Soresina (delete where not applicable) and very lovely was its Romanesque *pieve*, with an altarpiece by Divieto di Sosta and a fair ciborium carved by the hand of Orario Sportelli, and lo! the landlady of the Asino D'Oro bade me welcome, and very soft were the pillows &c &c.' They just aren't like that, these two-bit burgs of the great Cispadane and Transpadane flats, but in this absence, for me as for certain other perverse souls addicted to this part of Italy, lies the secret of their allure.

A place like Romano di Lombardia, on the way down to Crema from Bergamo, says it all. About such a town there is what the Edwardians used to call 'no side'. None of the older houses is conspicuously handsome, and if there is any architectural attraction whatever, it derives from the habit, prevailing right down the Po valley from Turin to the delta, of arcading the main streets, so that the relentless furnace heats of the summer months and the numbing autumn and winter fog-blankets will be kept out of the shops. These stores, what is more, are of the no-nonsense variety which, rather remarkably for Italy, sets small value on fancy window dressing and the subtler techniques of display. Useful things for the housewife – *casalinga*, a good Longobard word, 'houseling' – and the farmer and gardener and domestic potterer are flung together inside and out, like the wares of some dry-goods store in an American frontier town of the last century.

If the people here are certainly not poor (and the presence of the ubiquitous local savings banks implies that they aren't), there is no special effort made at ostentation. Now and then in a town like Romano I try to conceive the nature of existence for its inhabitants, the expectations and the terrors between which they gravitate, and the dreams which visit them asleep or awake. The kids don't look particularly restless or resentful, maybe because Milan is only fifty kilometres away, and the trains (for of course there is a station) take a mere three-quarters of an hour. Most of the adults have sorted out the dimensions and priorities according to which they will live, and the grizzled old men, with their faces weathered brick-red between their hat brims and their moustaches, and the white-haired old women in tidy cardigans and shawls, are not so much resigned to life as visibly at ease within the limits of their world.

Do I make it sound deceptively pastoral, the happy peasantry rejoicing in its lot, sitting in peace under its vine and fig tree? Is this what the Lega Lombarda longs to hear? If so, it is because you realize, in a spot like Romano di Lombardia, that small towns continue to flourish in Italy because people actually like living in them, like to feel embraced by their coddling littleness, like their comforting sense of the contained and the finite, and are perfectly ready, whatever metropolitan migrations they may make, to return to places whose quintessential provincialism offers the protection of guaranteed cosiness.

Italian life is full of such cyclic movements, and town after town has a local celebrity who, after dazzling the world came back to lay his bones among his own folk. Romano was not without such a lion, and his melodious roar was heard quite literally all across Europe. The finest tenor of his day, whom the Parisians called '*le roi des ténors*' and of whom the London music critic Henry Chorley wrote, 'As a singer and nothing but a singer, he is the only man of his class who deserves to be named in these pages as an artist of genius,' Giovanni Battista Rubini was the kind of star for whom even the greatest of composers could stretch a point or two. Bellini wrote *Il pirata* and *La sonnambula* with Rubini's soaring upper registers and tenderly expressive phrasing in mind, and would compose nothing for the hero of the *Puritani* until Rubini arrived in Paris to give him advice. Donizetti achieved international fame with the help of Rubini as Percy in *Anna Bolena*, where the aria 'Vivi tu', with its subtle infusion of melancholy, became the tenor's calling card.

The English adored him. At Her Majesty's in the Haymarket he reigned unchallenged for over a decade alongside the soprano Giulia Grisi and the basses Antonio Tamburini and Luigi Lablache, 'the great Burlybumbo who sings double D', a Falstaffian *basso* who gave singing lessons to the young Queen Victoria. The four stars were known as the *Puritani* quartet because that splendid piece, last and best of Bellini's works, was inconceivable without them.

What do singers do when they retire? Some go ungracefully and some, like those notorious divas whose 'last concerts' carry on over several seasons, seem reluctant to go at all. Others, like Callas, make such a pig's ear of the whole business that the resultant gossip enhances their already legendary aura. Certain among them become seriously domesticated, like the great Giuditta Pasta, who took to smallholding with her old mamma on the shores of Lake Como. And once or twice some of them actually go away and come back again, like Henriette Sonntag, who returned to the stage after fifteen years in retirement, so as to pay the debts of the impecunious Piedmontese count who had made a lady of her.

Rubini was a good man whom everyone loved, and a sensible fellow at that. Moving sideways from the stage to the concert platform, which he shared with Liszt and Pauline Viardot, the most outstanding singing actress of her day, he came home at last in 1844, from grand St Petersburg, where he had been court singing master to the Russian imperial family, to little Romano di Lombardia, where he was simply the son of a local horn player. Not content only to honour the town with his presence, the retired tenor built a palace for himself in impeccable neo-classical taste, its façade set off by a garden behind high wrought-iron screens, and endowed a school for local children, as though to perpetuate the dazzling trajectory which had carried him to glamour and success.

Out of Romano to the north, the plain is dotted with little castles and moated villas: at Vidolasco, where the fortress lies huddled among farmhouses like an old hunting dog asleep; at Castel Gabbiano and Ricengo, where the baroque manor houses have subsumed intriguing bits of former Sforza strongholds; and at Soncino, whose big, beetle-browed brick citadel glowers across the river Oglio at Orzinuovi on the eastern bank, the pair of them marking the old frontier outposts of Brescian and Cremonese territory in the days of the free communes during the high Middle Ages.

It comes as something of a shock to find, above the city gates of Crema, to the west, the white marble lion of Saint Mark, wings, book, '*Pax tibi Marce Evangelista*' and all. The Venetians this far into mainland Italy? In the intoxication of conquest on *tèrra ferma*, they pushed their empire almost to the gates of Milan. Crema, standing on the same longitude as Bergamo, was a political sugarplum offered as a *douceur* to Venice by Francesco Sforza in 1449 in return for its support of his claim to the Milanese dukedom.

Wherever the Venetians planted their scarlet and gilt masts, symbols of the Republic's dominion, they created a context of grandeur in which the full hierarchical stateliness of their government could show itself to the most impressive advantage. You notice this in cities like Verona and Brescia, where the profusion of white Istrian marble and the echoes of Palladio and Scamozzi sounding in the façades of churches and palaces emphasize Venice's unshakeable resolve that empire should be a visual as well as an administrative reality, that the image of hegemony is as important as its exercise.

The wonder is that there was much of Crema left when the Venetians arrived. Frederick Barbarossa – who else? – had commanded its total destruction in 1159 for remaining stoutly loyal to the Guelphs of Milan. So as to frighten the citizens into submission, he hung up his Cremaschi hostages outside the walls and devised a hideous form of siege engine, a movable tower to which a number of the town's children were bound alive and which was brought up close to the ramparts so that the anguished parents might call out to their offspring. Grimly the Cremaschi held on, fending off the dismal machine and killing nine of its wretched human attachments in the process. When, after a six-month siege, they finally gave in and retreated half-starved to Milan, Barbarossa put Crema to the torch. No wonder Hitler admired him so: the pair of them are shaking hands in Hell.

When the place put itself back together again in the thirteenth century, the citizens, helped by their Visconti overlords, built themselves a gothic Duomo of pink brick which, outside at least, is one of the sturdiest, most clean-lined of the smaller Lombard cathedrals. Its wondrously ornate west front, with loops of vine tendril around the ogival windows under the high crocketed gable, above a blind arcade of little marble columns, is a regional speciality known as a *facciata a vento*, a wind façade, because it is really a screen against the wind, the height of the nave roof behind being much lower than the illusion implies. John Addington Symonds, who wrote so feelingly of Lombard architecture a hundred years ago, went wild for the campanile and so do I. Entirely of baked clay, apart from the stone pillars of the lantern, it is the most umpompous, fanciful, truculently elegant belltower you ever saw, much more like a Moorish minaret in Spain than the adjunct to a Christian cathedral.

I like Crema, with its wrought-iron balconies and lines of shutters like something from a Bonington watercolour, its deep Venetian porticoes and nodding green cupolas, its Napoleonic Porta Serio by the Cremonese architect Faustino Rodi, a master of that megalithic neo-classical idiom which, from La Scala at Milan to San Francesco di Paola at Naples, is one of Italy's late architectural glories, its particoloured Augustinian cloister with a half perished but still beautiful frescoed Last Supper in the refectory, painted in 1498 by the Brescian master Giovan Pietro da Cemmo. I like the fact that the town has managed to hang on to so many of its palaces: the Vimercati, whose courtyard, its arches divided by chaste pairs of Doric columns under slender scallop-shell niches, looks more Parisian than Lombard; the Albergoni Arrigoni with its strange narrow windows glancing sidelong towards the box hedges of the grassy parterre, and, most dashing of all, Giuseppe Cozzi's unfinished Palazzo Terni de' Gregori, sheltered from the cobbled street outside by a swaggering baroque screen topped with sensuously posed muses in stone.

Above everything, what makes Crema memorable is its gardens and small sudden patches of green. You do not expect them, even in verdant Lombardy, but here they unquestionably are, glimpsed under gloomy archways and across dark courtyards – a fountain, a gravel walk, an ilex or a cedar tree, swags of vine and hibiscus, walls bearded with creeper and wisteria, a stand of hollyhocks, a lemon tree in a jar. There are always more gardens than you suspect in an Italian city, but they are of the *hortus conclusus* kind, to be enjoyed, like those of Crema, once you have shut the palace gates and are behind high walls with only the grating call of the ringdoves for company and a thin breeze twitching the scented tips of the syringa.

You will do well to avoid Cremona, the last great town in Lombardy, possessed of a big, glum Romanesque Duomo like an aircraft hangar, which somehow manages not to be quite interesting enough inside, and a gross communal museum which reminds me of Blake's mean, unjust but always memorable description of Sir Joshua Reynolds, 'this man was hired to depress art'. The picture gallery alone induces terminal wretchedness, and there is, or at least there was, one of those archaeological museums designed to make the whole science of recovering the remote past as rebarbative as possible. The people have the fame of being boorish, rude, unremarkable plutocrats, which is probably not fair, and Cremona's only claim to the world's attention, other than as the birthplace of Claudio Monteverdi and the centre of the nougat industry, has been as the nursery of the great fiddle-making school of Antonio Stradivari.

They have revived this art in the form of a technical research institute called ACLAP (Associazione Cremonese Liutai* Artigiani Professionisti – Italians are mad for acronyms), and the laborious old methods have been painstakingly recovered.

* *Liutaio* means both lute-player and violinmaker.

Violins came into general use at the end of the sixteenth century, so that the form of the instrument, retained to this day, is essentially that of an essay in baroque architecture. The volute and scrollwork of the head, the fluted edges of the sound box, the long f-shaped holes in the belly and the deeply indented curves at either side belong to the façades of churches or the decorated bands of carving around doors and picture frames among which Stradivari and the other great *liutai*, Andrea and Nicolo Amati and Giuseppe Guarneri, grew up. The first violin sonatas of any importance were written by a Lombard, Biagio Marini of Brescia, in 1629, and when you listen to them running through all their mingled currents of passion and energy, you hear a counterpart to the rhythms and dramatic contrasts of baroque sculpture and masonry, a music fashioned to match the form of the instrument.

These Cremona fiddles were cut from Lombard woods, spruce and maple for the belly and back, poplar, willow and pear for all the rest. There were forests all over Lombardy until the nineteenth century: in Roman times the historian Polybius commented on the very large number of pigs feeding in the oak groves on these plains. The pig has alas quite beaten the oak, and you may journey for miles among the pork-fattening farms of the Po without seeing much more than a coppice or two scattered here and there among the eternal files of poplars.

I was thinking about this woodlessness when, driving along the road out of Cremona, skirting the river towards Casalmaggiore, we suddenly broke down. For a moment we sat there staring at the dashboard and the steering wheel as if they were going to provide an instant answer to the mystery of why a nearly new Alfa Romeo should suddenly refuse to budge, and my brother, with his customary resignation, plugged away at the starter. After a while we gave up, got out of the car, and stood a minute or two looking about us.

It was just after midday on a warm spring morning. Off the meadow below the embanked road a pair of larks rose screaming into the air. There was a soft breeze curling up the pale undersides of the poplar leaves and rippling over the young maize stems stretching in military ranks towards the stream at the end of their field. Above us rose the frank, open-eyed sky of Lombardy, with its freight of scudding, heavy-bellied white clouds. The clarity of vision in the landscape, defining the shapes of trees and houses far into the distance, was matched by an extraordinary precision of sound. There was not much traffic on the road, and between the passing cars and lorries we could hear voices calling in the farm beyond the maize fields, a dog's barking and the fretful chirping of finches along the banks of the stream.

There was no obvious beauty in the scene. A country entirely devoted to the business of producing human and animal sustenance, it made hardly any concessions to casual aestheticism. Yet I found it then, as I still find it, lovelier than any other Italian landscape because of its absolute authenticity, its reassuring lack of compromise and the sense that it had not been scribbled and daubed over by waves of picturesque tourists. I was glad that it wasn't Tuscany, and that we shouldn't find, around the next corner, a villa with a swimming pool and a London merchant banker's family *in situ*, or an American poet, or a Swiss art historian, or a French costume designer, or an Australian novelist, or a German conductor, or a Scotch lord. There were just Italians here, this was just Italy, for good or ill, and I felt, as always on these plains of the Po, thoroughly happy and safe.

Perhaps that was why we had no scruples about abandoning the locked car and wandering down the road to the garage which suddenly seemed to appear, as if in a hallucination, from over the green horizon. There was a sort of roadhouse attached to it, with something like a restaurant and attendant scents of cooking in progress. The woman in charge of the place had one of those lopsided, bovine, motherly faces to be seen down here, where a certain sort of pawky kindliness in the Lombard countenance replaces standard-issue Italoid good looks. She laughed when we told her what had happened.

'It's always like that on this road,' she said, 'maybe we do it on purpose. Anyway you'll take some lunch while you're waiting.'

It was not clear what exactly we should be waiting for, or indeed for how long. Two businesslike men in seriously greasy overalls set off with our keys towards the car, and we sat down in the dark, cavernous restaurant with its coffee-bar counter stacked with boxes of Perugina and Majani chocolate, blue *panettone* cartons and gift-wrapped packets of nougat and macaroons.

'What's the name of this place?' my brother asked the woman as she laid the table.

'This,' she announced, 'is Motta Baluffi.'

Motta Baluffi – what on earth would Edward Hutton have made out of Motta Baluffi? 'Motta', by the way, is the same as the old French word 'motte', as in motte-and-bailey castle, a tump, a bump in the ground, but there was no visible bump here for as far as the eye could see, just a village of the *bassa cremonese** with a stuccoed brick church and a street of dull houses and the roads going on beyond to Scandolara Ravara and Torricella del Pizzo. 'And so, at noontide, I came to Motta Baluffi, and very joyful was I,' 'And lo! there at my feet lay little Motta Baluffi with her etcetera etcetera.' Somehow it wouldn't work, the place was stolidly resistant to Huttonish purple of any kind. Our feet were touching the ground, our eyes were unmisted with any enchantment, but there was something – it is hard to say exactly what, but Edward Hutton would have understood – about sitting down to a plate of risotto and a bottle of Barbera off a formica table in a roadhouse in Motta Baluffi on the waveless plain of Lombardy.

The men in greasy overalls returned with politely grinning faces. There was nothing wrong with the car. We should have guessed of course. It was just being a trifle cross and temperamental in that way cars have. So we went southwards, through Gussola with its neo-classical villas, and Casalmaggiore, which has a pompous nineteenth-century look, historical tushery in

* Bassa means the flat country around any town
in Lombardy or Emilia – thus the *bassa modenese*,
the *bassa pavese*, the *bassa reggiana*, etcetera.

brick and stone, to the river itself, Il Po, the great *raison d'être* of the northern Italian landscape, the frontier, the barrier, the father and god, Padanus or Eridanus as the Romans called him, who rises up in the mountains behind Turin, and after passing below Mantua and Rovigo, slides into the *bonifica*, the reclaimed marshlands of the *bassa ferrarese*, to meet the Adriatic in a triple-mouthed delta, Po di Venezia, Po di Goro, Po di Gnocco.

There is something dreadful about this river of the Po. It is not simply its vastness, turbid and inexorable in winter amid the impenetrable thickness of the fogs, sluggish and syrupy between shoals of mud in summer, or the uniquely unattractive stretches of grey stones that line its shores above the broad sandbanks. It is not even the scrubby little screens of undergrown poplars that screen it from the fields and roads on either side, or the more than faintly military-looking bridges that cross it, over which you expect even now to see the Wehrmacht and the partisans scrapping it out as they did all over this countryside in the desperate struggles of 1945.

No, it's the horrendous loneliness of everything – unpeopled, aching, voluminous and ghastly. You might now and then see a barge, or a man cutting reeds, the occasional fisherman, though most stretches of the river are now hopelessly polluted with fertilizers and industrial effluent (the money sponged off the EEC for cleaning it up having, in time-honoured Italian fashion, vanished into private pockets). In the remorseless glare of the dog-days there is even the odd sunbather along the sandbanks. Yet, as a river, as a component of the landscape, it is an awful thing, this Po. You imagine rapes and murders taking place here and the bodies not being discovered for weeks at a time. The poplar woods seem made on purpose to conceal headless corpses or mutilated torsos, and though Italy is a country significantly unhaunted by ghosts, these deserted riverbanks cry out with a spectral horror worthy of *Heart Of Darkness*.

Something always pulls me back, nevertheless, to the small towns along its winding margins, each of them a testimony to the pretensions and dreams of the ducal dynasties who commanded here. If you cross the river at Dosolo, for example, you find yourself inside the domains of one of the smallest duchies ever sewn on to the patchwork of mini-sovereignties which once made up the Italian peninsula. The little city of Guastalla was presented to Don Ferrante Gonzaga, brother of the Marquis of Mantua, in 1541 by the Emperor Charles V as a reward for his good government as Viceroy of Sicily. Officially detached from its feudal allegiance to the Milanese, it was turned into the capital of a tiny dukedom, and Don Ferrante and his successors began laying it out to a careful plan, with scientific fortifications, as a place which should do honour to a line of enlightened rulers.

Of course the experiment – for such it inevitably remained – did not work. Greedy neighbours were always wanting to get at Guastalla because of its commanding position at the river crossing, the Po itself had a tiresome tendency to flood the suburbs, and what with the ducal palace and the churches and the convents of the Theatines, Servites and Capuchins, and the Jewish ghetto crammed in behind the apse of the cathedral, life in the town was something of a squeeze. The tiny state never really made its mark in the region, and with the downfall of the greater Gonzaga duchy of Mantua after a fatal series of wrong political horses backed during the Hapsburg and Bourbon squabbles of the seventeenth century, it fell into the lap of the dukes of Parma, who with the best will in the world could do nothing to prevent the town from turning into a sort of grandiose village, a monument to overweening fantasy.

Places like Guastalla all found their chroniclers, generally learned local priests who, during the seventeenth or eighteenth century, sat down to write, with many a syntactical curlicue and much gilding and empurpling of the vocabulary, the annals of their city. One such is beside me now, the *Istoria della città di Guastalla, succintamente narrata dal Padre Maestro Gio. Battista Benamati, Servita, e consagrata all' Altezza Serenissima di Ferrando III Gonzaga Duca di Guastalla, Principe di Molfetta &c. In Parma, Per Mario Vigna, 1674, Con licenza de' Superiori.* Worms have eaten the title page and burrowed into poor Father Benamati's dedication to his Serene Highness, in which he

proclaims that 'my pen burned to recall to life those histories formerly dead and buried in oblivion, presuming only to
register in the temple of eternity, in immortal characters, the
glory of Guastalla.' The erratum sheet ('for "stimulation" read
"humiliation" ' and so on) is followed by an address to 'The
Benign Reader' ending 'Live happy and you will live long',
a Latin imprimatur from the General of the Servites and the
Consultor of the Holy Inquisition, and a pair of sonnets to the
Duke.

After all this, Benamati, once he has got down to business, is
really rather good, and the narrative canters briskly along, from
Empress Angiberta, Queen Adimandata and King Adelbert
(Longobards, you guessed) and Pope Urban II's proclamation
of the first crusade at the Council of Guastalla in 1094 to the
Duke of Ferrara's long siege of the city in 1557, aided by '*li
Francesi con Barche, e Bergantini armati, con alcuni pezzi di
Altigliaria*', a gift to the cathedral of the teeth of Saint Peter and
Saint Paul by the pious Cesare Gonzaga, the dreadful flooding
of the Po in 1618 'which seemed like another universal deluge',
and a visitation of the plague in 1630, in which three thousand
guastallesi died. As the little history draws to its close, the Jews
get a new ghetto, a theatre is built 'for the adornment of the
city, whose young persons may employ themselves in virtuous
actions', a miraculous Madonna causes the stump of an old plum
tree to bear fruit, and the good friar concludes with a tearful
prayer to God for long life to the Duke.

Guastalla has not changed that much since Benamati's day,
except that it is much quieter, less crowded, and houses have
been built in the seven star-points of the old bastions which once
marked the vanished city walls. The splendid Via della Posta,
now called Via Garibaldi, with an eighteenth-century synagogue
at one end, still draws its files of arcades and shutters down
the line of the old earthen embankment which the Lombards
built when they founded this place in 603 as a 'war stall', a
military encampment, from which the name derives. The Strada
Gonzaga still throws its arrow-straight course unimpeded across
the town, past the cobbled square in front of the yellow stuccoed

Duomo and the severe brick-fronted ducal palace. Leone Leoni's perfectly atrocious statue of Ferrante I dressed as a Roman warrior tramples for eternity on his supine enemy.

I could almost live here. I should go mad with boredom of course, but there are times when I've fancied the idea. Perhaps Gualtieri would be an even better spot to turn crazy in. Gualtieri, 'Walter's castle', lies three kilometres along the road westwards from Guastalla, and anyone who ever tells you that the Po valley is boring and has nothing worth looking at needs to be dragged here by the hair.

Even as you draw near it appears nothing out of the ordinary, another plain pink Padane townlet in the green sea of maize fields. Only when you get right inside does the nature of Gualtieri as the incarnation of a Renaissance ideal become apparent. For one or other of the two principal streets will throw you at last into a vast open piazza around which stretches a complete sequence of porticoed buildings, their lines broken only by a defensive-looking palace on one side, a muscular classical church on the other, and a tall clock-tower over the central arch. The effect is essentially that of the Place des Vosges in Paris: you wonder, indeed, whether Metezeaux, the architect of that square, had ever happened upon Gualtieri, or a plan or a picture of it.

The designer here was Giambattista Aleotti, who in 1580 began turning what was little more than a village into a habitation worthy of the Marchese Cornelio Bentivoglio, to whom Alfonso D'Este, Duke of Ferrara, had given Gualtieri as a reward for his share in reclaiming the marshlands south of the Po. The Bentivoglio were a family with taste as well as ambition, and Cornelio decorated his palace with frescoes by the Parmesan* Sisto Badalocchio depicting scenes from the *Gerusalemme liberata* of Tasso, who had dedicated the poem to

---

* In Italy a person from Parma is nowadays
called a *parmense*. *Parmigiano*, considered decent
enough once upon a time, has been banished to
the kitchen.

Duke Alfonso. After a bare fifty years, however, the marquisate of Gualtieri petered out, and the town became a backwater with one of the most sumptuous piazzas in northern Italy incongruously plonked in the midst of it. Nowadays old men in battered trilbies lounge about under the arches, boys play table soccer in the dark café and Gualtieri sits a little too solitary and forlorn since the dreams of Marquis Cornelio vanished into the winter mist which rises from the river.

The place that best of all sums up this sense of *tout passe, tout casse, tout lasse* lies farther west along the riverbank, across the old frontier of the Duchy of Parma at Colorno, where the ducal family, a branch of the Bourbons and much given to flaunting its French sophistications, created for itself during the eighteenth century a miniature Versailles on the marshy peninsula formed by the bends of the little river Parma before it runs into the Po. Very grand indeed was this summer palace of Colorno, '*il delizioso ed ammirevole Colorno*', designed by the French architect Ennemond Petitot, using the shell of an earlier villa built by the Bourbons' predecessors, the Farnese. Retaining the tall flanking towers of the original, Petitot and his assistants, Giuliano Mozzani and Ferdinando Bibiena, flung dignified façades across the sides of the palace facing the river and the park, and added a dramatic staircase sweeping up to the *piano nobile* from the garden.

A Gallic accent dominated the interior designs as well, with Gobelin tapestries, Sèvres vases and paintings specially commissioned for the great airy saloons from the artists Charles Lacroix and Adrien Manglard, then working in Rome. The church of San Liborio was transformed into 'Le Chapelle Royale', based by Petitot on Mansart's palace chapel at Versailles. The gardens were laid out in the manner of Le Nôtre, with a concession to changing taste in the creation of a *parco inglese*, where everything was charmingly 'natural', and there was a small deerpark attached. The Bourbons were utterly enchanted by it all, and when Johann Zoffany painted Duke Ferdinand's portrait in 1779 it was with his favourite hunting dog and the villa of Colorno in the distance.

This vision of an enlightened despot's paradise was all too speedily dissipated. Though Duchess Marie Louise amused herself with anglicizing the garden still further after the Napoleonic war (her garden architect and plantsman was a certain Carlo Barvitius, a member of the London Horticultural Society), the palace and its grounds soon afterwards fell into disuse, and in 1853 the deerpark was turned into rice fields. By the end of the nineteenth century practically all the fountains and statuary had either been destroyed or sold off; the grandest sculptural ensemble of all, a charming group representing Pluto carrying off Proserpina, was purchased by the Rothschilds of Waddesdon in Buckinghamshire, where it remains to this day.

The villa itself, stripped of its contents in 1862 by zealous officials of the royal house of Savoy, became successively an infantry barracks and a lunatic asylum. Only recently has it been reopened to the public as an elegant ruin, whose overgrown parterres and peeling state apartments sound the faintest of reverberations from a time when Colorno nursed its own little school of landscape painters, the music of the illustrious Ferdinando Paer, from whose *Leonora* Beethoven took a hint or two for *Fidelio*, sounded in the chapel royal of San Liborio, and the courtiers discussed agronomy and Diderot and English novels in the lime walks.

Colorno is still beautiful, its long, egg-yellow river front, topped with white statues and approached over a high-arching bridge, looking oddly un-Italian and not terribly French either, more like some Central European *Schloss* painted by Bernardo Bellotto. Opposite the gateway to the palace courtyard, in the café where an inscription tells you – as it tells you just about everywhere else in Italy – that Garibaldi halted there for an hour or two, the villagers sit gossiping at the plastic tables with their backs turned to the villa's superfluous elegance. Like most people, they do not greatly care about dead dukes and forgotten gardeners.

12 The Monkey and the Murderer

'Let's go,' said Tim, 'for a gire.' Tim is my elder brother and a gire is our word for a trip. Like so many siblings we have a family argot compounded of childhood misrenderings, invented words, terms extracted from books and deliberately misused, and ordinary locutions with entirely new meanings. Part of this private language consists of a whole set of anglicizations of Italian words whose sense is blunted by translation into English. Thus a busy street may be said to be 'formiculating' with people, or if they are crowded on to a staircase or into the foyer of a theatre, the place becomes 'stipated' with them.

A spineless person is 'abulic', a thoughtless character becomes 'acephalous' and if you wish to drive such creatures from you, it is necessary to find the right way of 'respingeing' them.

A gire is therefore not a Yeatsian spiral, in which those sailing to Byzantium are perne (whatever that means – Yeats in any case spells it 'gyre') but a jaunt, a *giro*, literally a turn or a bend but generally used by Italians to mean a journey for pleasure. My brother Tim is the ideal person to make gires with. I say this not just because I love him in that inexpressible fashion which transcends language or touch, but because it really is impossible for me to think of anybody else with whom I would rather travel.

If he were merely stolid and patient and an excellent driver, that would be enough, but in addition to this and to the fact that, in the manner of all younger brothers, I have made him my hero and protector since I first had any feelings on the subject, he has qualities which make him the perfect sightseeing companion. For one thing he never carries a camera. You do not have to dawdle about while he twiddles dials and finds correct angles and tells you to get out of the bloody way. For another, he is wholly without that exasperating readiness to linger for hours in front of a single work of art in a gallery or a church, gasping and mumbling about genius, while you're dying to get on and see as much as you can before the sacristan or the attendant comes jangling his chatelaine and shouting '*Si chiude!*' so that he can get off to his lunch. Tim, though naturally curious to see everything, is philosophical in the face of locked doors, restorations and eccentric opening hours. Together, in a fashion that would horrify more highminded tourists, we zip niftily through the *Sehenswürdigkeiten* of the various towns to which we girate, always making sure that there is a good lunch at the end of it. Tim, heavily built and portly as a Polynesian king, is a slow eater and a deep drinker, with an amazing instinct for finding some culinary elysium buried in the most unpromising environs, a Macchu Pichu or Palmyra of gastronomy where he can enchant the waiters with his knowledge of recondite vintages and inquisitiveness as to the preparation of local dishes.

So that day, with our friend William, who is also plump and bright and fond of his bottle, we set out for a gire into the Colli Piacentini, the range of green hills whose spurs run out into the well-watered plains west of the city of Piacenza, which stands on the frontiers between Emilia and Lombardy formed by the River Po. The thing about the Colli Piacentini is their unexpectedness. You have got used to the unvarying flatness of Emilia, with its roads laid from village to village like pieces of tape between drawing-pins, and then suddenly there are hummocks in the ground, clumps of trees, willow-fringed streams and gentle slopes of vineyard and pastureland running up to long level plateaux like the backs of recumbent cows.

We decided, I now recall, to save the climb into the hills themselves until after lunch, and cross first of all into western Lombardy, towards that delicious stretch of undulating country lying between the rivers Lambro and Ticino, which run south-wards into the Po. On the road towards Pavia we stopped to have a look at the castle of Belgiojoso, built in the fourteenth century by the Visconti of Milan to consolidate their hold upon the territory, and now rather pleasantly crumbling, though there are families living in the towers, the moat has been kept clean, the splendid neo-classical stables are used as workshops and a little cosmetic gardening has been applied to the seventeenth-century parterres behind the classicized west front.

I was glad to see Pavia again. Indeed I am always glad to see Pavia, which is one of the more remarkable Italian cities for being so pronouncedly un-Italian. If you have had the good luck to travel elsewhere in Europe, this singularity hits you as soon as you lock into the system of peripheric roads embracing the town. Perhaps it has something to do with the trees or the relationship of the pavements to the houses or whatever other detail you might care to fix on as an explanation, but the reminiscences here are those of Germany or northern France, anywhere rather than 'Papia densis turribus' where Saint Augustine lies buried, the ancient capital of the Lombard kings, the birthplace of Lanfranc, William the Conqueror's Archbishop of Canterbury, and the seat of one of the most venerable universities in Italy.

This impression of a foreign city which has somehow fetched up amid all the congruent incongruities of an Italian setting is confirmed as soon as you set foot within the line of the old walls (themselves long since swept away). There is a uniqueness in the architecture of Pavia which imprints itself indelibly on the memory, as if to correct any idea you might have been forming of a standard-issue Italian castle, an archetypal palace or a model church. The great fortress which the Visconti built in 1360, with its low-slung façade of double-arched Gothic windows between two tall turrets (there were two others at the back but they were destroyed in the sixteenth century by an ancestor of the painter Toulouse-Lautrec) and a huge colonnaded courtyard beyond, is one of the most elegantly conceived mediaeval buildings in Europe, yet it defies you to adduce imitations or originals elsewhere. There is nothing quite like it, just as there is nothing to match the brickwork of the Romanesque churches, San Pietro in Ciel d'Oro, San Teodoro, Santa Maria in Betlem, or the wide-arched bridge across the Ticino, resting on Roman piers and arcaded from end to end, with an oratory to Saint John Nepomuk perched in the middle. Even the Guelphs and the Ghibellines were known by other names in Pavia: here they called them Fallabrini and Marcabotti.

The true touch of singularity was given to Pavia by the Austrians during the eighteenth century, when the city and the university had their privileges confirmed by Maria Theresa and Joseph II. Perhaps after all it is not Munich or Cologne or Nancy or Lille of which this place reminds you, so much as some consequential city of the Hapsburg Enlightenment, a quieter, more studious version of Prague or Vienna or even Salzburg. There is a great deal of exceptionally handsome stucco facing on the walls of the colleges and faculty buildings, and those white plaster window frames against the washes of egg yellow, russet, cream and pink belong in some Styrian or Slovenian village, where the people eat gherkins and goose liver and there is more than a faint hint, in the profusion of moustachioes and the trousers and embroidered waistcoats of the peasantry, that the Turks have passed that way. If you had to name the composer of whom Pavia reminded you, it would be that quintessentially Imperial Austrian figure Josef Haydn, whose serenity, inventiveness and instinctive refinement match this place perfectly.

The wonder is that any of it has survived at all. You would hardly know that this grave, restrained academe, with its colonnaded university buildings, their courtyards adorned with togaed professorial statues, had been the metropolis of Theodoric the Goth, where the last great Roman prose writer Boethius wrote his *Consolation of Philosophy*, a final appeal from the nascent Christian world to the vanishing wisdom of pagan antiquity. Theodoric had Boethius put to death in AD524 by a mixture of strangling and clubbing. As well as executing the author of what Gibbon calls 'a golden volume not unworthy of the leisure of Plato or Tully, but which claims incomparable merit from the barbarism of the times', the Gothic tyrant killed Boethius's father-in-law Symmachus, who had complained rather too vociferously of the sentence.

But, as the magnificent Edward tells us, 'after a life of virtue and glory, Theodoric was now descending with shame and guilt into the grave: his mind was humbled by the contrast of the past and justly alarmed by the invisible terrors of futurity.' One evening at dinner in the palace, an enormous fish was brought to table. Looking at it, Theodoric was struck by its terrifying resemblance, as it lay there goggle-eyed and sharp-toothed on the dish, to Symmachus clamouring for revenge. Stricken with guilt he retired to bed, confessed his grief for the murders to his doctor, and died of dysentery. One is tempted to wonder whether he might not have sampled a bit of the fish beforehand.

Everybody wanted Pavia. Charlemagne took it by storm, a band of marauding Hungarians destroyed forty-three of its churches, and two German emperors sacked it almost to its foundations. Francis I of France besieged it unsuccessfully in 1524, and at the great battle with the army of the Emperor Charles V which took place under its walls, twelve thousand

French troops were slaughtered, and the king, bleeding almost to death, was taken prisoner. '*Tout est perdu, fors l'honneur*' he wrote to his mother, 'all is lost save honour'. As for Napoleon, having pillaged the city after a minor uprising by local dissidents understandably loyal to the Hapsburgs, he declared that had the blood of a single Frenchman been spilt, he would have turned the place into a new Carthage, leaving not a stone upright, and raising a column with the legend 'Here stood the fair city of Pavia'.

It was quiet in Piazza Vittoria where we sat eating rather a good fish luncheon served by self-effacing waiters with soft voices, and drank the slightly sparkling wine of the nearby hills. Pavia being what it is, this piazza has a peculiar shape and cast to it, a narrow oblong made up of ancient, flaking arcades of primitively gawky-looking pillars, with an odd jumble of medieval and early Renaissance façades strung above them on either side.

The talk at lunch was about murder. Tim and I had started on some of our favourite cases, Thompson and Bywaters, Mrs Rattenbury and the Armstrong affair, which involved two rival solicitors, a nagging wife and a box of chocolates seasoned with arsenic. Abstractedly, but quite coincidentally, William opened a newly-bought copy of *La Repubblica* at the *Cronaca* pages, and we decided, after a glance at them, that if the English murder really had declined as George Orwell said it had, then murder in Italy was alive and well and, all things considered, doing just fine.

The *Cronaca* section of *Repubblica* is a kind of light relief from the rest of the paper, which remains the most serious and intelligent of European public prints because it makes no compromises whatever with its readership. It has its faults, among them a London correspondent whose despatches are an embarrassing mixture of vulgar gossip and ludicrous inaccuracy, but it is for the most part adult, informative and responsible in a way that no paper in Great Britain can match. In Italy, a country whose manifold virtues include the fact that it has not a single trash tabloid of any description, *La Repubblica* is the journal for sensible people with liberal views. For rational conservatives there is a choice between *La Stampa* and *Il Corriere della Sera*. Oafs and bigots read *Il Giornale*.

Reading *Repubblica* regularly, you learn how to negotiate its various sections according to your mood. The front page is mostly an assemblage of and-now-read-on headlines, and I am afraid I nearly always skip the ensuing National Politics section, which involves a lot of snappily dressed and rottenly corrupt elderly men in Rome making Byzantine deals with each other to survive the forthcoming elections. The international pages which follow are outstanding in the detail with which they examine the issues behind the world news, and I admire the courage of a paper whose column inches are so closely printed and whose pictures are so few and so indifferently reproduced. It makes you quite long for the old *Times* with the hatch-match-dispatch on the front.

The four pages of sport at the back, written in a rather joky, urbane, sometimes positively baroque prose, are offset by the *Cultura* features, by now almost notorious in their unbending loftiness of purpose, enormous essays on obscure poets from the last years of the Austro-Hungarian Empire, German philosophers of the 1920s and the exchanges of letters (never as interesting as they ought to be) between famous Italian writers. There are no reviews as we understand the term, since the Anglo-American tradition of critical analysis is unknown in Italy. A critic reporting on a book will simply make a readable abstract of its contents, which perhaps explains why Italian publishers' blurbs never include the kind of gushing plaudits to which we are accustomed in Britain. An opera or drama reviewer will spend most of his column inches sounding off authoritatively on the work itself, devoting only a paragraph or two at the end to the performers, tagging each with a curt adjectival label. Actors come off a good deal worse than singers in this respect, and you understand why the stage has so limited a *réclame* in Italy. Who the hell would want to be an actor simply for the sake of seeing their name wrapped up in the standard form of words 'Good also in their various roles were A, B and C'?

Theatrical fame here is reserved in each generation for one or two outstanding performers and a small collection of atrocious hams who bawl and barnstorm their way through the classics in order to keep the audience awake.

The *Cronaca* pages offer you the drama of real life in a series of concentrated little articles forming a somewhat more sensational version of that entertaining third page of *The Daily Telegraph*. You wonder, indeed, after reading these laconic, yet intensely realized pieces, where on earth you have been living and breathing for the past few days or weeks. Northern Italy has a way of lulling you into a false security. The cosiness, the blandness, the relentless homogeneity of ordinary existence, are sufficient to persuade you that whatever you might be most afraid of just couldn't happen here, to such an extent that you try to imagine crimes of passion, child molesters, mass murders and raving psychopaths in order to dispel the miasmal air of normality which threatens to bury everything around you.

There is really no need for this. The *Cronaca* says it all, revealing a secret Italy of monstrous desires, arbitrary and inexplicable hatreds, grudges, jealousies and suspicions, of ferocious brutality and chilling callousness. It offers a much-needed corrective to the notion we like to entertain (and which Italians are understandably glad that we should entertain) of a country where people are kind to children and considerate towards the elderly, where violence, which among the less articulate sections of our own society acts like a system of rhetoric, is mercifully unknown, and where practical good sense will always defuse potentially explosive situations.

Up to a point this is so. Italians are fonder than we of the society of children, whose presence, however tiresome, is amiably tolerated, with the odd peevish slap or kick administered more out of absentminded bad temper than as formal disciplinary rigour. They do not, as a rule, bundle grandparents into sunset homes, and the still almost universal system of different generations living together as a family obviates any serious problem of loneliness, of 'unregarded age in corners thrown'. Nor indeed are they preternaturally violent towards each other in that morose, tattooed-forearm, pit-bull-terrier-keeping fashion which is the birthright of the English, a nation among whom happiness easily degenerates into boozy pugnacity. The Italians' instinct for survival, for keeping the feet firmly planted on the earth while others are hopelessly cloudborne, will always rescue them from a headlong rush towards maximum danger – and this, let it be said at once, in the teeth of a hoary national stereotype, is not cowardice but hard-headed realism.

The darker face of quotidian Italy, which seems to contradict all these assertions, is to be glimpsed in the little chronicles of *La Repubblica*. Northern Italians like to blame much of the crime which takes place in their cities on southerners and, by association with them, on the migrant African '*Vu cumprà*', and doubtless, where drugs and gang warfare are concerned, this is substantially true. Yet, putting the Calabrian kidnappings and the Neapolitan *camorrista* shoot-outs and the *mafioso* revenge killings aside, there is much else that belongs inalienably to the almost self-parodically provincial provinces of the prosperous north.

A single week will throw up a juicy fraud case in Bergamo, a festering squabble over an inheritance between the heirs of a Cremonese fertilizer king, a routine husband-shoots-wife's-boyfriend scenario in a Veneto village, a 'hunting accident' murder staged by a Piedmontese aristocrat desirous of paying off an old score with a neighbour, a horrendous tale of child-beating and starvation from some pelting farm out in the Po delta, and the slaying of a gay Tuscan policeman by his cheated transvestite lover.

The tone of these *faits divers*, whether northern or southern, is always mildly sardonic in its detachment, as though the authors were surprised at the degree of their own interest in the case under discussion and wanted, half-heartedly, to convince you of a less marked involvement. In certain items it is unashamedly amused. That day in Pavia, for example, there was a delicious example in just such a style about a group of young Sicilian aristocrats who had gone to the airport to meet a friend of theirs who was returning to Palermo from a month's intensive English course in London. Feeling that the occasion might be more auspiciously marked than by a mere onrush of hugs and kisses at the barrier, they had prepared, with a touch of fancy by no means untypical of Sicilians, a sort of charade or pantomime in which they had disguised themselves as the entourage of a certain 'Lord Themistocles Throb', expected hourly from England. One of the girls had got herself up as a chambermaid, in a black dress, cap and apron, the boys posed as footmen carrying cocktails on trays, and the most blatantly theatrical number of the lot had donned full drag to figure as a sort of vamp dowager with beads, cigarette holder and smooch lipstick.

The surprise, apparently, was not to be. In Italy as in Britain, there is a ridiculous old law which, for whatever reason, forbids you, except presumably during the carnival season, to wear theatrical costume in public places. It is seldom invoked, but on this occasion the airport police decided to be thoroughly mouldy spoilsports and poor Lord Themistocles Throb was greeted with the dispiriting spectacle of the bright young Palermitans being marched away in their gladrags as he emerged from the customs lounge.

After chewing over the *Cronaca* in the company of another bottle, we tonked off into the countryside to look at the Certosa, the stupendous Carthusian monastery founded in 1396 by Gian Galeazzo Visconti, Duke of Milan, in fulfilment of a vow made by his wife Caterina. Like everything else connected with Pavia, it is somehow particular in a way that transcends all the associations you might be justified in making with the Milanese Duomo, where the architects Bernardo da Venezia and Giacomo Campione had worked before embarking on the Certosa.

Jacob Burckhardt, in his *Civilisation of the Renaissance in Italy* (1860) judged the façade of the church, which you approach across a courtyard between broad grass-plots, to be the most splendidly decorative monument in Italy. Actually it is quite hideous, so preposterously over-adorned, so totally lacking in anything like a controlling idea of form or colour, such a mischmasch of classicizing doodles, a swag here, a mullion there, a band of marble inlay, a couple of blind arcades, and a set of crockets like things unpacked every Christmas from a cardboard box, that you are almost afraid to go inside the building for fear of something worse.

As it most happily turns out, the Certosa possesses one of Italy's more startlingly lovely church interiors. I say 'startling' because the lightness and brilliance of tone in the marble, the vault decoration and the glazing of abundant windows creates an all too unfamiliar beauty. Despite my undying love for the works of art they contain, my Protestant soul revolts against the dark churches of the Catholic communion. Whereas in Greek and Russian Orthodox churches the candles and incense and icons somehow conspire with the darkness to produce a sense of mysterious intelligence, a shadowed threshold to understanding, the same conjuration in Mother Church merely creates an unpleasant blend of kitsch and ignorance. I do so loathe the insistent windowlessness of most Italian churches,* which is why the Certosa captivates me by its fearless, confident brilliance of visual engagement.

There is a coherent handsomeness, a stately exuberance like that of some court dance, in every detail: the orange, black and white marble roundels and diamonds of the inlaid floor, Daniele Crespi's noble baroque scenes from the Life of Saint Bruno in the choir, the attitudinizing cherubs upholding the presbytery rails, the alabaster effigies of Lodovico Sforza 'il Moro' and his wife Beatrice d'Este brought here from Milan in 1564, the mesh of gold stars dotting the blue nave vaults, the walnut wardrobes in the sacristy and the altarpiece made by Baldassare degli Embriachi out of hippopotamus teeth.

Beyond this church lie two cloisters, called Piccolo and

* For a notable exception, try the cathedral at Pienza, radiant with south Tuscan daylight, built through the inspiration of that illumined romantic Aeneas Sylvius Piccolomini, Pope Pius II, in 1462.

Grande to distinguish one from another, but in reality both among the grandest in Italy. The larger of the two grants an amazing prospect of contrasted architectural patterns in the bands of arcading along the outer walls of the church, the thrusting white octagon of the lantern over the crossing and the line of marble finials above the cloister roof. In the Piccolo is the distinguishing feature of a Carthusian monastery, the range of cells like little houses, each with its bedroom and oratory and neatly-tended scrap of walled garden behind.

There is an *enoteca* next to the Certosa, beside a sort of weedy moat, made out of a converted mill and stacked with *vini pregiati* of Lombardy and Piedmont, the Oltrepo Pavese, the Gattinara and Ghemme and Nebbiolo, the Barbera and Barolo and Dolcetto, and my especially well-loved Franciacorta, the oak-smoke-flavoured vintage of the hills above the city of Brescia. The monks for their part will sell you, as is the way of monasteries, any number of soaps and aromatic waters and jars of honey and cakes of beeswax, besides a sort of low-alcohol aniseed drink called Gocce Imperiali, and a sticky black herbal elixir of a sort one imagines Friar Laurence in *Romeo and Juliet* preparing after a morning expedition with his basket.

The boot clinking with bottles, we set off across the Po, through Castel San Giovanni and Borgonovo into the Colli Piacentini, the Placentine Hills, with their comfortable green folds of farmland wrinkling up between the uncertain courses of the mountain rivers towards the grey ridges of the northern Apennines which break the horizon. We paused at that wondrous essay in the ersatz, Grazzano Visconti, a sort of Disneyland of romantic mediaevalism, a village whose noble proprietor, in the early years of this century, decided to improve upon it with many a merlon and machicolation, with sundry chevrons and bends both gules and argent, and luxuriant growths of that most unmediaeval of plants, the Virginia creeper. It was the age of Gabriele D'Annunzio's torridly Dantesque showcase dramas for Eleonora Duse, costumed with seemly pinching of wimples and bismotered habergeouns, to swooning, swooping, pinchbeck-exotic music by Respighi and Pizzetti, so the Visconti of the day felt free to install picturesque village folk in period costume doing characteristic things with looms and spinning wheels, and doubtless ready, at the drop of a coif or a biggin, to rattle off a strophe or a distich from Bindo di Cione del Frate, Guido Novello da Polenta or Frate Stoppa de' Bostichi.

As a corrective to the bogusness of Grazzano, there is always Castell'Arquato, perched up on the hillside above a little river called the Arda, which shimmies down into the plain to join the Po somewhere north of Busseto, where Verdi had his earliest music lessons. Castell'Arquato is the genuine mediaeval article, with a double girdle of ramparts and an exceptionally winsome piazza with a Palazzo Pretorio in crumbly ochre-coloured stone and a Romanesque church with a garden behind it in which, on fine afternoons like this one, you can sit and listen to the water of the fountain plopping agreeably into its basin, while you puff at a *toscanello* and watch the maize ripening on the flat bottom of the valley. Then, in an evil hour, we decided to go and have a look at Piacenza.

There ought to be a fine Emilian city down there by the bend of the river, in the incomparable tradition of Parma, Bologna and blessed Modena. Piacenza is as old as any of them, and was once just as important, having afforded one of the titles by which the Dukes of Parma were always officially styled. For a few months during the spring and summer of 1831 it was even the capital of the duchy, a place of refuge for Marie Louise, Napoleon's widow, who had been given the duchy as a sop to status by her Hapsburg relatives, while the citizens of Parma made a little revolution against her chief minister, the generally odious Count Werklein. As one of the more imaginative and intelligent of her increasingly dull and intellectually limited family, Marie Louise won back her capital city with relative ease, and though she closed the university and suppressed a newspaper or two, she was welcomed with three days of illuminations and a special cantata at the opera house.* She had the good sense to turn off Werklein for ever. As an answer to the pension application he impertinently addressed to her from Vienna, she merely scribbled the words 'Absolutely out of the question' across the letter and returned it to sender.

This was Piacenza's little moment of triumph over elegant, Frenchified, rich, snooty, pleasure-loving Parma. It has certainly never known another. Perhaps this accounts for its peculiar air of perpetual glumness, or maybe it was always a dour place and the experience of exile there made the duchess and her courtiers yet more eager to get home to swanky old Parma.

We arrived at Piacenza in the late summer afternoon, when the day-collected heat lifts off pavements and walls and you may generally expect a wisp or two of breeze to start freshening the streets. Usually this is the best time of all in Italy, an enchanted hour or so when the town, wherever you may find yourself, will begin turning out its people for the *passeggiata* and the cafés will throng with eaters of ice-creams and drinkers of *granita* and *frappé*, and the light on old stones will fall at its most subtly blandishing. There is something in this sacred time that inevitably exhilarates me, an unfettered sense of possibility which plays like a musician's hand upon the attuned emotions. It is my hour of feeling.

I wanted there to be something of this in Piacenza to which my senses could respond. I wanted it to look stately and vain of its grandeur. I wanted its inhabitants to have that superb complacency that irradiates the cities of the Emilian plain and derives as much as anything from the fact that their people represent the earliest surviving generations in this part of the world who have ever had enough to eat, good clothes to their backs and more money than they reasonably know what to do with.

* The Teatro Regio of Parma is the handsomest
of the larger theatres of northern Italy. Designed
by Nicola Bettoli, it opened in 1829 with the
premiere of Bellini's *Zaira*. Its audience is the
most captiously critical in Italy.

Instead here was one of the most insidiously creepy places I ever set foot in. A weird miasmal heaviness palled the streets, which even for midsummer were oddly without movement or crowds. Little knots of strollers moved up and down in a kind of fretful aimlessness, their lumpy, unformed faces bearing not the least hint of animation. Most terrifying of all, they were unfailingly silent. Those gaggles of girls and boys who in any other city would have fluttered the pigeons off the palaces with their cheerful row, wandered about muttering sullenly to one another, as if the stifling, waveless air were starting silently to choke them and in an hour or so we should find the piazza littered with their corpses like a new Pompeii.

A sort of vaguely defined horror began to possess us, a sensation accentuated by the appearance in the sky overhead of that dingy yellowish haze typical of the Po valley on a hot day, as if the sun had retired to bed with exhaustion. Through the noiseless, tomb-like lanes, between glum-looking baroque palaces and dog's-dinner façades from the early years of fascism when Mussolini was still wearing spats, we crept towards the square, the Piazza Cavalli, 'cuore storico della città', where, in front of the looming gothic Palazzo Comunale, two huge black equestrian statues by the Tuscan sculptor Francesco Mochi (1580–1648) of the Farnese Dukes of Parma Alessandro and Ranuccio advance at a high-stepping trot. Even in these there is something terrible, a ferocity, a merciless impatience in the swirl of their cloaks, the jut of their beards and their brandished swords, something perhaps of that terror the Netherlanders felt when Alessandro came among them as governor for King Philip of Spain amid the lacerating wars of Protestant and Catholic at the close of the sixteenth century.

We found a café under the shadow of the palace, and I set about demolishing one of those luxury ice-creams that arrive in a species of glass cornucopia with a parasol sticking out of the top, while Tim and William, each affected to the very bones by the indefinable ghastliness of the hour, sombrely drank long glasses of whisky. While we sat there, I watched two boys at work in the courtyard beyond, laying a telephone line. They were stripped to their shorts and, as it seemed, amazingly bronzed, well-timbered, agile and good to look at, the first aesthetically rewarding human creatures I'd set eyes on since we arrived.

Yet as my glance lingered on the pair, scrambling in and out of the trench, paying out cable and snipping wires, this ingratiating impression began to change into something more sinister. About their movements, the bends of the waist and twistings of the hips, the way in which now and then they touched one another, there was a curious kind of criminal knowingness, a collusion which might have been erotic if, in some inexplicable fashion, it didn't hint instead at a cynical professionalism, as though laying a telephone line were merely a cover for some far more felonious enterprise. Their beauty seemed without innocence, a cloak to menace, yet perhaps in that instant this was how I wanted them to look.

'What are you staring at?' asked my brother in his deep, rasping, accusatory voice.

'Nothing,' I lied, 'I was thinking about someone I used to know.'

On the opposite side of the piazza there is a gothic church of the Franciscans, with a high façade topped by three turrets, and a dreary interior got up in the most uninspired nineteenth-century style. As we wandered in, we were caught momentarily by the sound of organ music. There are fine organs in Italian churches, especially in the northern reaches of Lombardy and the Veneto, where the German tradition has stretched a finger or two across the mountains, but in a country so dismally ill-furnished for an adequate musical life, very few people exist who can play them at all well. To those nurtured on the magnificence of an English choral evensong, the lyric element in Italian church services is strangely flat and depressing. To find an organ going here, in tune what was more, seemed remarkable enough for us to want to know where precisely in the church it was and who played it.

There seemed at first to be nothing like a melody. A series of decorative semiquaver passages wound in and out of each other like basket-weaving, but as music it was wholly without interest.

Then, as we listened, we were aware of a most incongruous intrusion, for into this featureless texture of plaited twiddlings there was insinuated a clearly recognizable tune, none other than 'Colonel Bogey', to which as schoolkids we had sung 'Hitler has only got one ball'. And it was at that moment that I remembered The Murderer.

You would never have known to look at him that he was a murderer. That is of course the thing about such people. We expect them to appear louring and satanic, like the hero figures in Byron's verse tales 'marked with one virtue and a thousand crimes', and seldom acknowledge that their fascination arises precisely from their lack of any sort of *physique du role*. They frighten us with their ordinariness. Looking at the faded snapshot of some plain-faced housewife who has shot dead her two-timing lover, or at the photographic studio portrait of a pebble-spectacled wimp with a draggletail moustache who has cut his ladyfriend into manageable collops, we recognize in these commonplace countenances the spectre of our own readiness to do the deed.

The murderer I knew was a tall, bald, bespectacled man of about forty-five. He was not unhandsome: the leanness of his jaws, covered with a close-shaven beard, and the pencil-sharpness of his nose, gave him the air of a chronicler monk pictured in a Russian icon, an El Greco hermit or a portrait off a Fayyum coffin lid. To complement this impression, he had the stooping, slightly quizzical air of the true academic, which indeed he was, a professor at one of the Tuscan universities, engaged on an apparently interminable programme of linguistic research which had already involved the publication of three books and was about to yield a fourth.

We had met as a result of one of those paralysing one-day strikes organized by COBAS, the more extreme, or as some would say, less responsible of the Italian rail unions, under which the entire Italian railway system buckled, staggered and finally gave up. What turned out to be the last train from Milan, carrying us like a party of refugees vaguely in the direction of Rome, had made a vexatious point of stopping at almost every small station along the line until it halted for the duration at Bologna and we flung ourselves into a coach across the Apennines to Rome.

As the train jerked and dawdled its way southwards, with an increasing sense of screw-the-passengers in its maddening little halts at Cadeo, Casalpusterlengo, Sant'Ilario d'Enza and anywhere else that looked remotely inhabited on the Lombardo-Emilian plain, the professor, who saw me reading that morning's *Independent*, struck up a conversation. His English was so exceptionally good, so consistently flawless in its command of idiom, its sophisticated colloquialisms and its highly coloured vocabulary that there seemed no point in my trying to persevere in Italian. He was admirably unmoved by my congratulations on his expertise: this was a skill he took for granted, a nonchalant professional brilliance like that of a diva or an escapologist.

I was not especially flattered by his complete lack of interest in me, but I could not very well force him to ask me questions about myself; neither, since the train was crammed to the doors with fugitives from the Curse of COBAS, could I get up and move into the next carriage. In any case I should hardly have wanted to. Self-absorption is fascinating for the vulnerability it betrays. Bored to death though you may be with the egoist prosing on about his victories and triumphs, you want to stay the course so as to watch whatever might be revealed when he trips or stumbles. So I resigned myself to being merely a feed for his solipsism and began, in a thoroughly detached fashion, to enjoy it.

He made no secret of the fact that teaching bored him. His pupils were mostly faceless embryonic yuppies, whom he viewed with unashamed cynicism as simply the official guarantors of his job. It was not hard, indeed, to imagine them withering under the lash of his barely concealed scorn. What really mattered to him was the nature of language itself, not, I was interested to note, as a means of communication or as a vehicle for expression, but purely as a mechanism susceptible of adjustments and overhauling, yet so very nearly perfect.

When the professor began to talk in some detail of modal verbs, syntactical parameters and the use of the imperfect subjunctive, I contented myself with the occasional nod or hum of encouragement, though my grasp of his actual meaning, as he negotiated with terrifying precision the labyrinths of grammar, had deserted me early on. The manner was more enthralling than the matter. He spoke of the English language as if he were not merely its discoverer but its inventor, yet what seemed to annoy him most of all was its infuriating reluctance to submit itself to his will. Now and then I looked at him as he spoke. His long swarthy cenobite's face was suddenly heavy with the troubles of pulling recalcitrant grammatical structures into shape. I found myself almost wishing that there was something I could do to help, some formula whose casual imparting would show him the way towards that ultimate rationale with which he seemed so hopelessly obsessed.

Instead I stared out of the window and announced inanely: 'Ah, here we are at Lodi, where Napoleon fought the battle on the bridge. How well do you know England?'

He had only ever visited London, but his manner of describing it was just as bizarre as his earlier pronouncements on linguistics had been. Evidently he had no feeling whatever for its attractions as a city. Aesthetic considerations of any kind, from what I could gather, meant nothing to him – his acquaintance with English and American fiction went no further than Agatha Christie and Raymond Chandler – and the beauty and singularity of London apparently left him unmoved.

What preoccupied the professor was the indescribable filth in which the English, even those with sufficient money and status, chose readily to live. He talked with eloquence of the middle-class families in Highgate and Streatham with whom he regularly boarded, the smell of the bedroom curtains, the mark on the enamel of the bath made by the dripping tap, the ring round the lavatory basin and the layers of encrusted grime in the plughole of the kitchen sink. With something like relish, he described an attempt by his landlady to make him what she called a casserole, which he had watched entranced as much by the unhygienic methods of preparation as by the unspeakable horror which resulted.

'And did you eat it?' I asked.

'Oh yes,' said he, a smile breaking the mournful composure of his features, 'but not out of politeness. For an experiment.'

It was clear that he liked neither England nor the English. He had travelled elsewhere, to France and to America, with far greater pleasure, and his resolute incuriosity about a country he visited so regularly was mystifying to me. He had discovered an unfathomable satisfaction in connecting the disobedience of the English language with the unregenerate foulness and disorder of domestic England, and the antipathy created by both these things seemed to nourish him like a vitamin. By the time we crawled into Bologna I had buried altogether my irritation at being made no more than a stooge, and began to feel quite disappointed at having to say farewell to him.

In the shadowed booking halls of the station we shook hands and I hurried away towards the waiting '*pulman*'. There was no special warmth in the professor's goodbye, and I wondered if he had been remotely aware of me as a sentient individual to whose scrutiny he had subjected his distinctive personality. I suppose I did wonder briefly whether he were mad, but his quirks and obsessions were easily explained by the kind of life he led.

How little I had actually guessed was revealed to me two years later in the Tuscan town of Montepulciano, where I had stopped to lunch with some friends. That morning I had bought *La Repubblica*, but there was no time to do more than glance at the headlines as we coasted through the Crete Senesi towards Asciano, Buonconvento and the delights of San Quirico and Pienza. We went and had our coffee at a bar in the square amid those palaces whose masonry of golden tufa makes them look as if sliced out of ginger-cake, and it was there that I was able to flick forward at last to the Cronaca pages. There was the usual heady cocktail of folly and vice, and I was all set to read a juicy-looking story about a man in Rovigo who had made a porno video of his wife *in flagrante* with the family lawyer when I noticed in the adjacent column a face I could never have forgotten in a million years.

The mugshot enhanced rather than diminished those antique lineaments, whose expression had lost nothing of its donnish puzzlement. On either side of it were two other portraits, characteristically blurred and unflattering, of his female victims. For the professor had killed twice, in a manner strangely unscientific and amateurish, so that the police had little difficulty tracking him down. Both women were young and unmarried, and in each case he appeared to have established their movements to and from the offices where they worked before stabbing and strangling them. On neither had he attempted a sexual assault. Such fastidiousness seemed somehow typical.

His domestic life and professional character, said the article, were both exemplary. Though his colleagues testified to a certain limited celebrity in the world of linguistics, none of his books had made him famous. Somewhat ironically, he was judged a sound if rather severe teacher and an admirably concise and methodical lecturer. Out of term he went home to his mother in Piacenza, where he had the reputation of being *un bravo ragazzo*, punctilious in his attentiveness to family duties and unexpectedly pious in attending mass. He was unmarried, a detail which would doubtless have been made to account for something if anyone could produce a motive, but he had kept silent on the subject, and the reporter in desperation offered a few woolly hypotheses about homosexuality or a Jack-the-Ripper 'down on women', though there was no definite evidence of either.

I read the whole piece with understandable amazement. To meet and talk with a live murderer is, I imagine, a distinction craved by many, and I basked for a while in the dubious rays of reflected glory. My friends, at any rate, were exceedingly envious, wanting to know whether or not I'd received the slightest sinister inkling from our long conversation. It was the fact that I hadn't which, when I pondered the whole business later that day, made me shudder slightly. With that wisdom after the event which in such cases everyone loves to display, I could have said that the professor's monomaniacal preoccupation with cleanliness and his obsessive hankering after linguistic precision both pointed in some way or another towards an unbalanced mind, but it could as easily have been a simple case of academic quirkishness as any indication of a dangerous psychopath. What frightened me in retrospect was his articulate coolness and total absence of passion.

I thought about it now, in this gimcrack church of Piacenza, where perhaps he had dipped his long fingers with their cushion-capped nails into the holy water stoup and turned his sad hermit's eyes in prayer to the altar. I imagined him at home, alone with his mother and her knitting and the telly, a murderer's mother like the Kray Brothers' mum or the mother of my ancestor William Palmer the Rugely poisoner who swore by her 'saintly Billy' to the last. A motive had simply not emerged, neither was any former connection established between him and his victims. He had done it perhaps in order to prove a point, to establish the culminating element in some extended theoretical process which had engaged him to the exclusion of everything else. The more convinced of this I became, the more I felt I should have liked to ask him, not *why* he had murdered but what exactly he meant by it. From a professor of linguistics the explanation would have been an interesting one.

In the church the weirdly arabesqued melody, mysterious as Caliban's airs, ground on:

> Hitler has only got one ball,
> Goering has two but very small,
>   Himmler
>   Is rather sim'lar,
> But poor old Goebbels
> Has no balls
>   At all.

There was no instrument anywhere to be seen. Then, through an opened side door, we found the music. Outside in the street, a man of uncertain age, with greying sandy curls, a sort of senescent hippy in dingy mauve harem pants, was playing a barrel-organ. You could tell from his spectacles that he was a

German. On top of the organ a mangy-looking brown monkey gambolled to and fro, less from enthusiasm than sheer force of habit, and a cap with a few loose lire lay at the grinder's feet. It must have seemed a splendid wheeze to tramp round Italy with an organ and a monkey, Being Picturesque. In the present context there was something decidedly ghoulish about the whole ensemble, the skinny, motheaten marmoset, the creaking squeezebox and the whey-faced alternative leering myopically at us across the pavement. His spectacles were round, with narrow black rims, just like the professor's.

A few drops of rain fell as we crossed the square. Lurking under their arch, the telephone boys were rolling cigarettes, a brace of spies handing on the papers.

'Beastly place, isn't it?' said Tim, as the thunder rolled towards us across the Po. We fled southwards to Fidenza, where they drink their Lambrusco out of white china bowls.

13 Emily Street

After a few years of jaunting up and down Italy, the traveller begins to claim some part of it for his own. The country becomes 'my Italy', staked out with no right other than the dubious freedom guaranteed by familiarity and enthusiasm. Something in a landscape or a city will clinch his loyalty, he will start picking up a smattering of regional history, acquire a few dialect phrases or a spot of the local gastronomy to make him feel he really belongs, and make vague resolutions to buy a farm or the attic of a palace or the window of an abandoned monastery.

Other people's knowingness is insufferable, and there are few things more wince-making than the I-got-here-before-you act indulged in so thoughtlessly by those of us who tend to return to the same place year after year. This book, I suppose is neither more nor less than a manifestation of the same phenomenon. Once, on a very small Mediterranean island, I spent a week trying to escape from a desperately seen-it-all-done-it-all Swiss, who greeted my innocent reactions to the charm of scenery, local building styles, rhythms of peasant life, religious festivities etcetera with a series of little lectures calculated to show that none of it was new to him and that I need not look any further for compendious and exhaustive illumination of the topic in hand.

Yet as soon as the vital link is made, once 'the land of lands' lays its fingers, as it were, to your throat, you can scarce avoid the sense of presumed intimacy which the suddenly-mastered rhetoric of the place affords. It is not simply a question of knowing which restaurant will serve the best risotto, whether the local white wine goes best with cheese or fruit, where the shop is that sells handmade paper, or the exact half-hour in the late afternoon when the little oratory with the frescoes opens for mass, so that, unbeliever as you are, you can slip in for a look while the old women are murmuring cosily through their rosaries. It is the feeling that you and this place have marked each other, that between you there is some perpetually unfinished business, 'an old contracting', which will not be successfully concluded until the pair of you are inextricably fused.

In my case, it is perhaps a little worse. I have this fantasy about being the people I desire, imagining myself inhabiting them physically, walking with their legs, speaking with their mouths, touching with their hands. Simple lust becomes envy to the extent that I sometimes wonder whether, possessed with a consummate insanity, I might not end by flaying them for their skins or even eating them in order to achieve the desired transformation.

My reaction is exactly the same towards places. If true passion is, as I've always taken it to be, a longing for self-extinction, a release of the imprisoned identity from the delusive essence created for it by those who surround us, a freeing of the soul which prefigures the experience of immortality, then something of this kind, a union with a lover, is what I feel about certain places in Italy. Milton, in *Il Penseroso*, has a wonderful line about 'forget thyself to marble', and it is in these towns and villages and prospects that I can forget myself until I am the stones and bricks and earth and water and trees of which they are made.

This ought to happen in Tuscany, but precisely why it doesn't I'll explain in another chapter. Venice, where it might so easily occur, is too closely identified with ardent sentimental experience for me to be able to achieve the desired fusion, nor, for all my love of it, do I greatly wish to. One territory, however, has become my own to the extent that my heart starts to race and an exhilaration beyond all language overcomes me in the yearly renewal of our acquaintance.

I love it precisely because it has been so conspicuously unloved and unvisited by other travellers to Italy. It has had its great painters, sculptors and architects, but they are not what the wise and good among art historians choose to term great, and several of the very best spent no more than a few years of their early lives here. The cooks are the finest in the world, acknowledged as such by their fastidious compatriots, but the popular idea of Italian cooking does not immediately summon up the special delights of this region, and the single wine of any note neither travels well nor is considered among the nation's most prized. The landscape is uniformly flat, the domestic architecture of the villages, always charmless, is nowadays irredeemably hideous, and the small towns are without much in the way of castles, churches or palaces to detain the traveller. At first glance it is scarcely any wonder that nearly everybody with leisure to wander hurries across this country on the railway or the *autostrada* and feels no special temptation to turn aside from their journey.

It is the province of Emilia, that broad river plain stretching southwards from the Po to the foothills of the Apennines. This has not always been its name*: a label of convenience stuck on after the Risorgimento, it was derived from the Roman Via Aemilia, running northwest from Ariminum to Mediolanum, laid out in 187BC by Marcus Aemilius Lepidus. He was the ancestor of Shakespeare's Lepidus, that 'slight, unmeritable man, meet to be sent on errands', the makeweight in the triumvirate with those historical megastars Mark Antony and Octavius Caesar. You can see the island in the river where they formed their fatal pact if you take the Via Emilia north through the suburbs of Bologna.

Before 1860 Bologna and Ferrara were governed by the Pope's legate, everything to the northeast belonged to the Duke of Parma, and the territory of the Duke of Modena, owing to a shrewd dynastic marriage with an heiress of the Cybo family of Massa, extended right over the mountains to the Carrara marble quarries and the Gulf of Genoa. Travellers complained incessantly at the cost of having to cross so many frontiers, what with the official bribes to the customs officers on either side (failure to pay meant having your entire luggage ransacked with elaborate disregard for its contents) but there was no help for it if you wanted to stay on the only decent roads down to Florence and Rome.

Victorian tourists, even now more influential on our attitudes towards Italy than we are willing to acknowledge, found nothing to detain them in these cities of the plain save the common accidents of the journey – a lame coach horse, a portmanteau gone astray, a wrangle with the authorities over a visa. If they turned aside to inspect the ducal galleries of Modena and Parma or the great mediaeval basilicas of Bologna, it was more from duty than interest, and in their *carnets de voyage* – 'sombre', 'dusty', 'indifferent', 'dull', 'drab', 'poor', 'dirty', 'ugly'.

---

* Italians anxious to exhibit their prowess in English sometimes quaintly and charmingly refer to it as 'Emily': thus Via Emilia becomes 'Emily Street'. A Bolognese pop group in the early 'seventies was called 'The New Emily Jazz Orchestra'.

Of all these scorned and slighted cities, the most consistently unvisited is Modena. Apart from a glance or two at the ducal Correggios and a peep, perhaps, at the fabulous collection of mediaeval codices in the Biblioteca Estense, nobody has ever bothered much about it, and Italians, who would far rather be windsurfing in the Maldives or tripping on opium in a Phuket beach-hut, never go there if they can help it. You can catch a glimpse of Modena as you whoosh along the *autostrada*, an ash-grey profile of church towers, modest high-rise blocks and the squat cuboids of local light industry, spectral and illusory across the fields. Or the train that is carrying you down towards the lands of Giotto and Bernini will stop there for a minute or two, a door will trundle open and one of those melodious station tannoy voices will echo down the platform, 'Modenaaa, stazione di Modenaaa', but you will not get off.

And why not? You are closer here than ever you will be at Florence or Venice or Rome to the Italy of the Italians, the ordinary humdrum core of life among the indigenes, who for the most part do not greatly care about frescoes and tactile values and predella panels, but are perfectly happy to acknowledge them as a portion of their inheritance, like the boring chunks of Manzoni mugged up for school exams or the tune of '*Va pensiero sull' ali dorate*', in *Nabucco*. And they will tell you with pride that their city is the fifth richest in Italy, that there are no slums, no beggars, a murder maybe once a year, and an overwhelming, positively stifling air of comfort and prosperity.

After its no-nonsense fashion, Modena has contributed to the sum of human happiness. It was the home of the great Enzo Ferrari and still makes his racing cars at Maranello. Gabriele Falloppia, the sixteenth-century anatomist who identified the workings of what the English choose to call 'the fallowpian tubes', was born here and spent much time examining the city's poxed, which explains why Italy's national *Enciclopedia Treccani* can quaintly refer to him as '*sifilografo*'. A hundred years afterwards, Bernardo Ramazzini, the Duke of Modena's physician, was among the first doctors to make a scientific study of the diseases of the poor, publishing demographic surveys of the yearly epidemics sweeping through the wretched villages of the *bassa modenese*, making shrewd connections between nutrition and disease resistance and observing the ways in which certain maladies attached themselves to specific trades.

Modena was never a literary city (the university is conspicuously without a proper faculty of letters) but there, as wherever not, were local poets, among them Fulvio Testi, who was almost, but not quite, a very great writer indeed. He became the Duke of Modena's secretary of state and artistic adviser, and was sent as ambassador to Vienna and Madrid, but his restlessness set him intriguing with the French for a plum job at the papal court, so the duke clapped him in gaol, where he died of a fever in 1646.

Testi's poetry is good not just because it transcends the usual self-regarding fancywork of European baroque, but because it's so much more nakedly autobiographical than that of his contemporaries. This is the writing of an essentially unhappy man, who wanted to spend less time playing the courtier and the diplomat, writing odes on Prince Luigi D'Este's success in the tiltyard or the Duchess of Savoy's attack of yellow jaundice, and more on the pleasures of the countryside and the cosmopolitan society of Roman cardinals, among whom he could set aside the epic poems on the Emperor Constantine and the Conquest of India which the duke kept nagging him to get on with, and write instead of his love for the legendary Neapolitan soprano, Leonora Baroni (Milton adored her too – did he and Testi ever meet to compare notes?) or send wonderful poetic letters of advice to friends, advice which he himself would have been too rash to follow.

One of these is an angry, melancholy warning to a fellow diplomat, Count Giovanni Battista Ronchi, entitled 'That the present age is corrupted with sloth', in which he imagines him wandering among the ruins of Rome scattered along the Aventine and Caelian hills. 'Where once there were temples and theatres,' says Testi, 'I hear the lowing of oxen and the clank of the plough, and I hear you sigh from the depth of your heart for the city that is no more.' He senses idleness and sterile foppery enfeebling Italy at the fag-end of the Renaissance, and sees amid the broken columns and limbless statuary a portent of foreign invaders trampling yet again on the supine, helpless peninsula.

Testi was right as regards Modena, though the dismal turns of great-power politics which eventually made the place a byword for tyranny at its most sordid and petty lay two hundred years away. His masters, the dukes and princes of the Este family, ruled shrewdly after their fashion, wrestling with those incurable ills to which small seventeenth-century sovereigns were heirs – too many nobles, too much banditry, not enough cash – and trying, more or less successfully, to hedge their bets with Spain, France, the Emperor and the Pope. From their canny, ruthless forebears, who had ruled from Ferrara until the insatiable greed of the popes invoked a kink in the line of succession to fob them off with Modena while their former duchy was clawed to Mother Church, the Este inherited, along with prudence and acquisitiveness, a louche, lingering sexual allure which comes out in their portraits and busts, a sort of erotic danger whose power can still be sensed faintly under the slashed doublets, pinked sleeves, shoe-roses, panniered skirts and curled moustachioes.

It was something they passed to the young Modenese princess who in 1673 was escorted to London to become the bride, at barely fifteen, of the forty-five-year-old James Duke of York, the future James II. Maria Beatrice D'Este, daughter of Duke Francesco I and a great-niece, on her mother's side, of Cardinal Mazarin, was one of those attractive and intelligent queen-consorts who do whatever they can to make up for the obtuseness of their royal husbands. 'I thinke you will finde this young princess,' wrote Lord Peterborough, the ambassador sent to Modena by Charles II to arrange the match, 'to have beauty in hur person, and in hur minde; to be faire tall, well shap'd and healthful,' though another diplomat warned that 'shee is a stiffe Roman Catholique'.

Known to school history books and royal pedigrees as 'Mary of Modena', she set about making friends with everyone in the hostile, xenophobic world of Restoration London, playing interminable card-games with her stepdaughters, having snowball fights with her ladies-in-waiting, going in disguise to Bartholomew Fair, and bringing painters and musicians from her father's court to assuage the English passion for novelty.

Among them was Benedetto Gennari, nephew of the great Guercino and one of the most accomplished masters of the late Italian baroque. Arriving in London a year after Mary, he settled down to a remarkably prolific career as a painter for the royal family and the nobility. In the space of sixteen years he completed over a hundred canvases in every style from the intimate miniature to the lavish altarpiece, with a wit, delicacy and sophistication worthy of his squint-eyed genius of an uncle. There were saints and Madonnas for Queen Catherine's chapel, their faces grave and tender yet touched with a sensuous glow from the sheen of brilliant robes and the burst of sunlight through a scramble of cloud-borne *putti*. There were portraits of 'Miledi Ogle' clutching a green kerchief to her white bosom, of 'Miledi Beti Felton figurata da Cleopatra', of 'Signor Carlo Sidni' and 'Madama Niuton'. There were scores of erotic mythologies, a Danae, a Galatea, 'the Genius of Poetry' like a mistress *en déshabillé*, and a frankly pornographic piece involving two shepherdesses and the manly attributes of a sleeping shepherd, for King Charles's new dining room 'nel Palazzo di Windsor' and for his 'nuovo apartamento in Weteal'. From his self-portrait, painted for the Grand Duke of Tuscany's Uffizi collection in 1686, Gennari turns to look at us from mixing colours on his palette, his sidelong glance quintessentially Italian in its knowing, confident alertness.

We never honestly deserved him, and even if there had been a native painter remotely versatile enough to absorb his influence, religion and politics between them had already determined that the warm breeze of Italianate elegance should prove little more than a fugitive gust. Once her husband ascended the throne as James II, even Mary of Modena's inherited resources of tact and suavity were unavailing against his malign genius for making himself the most unattractive monarch ever to occupy the throne of England. A merciless propaganda war waged against her by the Protestants accomplished the *coup de grâce* with the notorious libel which declared that her infant son was really a child smuggled into the bedchamber in a warming-pan after a phantom pregnancy.

We never deserved Mary either. Italian blood has returned to the British royal family in the person of the Princess of Wales, descended from the Medici through a bastard son of Charles II. The king's grandmother was a Florentine princess, and Charles himself was a perfect heir of Cosimo Il Grande and Lorenzo Il Magnifico in his swarthy Medicean ugliness. But in 1688 the only Italian Queen of England accompanied her husband into exile, and it was her initiative and common sense which kept his cause alive. Mary's descendants inherited good looks from her but nothing else: in their pigheadedness, vacillation and dishonesty they were perfect Stuarts.

Gennari, who followed the royal refugees to the château of Saint-Germain en Laye outside Paris, left us two portraits of the Queen, fascinatingly unlike the standard images of her purveyed by the routine talents of the court painters of Saint James's – Lely, Wissing and Verelst – all sullen pouting and poached-egg eyes. This Mary has the long, narrow Este nose, a curious, slightly twisted mouth and a gaze clouded with cynical resignation to the thirty years of baffled hopes which lay ahead of her. When she died in 1718, a widow of fifty-nine, even the notoriously waspish Duc de Saint-Simon could find it in him to record that 'with much natural sensibility, great spirit and a pride which she had learned to control and humble, she had the most noble bearing in the world, regal and impressive yet gentle and modest. Her death was as holy as her life.'

In Modena Mary had grown up amid a little sunburst of art and learning. The Este court had listened enraptured to the violin sonatas of Marco Uccellini, their sinuous instrumental lines charged with a sobbing, passionate insistence, like the pleadings and wheedlings of a lover, and they had thronged to the church of San Carlo to hear the oratorios of Alessandro Stradella, the brilliant young son of the governor of the ducal fortress at Vignola. There was nobody in Europe to rival Stradella: the potentates of Italy, from the Pope to the self-exiled Queen

Christina of Sweden, jostled for his works, which rank him among the greatest musical dramatists between Monteverdi and Handel, but a taste for glamorous adventure was his undoing. Eloping with a Venetian patrician's daughter, he was set upon by hired bravoes and left for dead on the road, while the unfortunate girl was hauled off to spend her days as a nun. Managing to get to Genoa, the philandering maestro embarked on another affair, this time with one of his aristocratic pupils. Her brothers got to hear of it and swiftly had him murdered. One feels he would have relished the fact that at least a dozen operas have been based on his tragic history.

Among his librettists was Girolamo Graziani, who had taken over from Testi as the duke's chief minister and been instrumental in arranging Mary's marriage. Few are likely to want to stagger through his epic poem on the Conquest of Granada (ducal nagging here was rather more successful) but *Il Cromvele*, a tragedy based on the execution of Charles I, is definitely worth a look, if only because of its bizarrely imaginative handling of the subject. Real characters, some of them, like 'Anna ora Duchessa di Iorch', still alive when the play was written in 1662, are mixed with fictitious inventions. The names of the Parliamentarian regicides are all italianized – Harrisone, Lamberto, Iretone – and Cromvele is given some really rather moving soliloquies, in one of which guilty dreams torment him ('*Cessate, horridi mostri, cessate, ardenti fiamme, a tormentar me solo!*'), and in another, a sort of 'it-must-be-by-his death' affair, we can feel the obvious influence of Shakespeare, whose works Graziani probably knew through his contacts with English diplomats.

The play takes off with the appearance of Queen Henrietta Maria in male disguise and of Cromvele's wife, Elisabetta, who falls in love with King Carlo and tries to get him out of prison. Unknown to her, the little pageboy Edmondo, who has been hanging around throughout the play with nothing more useful to do than launch into a song or two, is in fact her long-lost daughter Delmira. Carlo's decapitation is reported to the Queen by a messenger in a 'nothing-common-did-nor-mean' speech which suggests that Graziani had studied accounts of the actual event, and Cromvele runs off distracted with remorse, having discovered Edmondo/Delmira's true identity. Until the very end, which is a complete let-down, with Lamberto and Iretone as a moralizing Tweedledum and Tweedledee shaking their heads in an ee-there's-nowt-so-queer-as-folk fashion, *Il Cromvele* is quite punchy as tragedies of this sort go, though I haven't yet discovered if it was ever acted and what the audience thought of it.

Most of all, the Modenese of Mary's day were still chuckling over the devastatingly mordant satire on the pretensions and rivalries of the various little states of Italy written in 1622 by the courtier Alessandro Tassoni and entitled *La secchia rapita*, 'The Rape of the Bucket'. A mock epic account of a small mediaeval war between Modena and Bologna, in which the Modenese carried off, as their principal trophy, a wooden bucket from a Bolognese well, the poem gave the notoriously quarrelsome Tassoni a chance to air his private grudges against the enemies he had made all over Italy, and this in the end explains why the work isn't quite the masterpiece it ought to be.

Yet the whole rambling affair is vitalized by a wonderful mischief. Tassoni, whose polemic prose – whether against Spanish imperialism in Italy or blasting the overweening ambitions of the Duke of Savoy – is some of the most potently vitriolic ever written in Italian, was more than a mere mudslinger in poetry. In an age and a culture so neurotically obsessed with trying to create an epic dimension to life even while it was forced to acknowledge that a modern Homer and Virgil were impossibilities, he mocks the genre with an affectionate realism. The grandly Homeric council of the gods, for instance, breaks down when it's discovered that many of them have better things to do: Diana has got up early and gone to a well 'somewhere in the Tuscan Maremma' to finish her washing and won't be back before sunset, Juno is busy with the hairdresser, the Fates send their apologies but they're making bread, and Silenus is discovered watering down the wine. On earth, meanwhile, the heroic warriors dawdle over absurd bawdy intrigues worthy of

Boccaccio, and consistently fail to carry out the doughty deeds expected of them.

'The Rape of the Bucket' was wildly popular for the next hundred years and produced a score of imitators. In France Jacques Boileau wrote *Le Lutrin*, 'The Rape of the Lectern', while in England a handsome, crippled dwarf composed a little mock-epic about a party of Catholic aristocrats at a picnic by the Thames and of what happened when they all sat down to play cards and the Baron cut off a tress of Miss Fermor's hair. Alexander Pope's 'The Rape of the Lock', which some think the most perfect poem in English, has its roots in the cobbled alleys of old Modena.

The bucket still hangs in its place of honour, high in the marble cage of La Ghirlandina, the great white belltower of the cathedral, with its octagonal spire added to the Romanesque campanile early in the fourteenth century. Perhaps the balustrades decorating it really are the original garlands which gave the tower its name, but a more affecting folk etymology says that when Jewish exiles from Spain sought refuge here, they sighed and wept when they beheld the belfry for the first time, because it reminded them of La Giralda, the erstwhile minaret which stands so gracefully beside the cathedral at Seville – thus 'Giraldina', 'Ghirlandina', well why not?

In the first cathedral church of Modena, a little Roman basilica, they buried the town's patron, Saint Geminianus, born in the very year, AD312, when Constantine defeated Maxentius at the Milvian Bridge, after his famous vision of the Holy Cross. Geminianus had never wanted to be a bishop: when he heard the news of his election, he fled into a wood outside the city and tried to set up for a hermit, but angelic guides led the anxious citizens to his hiding place, he was induced to accept the responsibility and excellent he turned out to be. When, after an encounter with a demon whom he sent packing with the sign of the cross, Geminianus's fame reached Constantinople, he was summoned to draw a devil out of the Emperor Jovian's mad daughter. During the barbarian invasions of Italy in the century which followed, the bishop, who had died aged eighty-six in the odour of sanctity, was invoked as sovran protector of beleaguered cities against marauding Huns and Ostrogoths, but for most travellers his name is enshrined in that archetype of Tuscan hill towns, San Gimignano. In Emilia, somehow typically, it has been given to a regional bank, along with that of another local saint, Prospero – the equivalent, as it were, of 'Save and Prosper'.

Oldest of the great Romanesque cathedrals of Europe, the Duomo of Modena was built as an act of faith in the idea of the city, considered not simply as a place of walls and houses and towers (and, in the case of Modena, canals, for in mediaeval times it was a sort of inland Venice) but as the incarnation of freedom, safety and prosperity. It was, and remains, the ultimate cohesive element in that abstract townscape created by every Italian, in which the piazza, or the nave of the principal church, or the arms of the main thoroughfares, become the womb, the cradle, the lap, the embrace to whose shelter he may always return. The word for this gut parochialism, transcending all other loyalties, is *campanilismo* – 'belltower-ism' – and La Ghirlandina stands for every other campanile in Italy.

For their architect the Modenese chose Lanfranco, of whom we know nothing beyond the praises given him in the inscription chiselled on the apse, which calls him 'famous, learned and versatile, the prince and master of this work'. A little picture of him in a contemporary manuscript shows him holding what looks like a cudgel, supervising the builders as they carry their hods to the site. His was the grand design, from the bulbous apsidal conches, the conical turrets and the raised presbytery to the serene sequences of blind arcading along the outer walls of the nave and the varied shapes of pediments and porticoes. His is among the earliest known names of Italian architecture, but of course we are at Modena, the forgotten, the neglected, the ignored, so you will not find it in any dictionary, because nobody has bothered to look closely at his handiwork.

Beside Lanfranco, adorning arches and doorways and pillars, worked one of the most prodigally gifted of all mediaeval sculptors, an artist with an unrivalled sense of the pliable, vibrant energies of stone: the great Wiligelmo, himself the prince and master of this work. His figures, amid their friezes of trailing vineleaves, griffons and dragons, peacocks and doves, have that sturdiness, that unbudgeable strength which makes the images of Romanesque sculpture so much more compelling than those of later ages, with their greater suavity and finish. These thick-limbed, fork-bearded, lumpy, slabby people are governed by the overpowering singleness of their immediate impulses – towards tenderness, brutality, envy or shame. In the free play of Wiligelmo's visual fancy, and in that of the unknown 'Master of the Metopes' working alongside him, there is no sense of an anxious backward glance towards some reproving religious authority, likely to rap them across the knuckles for heresy, worldliness or faulty iconography. The exuberance here is that of a paganism not yet suppressed, bringing memories of an ultramontane northern world of Celt, Saxon and Viking, of fogs and fens and loathly worms guarding the gold-hoard, of dragon-beaked ships on grey, choppy seas and the skald praising the ring-giver in the mead-hall.

Romanesque acknowledges two elements quite alien to Italian consciousness – terror and romance* – and welds them into a language fit for expressing the legendary or the irrational. It comes as no surprise, then, to find staring at us from one of Wiligelmo's carved capitals a jack-in-the-green, a leering face made out of leaves, of a kind we are more used to seeing on the corbels and gargoyles of English country churches. Among the metopes, including a fish-tailed man with a Norse beard and a three-armed woman scratching her bottom, is the strange hermaphroditic figure, with thighs splayed blatantly apart, called Il Potta di Modena, and nothing else but a variation on that age-old Celtic fertility symbol known as a *sheela-na-gig*.

The ultimate proof of all this foreignness is to be found on the

* Is it purely accidental that the two great Italian verse romances, Ariosto's *Orlando Furioso* and Tasso's *Gerusalemme Liberata*, are rooted in the Germanic myth-history of the princely families they celebrate?

frieze decorating the north porch of the cathedral. Chainmailed knights with pennoned lances attack a moated castle whose towers are still covered in scaffolding. The sculptor had a cruder hand than Wiligelmo's, but took care to identify these galloping paladins. And who are they? Their names – Isdernus, Mardoc, Burmaltus, Galvariun, Carado – are certainly not Italian. One among them, 'Artus de Bretania', tells all, so Galvaginus must be Gawain and the woman labelled Winlogee peering anxiously from the castle is Guinevere. The story of King Arthur, 'The Matter of Britain', has made it across the Alps to find its first known pictorial representation under the shadow of La Ghirlandina.

The tower, like a diacritical mark, punctuates the line of the Via Emilia, Emily Street indeed, the main drag of the city, up and down which, on winter evenings when the air is full of a smell like wilting daffodils from the tobacco factory, Modena parades, first one way then the other, in a ritual which for obvious reasons has become known as *la vasca* – the swimming-pool. '*Facciamo due passi*', 'let's make two steps' as the Italians say, '*facciamo un giro*', 'let's make a turn', and before dinner the elderly in their furs and lodens and the young in their bomber jackets and designer jeans wander contentedly up and down, poking into the shops, dawdling at this or that bar, staring mesmerized at the windows full of Fendi, Missoni, Trussardi and Valentino which have taken the place of the wonderful old grocers, bakers, cheese and sausage sellers which used to line the arcades when the town cared more about eating and a little less about image.

They are the most elegant in Italy, these arcades of Emily Street. If they have none of the grandeur of their Bolognese cousins or the *ancien régime* symmetry of those at Turin, there is a venerable grace to their curves and verticals which confers unquestioned supremacy. Their colour is the prevailing hue of the city, an egg yellow fading to lemon and cream, set off, in the side streets, by washes of russet and ochre and dull orange above the cobbled kennels of Via Balugola, Rua Pioppa and Via Mascherella, bending away from Via Emilia in narrow, furtive little arcs like the strands of a spider's web.

The dukes never thought, as other rulers might, to drive grandiose thoroughfares up and down the town and make squares full of cafés and prancing equestrian statues surrounded by allegorical bosoms and buttocks. Nothing in Modena really passes for a piazza in the true Italian sense, and the houses of the nobility are as unassuming as the most obsessive framer of sumptuary laws could wish. Apart from the cathedral, almost the only grand buildings in the city are the synagogue and the ducal palace – either end, as it might be, of the social scale in the old order of things.

The Jews were kept pent up in a ghetto formed by three narrow lanes, over which the Ghirlandina kept watch. Numbering more than a thousand, they were locked in each night with chains stretched across the ends of the street, and rather to the credit of the modern city fathers, the darkest of these alleys has kept its inglorious name – Vicolo Squallore – as a memory of the festering degradation it once nurtured.

Released from imprisoning squalor by the Risorgimento, Modena's Jews started up a Zionist magazine and built a magnificent synagogue, its architecture vocal with defiant confidence. Actually, in a charming and humorous fashion, the whole affair is a stylistic dog's dinner. There is a touch of Palladianism in the pediment, shades of old Rome in the marble columns, some utterly incongruous Romanesque fenestration, a sprinkling of coloured glass and garlanded reliefs surrounding chaste symbolic confections of scrolls, tablets and candlesticks. If the architect Ludovico Maglietta was hardly a genius, he made the Modenese take notice of their Jews.

Behind the ghetto, across a broad open space that ought to be a classic piazza but is more like a large car park, stands the ducal palace, begun by Francesco I in 1634. Imposing rather than beautiful, with an austere grandeur appropriate to a ruler who flirted politically with Spain and had his portrait painted by Velazquez, it has been for a century or more the Italian Sandhurst, a training academy for army officers, where even the civilian teachers are given military rank (my brother, who taught there for ten years, was a lieutenant-colonel: anybody less like a lieutenant-colonel it is impossible to imagine). The place is run along lines not dissimilar to an English public school, with prefects and a head boy.

The cadets, as might be supposed, are an exceptionally handsome crew, the more so because of prevailing origins in two areas of Italy noted for the beauty of their males and an atavistic loyalty to military tradition. For the most part these boys are either lustrous-eyed, blue-chinned Neapolitans, minor aristocrats from among the crazy superfluity of titles in the erstwhile Kingdom of the Two Sicilies, or else they are strapping, blond-hued Piedmontese, immemorial uniformed servants of the state, out of Alpine castles and dark palaces in Asti and Alessandria, from whose portrait frames epauletted generals and beribboned field marshals reproach them with the family call to the colours.

Their winter uniform, navy with maroon facings, a tall cap with a glazed peak and cockade, and a pleated cape to finish it off, is incomparably dashing. I remember riding on a bus one foggy October evening through a peculiarly drab suburb of Rome when, along with the housewives with their supermarket bags and the schoolkids clutching their satchels, a solitary academy cadet climbed aboard, immaculate from black boots to braided collar. He wasn't in the least good-looking – his face had a kind of boyish plumpness which told of a *mamma* waiting at home with a savoury panful of *gnocchi alla romana* – yet standing there in the dim light of the trundling bus he became our cynosure, envied, desired, adored, a solemn, dignified little creature whose arrival from the nineteenth century made us feel shabby and commonplace. It was only when he got off about four stops later that we realized nobody had said a word since his appearance.

In the summer, together with the rest of his classmates, he would change into a yet more elegant costume, cream with a magenta stripe and a little gilt dagger on the swordbelt, like a soldier out of an operetta. Catch a Sandhurst lad wearing anything like this!

The palace's destiny was a good deal more appropriate than some. In the Napoleonic era the Modenese troops were considered second to none, and after the 1815 restoration the army was beefed up with the help of Austrian money and expertise to create a loyal praetorian guard for the duke and his ministers. When, on 11 June 1859, Francesco V reviewed his troops for the last time before leaving for perpetual exile in Vienna, he was greeted with rousing cheers by the soldiers and – unique in the annals of the Risorgimento – the entire force followed him across the frontier into the Austrian province of Venetia, where three years later nearly all of them, officers and men, chose to join the army of Emperor Franz Josef.

This story is the more touching because Francesco was so manifestly unworthy of such devotion. He and his father, Francesco IV, represented for many in Europe the final incarnation of despotic tyranny – blinkered, dogmatic, inflexible in the ultimate egoism of sacrosanct convictions. Alone among the rulers of Italy during the early nineteenth century, neither man has ever found a significant champion: while Sir Harold Acton has made it possible for us to love King Ferdinand 'Bomba' of Naples, and the Austrian historian Franz Pesendorfer has offered a convincing case for the virtues of Tuscany's last Grand Duke, apologists have stayed silent as to Modena's two *fin-de-ligne* specimens, whose strong Este blood was washed thin with the tepid water-gruel of the Hapsburgs.

They meant well, that was the awful thing. Theirs was that negative goodness not unknown in certain politicians of our own day, which believes that consistency to principles, regardless of their intrinsic moral value or of their application to the lives of ordinary people, justifies any sort of oppression, intolerance and cruelty. In their dim, plodding fashion they loved their subjects (those who were not conspiring to murder them or topple them from power) and showed them the kind of fatherly benevolence it behoves a despot now and then to display. It seems never seriously to have occurred to them that they might not be loved equally in return or that their ministers – a mixture of corrupt timeservers, legitimist bigots and a few wholehearted loyalists – might actually be detested as the agents of relentless obscurantism.

Anything that looked like a liberal initiative was instantly crushed. The municipal communes set up by Napoleon were dismantled, education was returned to the dead hand of Mother Church, the Jesuits, exiled decades earlier, were recalled, special civil disabilities were revived to make life difficult for the Jews, the faculty of law at the university, an obvious hotbed of political dissent, was limited to a tiny number of carefully screened students, censorship of the most indiscriminate type was imposed and the single permitted newspaper was an official propaganda sheet entitled, with an irony which speaks volumes for the essential humourlessness at the heart of the régime, *La Voce della Verità*, 'The Voice of Truth'.

Even their sternest critics, however, tried to find something good to say about the two Hapsburg Francescos. Turning over the pages of *I Ducati Estensi*, the passionate, often wildly exaggerated chronicle of their misdeeds published in Turin in 1849 by the exiled revolutionary Nicomede Bianchi, we can feel behind his indignation a sense of shame that Modena should have sunk so low and an anxiety that even at its worst it should not appear too thoroughly contemptible in the eyes of the enlightened world.

The place inspires that sort of unostentatious loyalty. In front of the ducal palace stands a somewhat forlorn-looking bleached marble statue of the patriotic martyr Ciro Menotti, executed for his part in the revolt of 1831. He was an enterprising industrialist from the little town of Carpi, who, having started out in his father's business as a maker of straw hats, diversified by establishing a silk mill powered by a steam engine, the first seen in Italy. Devoted to Modena, Menotti, for all his commercial acumen, was extremely naive and genuinely believed that the Duke's paternalism reflected a more profound concern with Italian independence. Few causes could have been further from Francesco's thoughts. It was simply that, equipped with a vast personal fortune, he was also insanely ambitious and toying with the prospect of becoming King of Italy. Since his machinations needed to be conducted in secret, Menotti seemed the ideal fall-guy.

The story of the duke and the hatter is one of the more

bizarrely tragic episodes of nineteenth-century history. While Menotti engaged Francesco with his patriotic moonshine, his friend the lawyer Enrico Misley was busy rounding up a rag-tag-and-bobtail force of exiles and malcontents among the Italian communities in Paris and London with the object of invading the Savoyard territories of the King of Piedmont. Help was supposed to be coming from Louis Philippe, newly installed on the French throne, and it is just possible that Francesco, who either hated or envied his fellow Italian rulers (including the Pope, who was, if anything, even more reactionary than he), genuinely believed that the hour was at hand for making them lick his boots.

Altogether more touching was Menotti's simple faith that the whole ramshackle scheme would work. Louis Philippe, needless to say, was far too sensible to compromise his new-found eminence by committing France to an international scrap, and Misley's little army faded into thin air. For his part, Menotti was supposed to begin the Modenese end of the revolt during an opera gala at the Teatro Ducale on the fifth of February, at which, entering the ducal box, he would announce the dawning of a new epoch and offer the crown of Italy to his complaisant master. Opera houses are the classic flashpoints of revolution: only a month or so later the independent state of Belgium was to be established as the result of an uprising which broke out during a performance of Auber's *La Muette de Portici* (itself based on a revolutionary theme) at the theatre in Brussels.

Nothing of the kind took place in Modena. On the second of February Francesco ordered a number of tactical arrests and, with his customary meticulous attention to official documents, signed several decrees of banishment. On the following evening soldiers were sent to Menotti's house in Corso Canalgrande to arrest him. There was armed resistance and two of the troop were killed. When news of the incident reached the palace, the duke hurried on foot to the scene, dodging behind the columns of the arcades as marksmen from Menotti's windows tried to pick him off. The deaths of two more soldiers underlined the serious intentions of those inside the house, and a cannon was dragged up to the entrance of Via Fonteraso opposite to force a breach in the wall. After the first shot the defenders offered to capitulate, but since their terms proved unacceptable, Colonel Stanzani, commanding the besiegers, resumed the assault, and it was around one o'clock the next morning before they finally gave in. Menotti himself, trying to escape by climbing down a rope into the lane behind the house, was hit in the shoulder and arrested.

Francesco was too well aware of his prisoner's value to have him executed on the spot. The rebellion had been far more successful in other towns throughout the duchy, and on the principle of *reculer pour mieux sauter* the duke deemed it prudent to retire with his family into Austrian territory across the Po, taking Menotti with him as a potential bargaining counter and waiting on events in the safety of the fortress at Mantua. A month later the provisional government yielded to the imperial troops and the hatter and his master returned to their beloved city, bracing itself for a renewed dose of aggrieved, reproachful paternalism, like a naughty child who is told that it doesn't know what's good for it.

Resolved to make examples both of his own benignity and of others' refractoriness, Francesco imprisoned or exiled all the revolutionaries except two. One of these was the notary Vincenzo Borelli, who had drawn up the document declaring the duke's authority to be null and void. The other was the wretched Ciro Menotti, executed, as the Austrian authorities were quick to perceive, as much for what he knew of the duke's secret *folies de grandeur* as for his part in the revolt itself. The sentence was carried out on 26 May 1831.

Menotti had been allowed to write a last letter to his wife Cecchina, an appeal to her fortitude couched in eloquently simple terms.

> Live for your children and be a father to them. The sole demand my love can make upon you is that you should not give way to grief. Do not let the thought of my untimely death make you afraid. God will give me strength and courage to confront the fatal moment itself. I send you a lock of my hair

as a memory of me for my family. God knows how much I blame myself for their misfortunes! One more tender kiss to you and the children, while I still hold a part among earthly things. Farewell, farewell for ever, your Ciro.

Almost as soon as Menotti's confessor left the prison with the letter it was seized by the odious Advocate Zerbini, president of the state tribunal, and placed in the official police dossier on the destined revolt. Cecchina was not to receive it for another seventeen years.

One prisoner at least might almost have envied Menotti's swift end. Countess Rosa Rangoni was a member of the most illustrious noble family in Modena* and descended on her father's side from Fulvio Testi. Her crime, according to the tribunal, had been 'to sew, at the orders of the rebel ringleader Ciro Menotti, a flag of silk in the colours, white, red and green, in full knowledge of the use to which it would be put', and for this heinous offence her judges invoked 'the application of a punishment neither unbecoming nor inconvenient to her position'. Sentenced to three years imprisonment, she was confined, at the duke's express wish, in the Carmelite convent at Reggio – all for her patriotic needlework.

Does any of this really matter? Not to the Modenese. The irony intrinsic to this city lies in its reflection of an essential Italian paradox: that a country so profoundly dominated by the presence of the past should be even more strongly characterized by profound lack of interest in that past. The Romanesque portals of the Duomo were obscured by scaffolding and corrugated metal sheets for more than a decade during the 1970s and early 1980s, but nobody complained very much or expressed any particular amazement when the rusty old iron was at last peeled away to disclose the beauty beneath. Few either know

---

* One of them, a Jesuit envoy to Poland, is the villain in Mussorgsky's *Boris Godunov*, scheming to seduce Holy Russia away from orthodoxy to popery.

or care about the bucket at the top of the Ghirlandina or the prismatic brilliance of the illuminations in Borso D'Este's fifteenth-century Bible in the Biblioteca Estense, where students gossip and gum-chew their way through *tesi di laurea* on useful subjects like macroeconomics and company law.

Strolling in the summer nights along the leafy diagonals of the boulevards on the southern side of the city, where your chums are eating ices or coconut or sucking deliciously tooth-numbing grapefruit *granita*, will you care that where you tread was once a fortified rampart, torn down less than a century ago? Will you ever set foot in what remains of the duke's galleries, with their exquisite small Flemish panels by Bouts and Van Cleve, their sumptuous Guidos and Procaccinis and the ugly, menacing libertine Francesco I by Velazquez, or will their echoing loneliness frighten you out again on to the stairs, where some wag has stuck a cigarette butt between the blubber-lips of the extravagantly periwigged Duke Rinaldo?

They could not really give a toss, these Modenese, quiet-living, well-to-do, not especially sophisticated, with their contagiously slippery speech inflection lilting up and down the musical interval of a major sixth. Theirs is the imperative now, the decisive today, without a Testi or a Tassoni or a Gennari to stir the imagination too actively to life. This is Middle Italy incarnate, the most unrelentingly consumer-orientated society in Europe, its preoccupations those of clothes, cars, holidays and fashionable gadgetry, the bread-and-circuses of Italian capitalism.

For them there is little or no life of the mind or spirit. Their education has been of that elementary variety which implants a little mathematics, fundamental literacy and the knowledge of a foreign language. Their religion is a lackadaisical Catholicism taken out of mothballs at christenings, first communions, weddings and funerals, the religion, in short, of the photo-opportunity. There is little anguish or doubt or stress, because the *piccolo mondo moderno* they inhabit is so full of certainties. The shops will always bulge with acquisitive lures and promises, the appalling television channels will be there to offer the bromide and novocaine of endless game shows and tit-and-bum variety spectaculars, the news mags will order their graver thoughts on matters a little more global than the thousand different ways of preparing a risotto or the chances for Juve and Samp in the league championships.

The delight of living in Modena derives, in large part, from knowing that everything will be taken care of. There is no serious poverty here, no housing crisis, no violent crime on any significant scale. The streets are spotlessly clean, the properly subsidized buses are frequent and punctual, the city subscribes without demur to an opera and concert season at the old ducal theatre, patronizes local exhibitions and flatters the wellbeing and civic pride of its inhabitants to a degree unparalleled elsewhere in Europe.

So the Modenese rest content, the more so perhaps because their freedom is so singularly restricted. In a country whose rulers – a collection of sinister, gerrymandering old men in suits – have designed prosperity and material happiness as a sedative to original thought and impulse, true freedom, the freedom of restlessness and social initiative and passionate polemic, can hardly gain a foothold. What use has it after all? Where it exists, its growth is like that of plants seen from time to time burgeoning desperately on the top of ruined buildings where some bird has let fall a seed or the wind has blown a flower. Otherwise placidity remains untroubled. An inner life, whether of anxiety, neurosis, imaginative desire or spiritual ecstasy, is practically nowhere to be found.

Certainly the notion of another Risorgimento sweeping the land is hard to entertain. Now and then, walking through the cobbled lanes of old Modena in the sticky darkness of a summer night, I glance up at a window veiled by shutters, with light glimpsed through the lattices, and wonder whether in that room something eloquent of genuine, obsessive, monopolizing emotion might not at this moment be taking place. A pair of lovers perhaps, their limbs glistening with sweat, has entered that phase of sensual intensity in which the world no longer exists beyond the palpable physicality of the beloved. A writer has, at this crucial instant, completed that chapter of her novel which provides the moral and structural climax of the entire work: for a second or two she confronts the reality of her genius. A murderer has just cracked his victim's head open like a walnut, and stands for a moment surveying his achievement. If you listen carefully you will hear him breathing.

It might be so, it just might. But the cynicism of experience conjures up a far more probable scene, of little Cinzia reaching into her Snoopy satchel for her *block-notes* on which she will scrawl her homework while Mamma finger-licks her way through this week's *Gente*, with its umpteenth picture-spread of the Monegasque royal family, Papa broods on the season's chances for his favourite team in the *Gazzetta dello Sport*, young Marco chats on the telephone to a mate about *il computer*, and the telly prattles on, cosy and acephalous as ever.

Nothing will trouble the surface of this bourgeois idyll. It is, of course, faintly possible that Mamma is having an affair with the dentist she seems to have been visiting rather too often, that Cinzia will go seriously into green politics and that Marco will start a new life as a drag-queen. Thoughts like these have now and then haunted Papa between Gullit and Maradona, but they remain mere phantoms. The desperate idealism of Menotti and satirical snarling of Tassoni are distant almost as if the past they inhabited were a remote planet and their earthly reality reduced to the lichened irrelevance of marble statuary.

This insouciance in the face of a historical legacy is not particular to Modena, and for Italians in general it is very easily explained. They will tell you that the subject is badly taught at school, that much of it, especially those parts which concern the great national drive towards unity in the early nineteenth century, can be easily perceived as a simplified myth of nationhood, and that in their recent past, from 1870 onwards, they have very little to be proud of.

The first two assertions are doubtless true, and the last certainly is. Maybe it is not a distaste for looking back, so much as a protective incuriosity, the legacy of an age-old feeling that it is better, or at any rate safer, not to know in case the agents of some tyrannical pope or emperor or duke catch you in the act of trying to find out. Yet if I sense this cocooning ignorance more strongly in Modena than anywhere else, it isn't just from pleasurable familiarity with the place itself.

For in this city, from 1700 to 1750, there lived and worked the man who, more than anybody else before or since (yes, even more than Benedetto Croce), laboured to make the Italians understand their past so that they might show themselves worthy of inheriting it. Lodovico Antonio Muratori is not a name known much outside Italy, yet he richly deserves to be up there with Dante and Michelangelo and Verdi and Enzo Ferrari forsooth, as somebody who gave Italy to the wider world. Trained as a lawyer and philosopher, he took holy orders, and at the age of twenty-three was given charge of the great Ambrosian Library at Milan, where his fame among scholars brought him an invitation from the Duke of Modena to return to the city and become his librarian. Settling here for good, Muratori began on the serious business of astonishing the world. His energy, diligence and total mastery of all he turned his hand to seem even more phenomenal when we consider the difficulties he faced in getting hold of what he needed to create his stupendous series of historical collections.

Sordid greed and mendacity characterized papal government then and since. The Pope was currently angling for the valuable port of Comacchio in the Po delta, which the Este dukes had developed a century earlier. When papal propagandists tried to rubbish the Este's respectability, Muratori weighed in with the *Antichita estensi* (1717), no mere piece of historical whitewashing but a huge perspective of the rise and exploits of a single great family in an Italian context about which, until then, almost nothing was known.

Enthusiasm led him indefatigably on. For thirty years, from 1723 until his death in 1750, he issued volume after volume of the *Rerum italicarum scriptores*, the first published collection of chronicles and documents for Italian history from AD 500 to 1500. As if this were not enough, there followed the six volumes of *Antiquitates italicae medii aevi* (1738), the earliest attempt by any scholar to present mediaeval life through original sources, and in 1744 Muratori began his most famous work, the *Annali d'Italia*, twenty-one volumes setting out the fortunes of Italy from the reign of Augustus Caesar to the Peace of Aix la Chapelle in 1749.

To track down source materials for these various works was a phenomenal achievement in itself. Muratori was constantly being harassed by hostile theologians, instinctively suspicious of his quest for buried facts, by partisans of the papal cause who felt that this priest, however devout his day-to-day conduct, was bent on betraying Holy Church, and by haughty, arrogant sovereigns and nobles, fearful lest the truths unearthed by historical enquiry should besmirch their family honour.

Fearless and determined, Muratori pursued his search, maintaining a colossal network of learned correspondence which stretched from Paris and London to Warsaw, Copenhagen and Prague. He became one of the most respected figures in enlightened Europe, and every historian who has ever written since, in whatever language, owes something to his scrupulous regard for veracity and authenticity. His monumental achievement was, first of all, to show his countrymen that they *needed* to know about their history as a sequence of connected movements, events and causes, so as to have a standard against which to measure themselves. More significantly for us all, he had used the evidence of history as a weapon with which to counter corruption, hypocrisy and lying. The past was to be the ultimate impartial arbiter of the present. 'The love of truth alone,' he says at the end of the *Annali*, 'or of what I believe to be the truth, that is what guides my pen: and truth,' he adds sarcastically, alluding to the famous quarrel between pope and emperor which tore mediaeval Italy in half, 'cannot yet call itself Guelph or Ghibelline.'

That his tremendous enterprise should have been pioneered in Modena is the final paradox. Italy is seldom philistine in the name of expediency, and the old city need not fear, as it might so easily in Britain, a fatal gashing and stabbing by a multi-storey car park, a four-lane highway or a shopping mall. The past has settled down comfortably beside the present. Something really exciting will happen in Italy when Italians start wanting to know about it. Till then Muratori's ghost walks unquiet.

14 Hunting the Stockfish

A traveller in Italy gets into the habit of carrying two sorts of map. One is of course the excellent green Touring Club series, with its helpful indications of kilometric distances along the roads between the various towns and villages and its discreet underlinings of those places you might not otherwise have fancied visiting but which might turn out to be, as the French say, 'worth the detour'. There is no such thing as an Italian equivalent of the British Ordnance Survey; if there were, it would probably create legal mayhem among landowners and those with claims to the inheritance of property, so it is probably a case of leaving well alone rather than simple inertia. Unless you are a walker – still a very eccentric thing to be in this land of car-drivers and scooter-riders – you will need nothing better than the Touring Club sheets, and if you discover some new treasure in the form of a church or a villa or a view, you can always scribble it into the margin as part of that archaeology of travel which makes the possession of old maps and guidebooks so poignant an experience.

The other kind of map doesn't, strictly speaking, exist. That is to say, you make it for yourself and unfold it in your associative memory, where it lies bundled up together with other people's recommendations and caveats and your own past experiences, bitter or delectable. This is the cartography of individual desire, the chart whose points of orientation are determined by the notional fulfilment of a particular craving. You might, for example, map out the Veneto as a trail of Palladian villas or Tuscany in terms of Medicean fortresses or Umbria according to the number of saintly relics stored under the altars of its principal cities. Shunning these as too orthodox, the more blasé traveller may (indeed often does) survey Italy beneath a grid of human latitudes and longitudes, formed out of such factors as the proportion of hospitable expatriates per region, who isn't speaking to whom in southern Tuscany, has the local aristocracy enough snob appeal and so on. As for the chances of sexual adventure for which Italy once enjoyed such celebrity among travellers, nowadays we are all far too smugly hypocritical to admit to a thought of that.

There is one plan of this sort which Italians all carry in head and heart, and which they readily help you to draw, the Great Gastronomic Map of the peninsula, the pirate's chart, the x-marks-the-spot, the grand atlas of a thousand sheets crammed with *ristoranti, trattorie, osterie, alberghi* and *taverne*, the realm of the crossed knife and fork, the bottle and glass and the bunch of grapes.

The sacraments of the table in Italy, once apparently immutable and cut in stone, are now in all probability doomed. A generation or so back, Italians cared more about the nature, quality and preparation of food than any other people on earth. Had one been asked to name the single subject which, more than all the rest, engrossed conversation in Italy, there would have been no competition. Everywhere, given half the chance, the nation talked about eating, praised and dispraised, commended and deplored, disputed the merits and elaborated the ingredients and detailed the various phases in the making of a thousand dishes. They knew about consistency and thickness in a slice of mortadella, the differing piquancy of one salame compared with another from a nearby village, the ageing of wines and the ripeness of cheeses and the sympathy between a pasta and its *sugo*. When you heard them talk thus, it was with the fantasy and exuberance of a race to whom centuries of peasant poverty had taught that miraculous resourcefulness which made their 'poor' cookery into one of the adornments of civilization.

Wealth or, more significantly for the Italians, a desire for wealth to be visible, has begun dangerously eroding the integrity of the kitchen. Restaurants are now frequently dispiriting in their fussiness, their disgraceful pandering to faddism and a ridiculous overemphasis on the performance rather than the substance of eating. Waiters appear dressed in black coats, trolleys whirl furiously to and fro like something from *Ben Hur*, and there is a dangerous daintiness in the glasses and napery. Even the name of the establishment has to have a gloss applied to it. One restaurant, in a small country town west of Modena, having achieved local celebrity as the Vitello d'Oro, serving plain, genuine Emilian dishes to plain, genuine Emilian folk, has recently transformed itself into an amazing velvet-and-chandeliers Lucullan pleasure dome, with the grandiose title 'Clinica Gastronomica'. Forsooth!

The Clinica Gastronomica syndrome has filtered down to far smaller enterprises that have no business to be poncing about in this mutton-dressed-as-lamb fashion. One summer morning I stopped in Orvieto to look at the cathedral. Apart from the Pozzo di San Patrizio, Antonio da Sangallo's amazing Renaissance well, and a handful of distinguished palaces, there is really not much else to see in Orvieto, and just then, since the Palazzo Soliano, where they keep the picture gallery, was in the process of being gutted for restoration and the Signorelli frescoes in the Duomo were completely masked by scaffolding, there was even less. The buses to the railway station, which, as in most Umbrian cities, lies at the foot of a very steep hill, ran every two hours, and I fancied I might cram in a decent luncheon before catching the afternoon express to Florence.

In a place so popular with tourists, the various restaurants seemed strangely reluctant to open, and I wandered to and fro desperately seeking somewhere in which I should not be conspicuous as either the first or, what might turn out to be the case, the only customer in ages. The church clocks struck one. The little *trattoria* advertising 'sane* and genuine cooking' which I rather liked the look of remained firmly closed, and the presence of two gossiping waiters outside another halfway decent *osteria* instantly raised the hackles of my embarrassment. When the deuce did the *orvietani*, let alone the knots of Germans, French and English drifting among the majolica shops and the *enoteche*, actually sit down to eat?

Finally, I happened on what seemed a quiet, invitingly dark spot set back along an alley off one of the main streets. I was beginning to faint with inanition, there was a thunderstorm gathering over the bosky tufa plugs which form such an attractive backdrop to the town, and one and a half hours might very pleasantly be killed with sampling a local *sugo* on the pasta, a glass or two of an Orvieto that was bound to be a sight better than the chalky lemonade which gets exported to England under the name, and a reading of the legend on the mineral water bottle which would tell me that the *sorgente* was recommended for liver and kidney complaints, and might have diuretic effects, and that Professor G. Rossi of the University of Perugia had certified it, on a given date, as containing 23.4

---

* '*Cucina sana e genuina*': *sana* of course means healthy but 'sane' is quite as valid a translation in this context.

ions of calcium, not to speak of other enriching salts and chemicals.

I cannot recall when lunch in Italy was quite so unnervingly dismal. On my gastronomic map, this place, whose name I now infuriatingly fail to remember, is to be indicated with a skull and crossbones. For a start it was endowed with an overdressed elegance entirely out of keeping with its status, at least as it appeared from the street, that of an agreeable small *trattoria* without too many frills. The walls were decorated in ever-so-tasteful shades of pink and grey, employing that 'dragged' effect much cherished by interior designers in London and New York during the early Eighties. Above the pearl-hued dado ran an extraordinary frieze made of modernistic woodcarvings, representing, as far as I could make out in the aerosol-fragrant gloom, an energetic sequence of nude figures, generously developed, running after one another under a ceiling which a thoughtful painter had adorned with puffy clouds under a smudgy blue sky.

There was music. There ought never to be music in Italian restaurants, and you must promise faithfully that if you ever enter a restaurant in Italy in which there is music, you will turn round and walk straight out, as I did not. It was Mozart. I have nothing against Mozart. Indeed, I must confess to a secret fondness for him, but so much has he become the musical wallpaper of the not terribly musical that nowadays one would rather forget about him altogether than be forced to listen to 'Eine Kleine Nachtmusik' in a gloomy trat in western Umbria while one awaits service.

It was an exceedingly long wait. The only evidence of life in the whole place was the mournful-looking proprietor, a youngish man with a pepper-and-salt beard who seemed from his accent to be not quite authentically Italian. While he took my order and described to me the components of the various dishes, he stared fixedly at me as though something was missing in our exchange which I was expected to supply. Since I had nothing whatever to say beyond my request for lunch, his face assumed, not surprisingly, an expression of even more profound sadness and he retreated, in this mysteriously baffled state, to the kitchen.

I sat there for half an hour. A strange horror began to grip me, a species of almost tearful unhappiness induced by being utterly alone in this fancy little box down a backstreet in Orvieto with the earliest rumblings of thunder advancing towards the city. Mine isn't that courage which, declaring 'this lousy place sucks!', can arm a determination to get up and leave. So I sat and listened to the clattering and chat which had suddenly started in the kitchen, and took nervous sippets of wine and water while the A major piano concerto mocked me with its serenity from speakers concealed behind the *boiserie* of jogging nudes.

When at last the sad beard brought my pasta, I was, for whatever reason, on the edge of hysteria, and the spoon shook in my hand as I tossed cheese over the ravioli. I should have guessed there wouldn't be many of them, but four exiguous envelopes surrounded by a frieze of carefully arranged sage leaves said it all. When, after a further twenty minutes, my dish of veal appeared in the form of something as spectral-looking as a papyrus fragment, decorated on either side with *fauviste* smears of a strange green liquor, I heard the passing bell of Italian cooking. The coffee arrived in a little black cup shaped like a greek vase. The bill came to 50,000 lire.

I tell this as a cautionary tale to anyone misguided enough to believe that influences from beyond the Alps will somehow prove beneficial to the development of Italian cuisine – supposing in any case that development is in any way desirable. In fact, like much else in modern Italy, eating habits are all too easily conditioned by a fatal susceptibility to the charm of whatever is foreign and new. Along with the meretricious flimflam of *nouvelle cuisine*, the country is now being ravaged by the ruthless opportunism of fast food, and any number of pseudo-Macdonalds are to be found obtrusively making their point in the midst of the various *centri storici*.

Much of this craze for '*gli hamburger*' (Italians stress the second syllable: 'amBoorger') and '*patatine* regular' derives less from actual pleasure in their consumption than from the amazing, almost obsessive desire of young Italians to be as like one another in their tastes and attitudes as possible. Perhaps that is why so many of them, in comparison with their counterparts elsewhere in Europe, appear painfully uninteresting. Whatever is to become of Italy in a decade or so, when these flavourless cardboard cutouts are in positions of executive authority?

I can't believe, however, that anything so deep-rooted as the Italian passion for the table will perish this rapidly. I still remember with pleasure the face of the sixteen-year-old daughter of some friends in Rome lighting up with envy when I told her that I was off to Bologna. There are, of course, a thousand reasons why any of us should be envied a trip to Bologna, that abode of the blest to which all certified Italophiles go when they die. She wasn't, however, jealous because of the Renis and Domenichinos and Carraccis in the gallery, or the cloister of Santo Stefano, or the shops of Via Ugo Bassi and Via dell'Indipendenza, or the incidental delights of being in a place whose perfectly-drawn dimensions justify the entire abstract concept of the city against all the pompous, sentimental, accusatory rhetoric of green ruralism. 'Ah, Bologna!' she exclaimed, 'There you can eat a whole plateful of tortellini!'

Everybody knows about Bolognese *tortellini* (which you are always told are modelled upon the navel of Venus) as they know about the city's splendid *mortadella*, which should be cut and eaten thick rather than in the paper-thin slices we are accustomed to find outside Italy. But she was right, of course, because Bologna the Red and the Learned is also Bologna the Fat, a town where food is understood as integral to a cultivated existence as opposed to a wedge of nourishment crammed into the maw to palliate hunger.

When I think of Bologna in this context, I think of a certain cake shop in the centre of the city, where the beauty of what is displayed on stands and under glass, of frosting and icing and glazes of chocolate and jam, and sprinklings of nuts and dustings of coffee and mosaics of angelica and candied fruit, is complemented by a remarkable ceiling adorned with a frieze of red and grey garlands in the Liberty style – which is what

Art Nouveau is called in Italy, because the earliest examples
came from the famous emporium in Great Marlborough Street.
Around this ceiling runs a sequence of quotations in Greek
and Latin from the works of Homer and Virgil. I can't recall
their purport, but that is not the point. What matters here
is the notion, wholly without offence against decorum, that
The Odyssey and *torta alla meringa* should go together, the
sense that to these sticky sweetmeats belongs a kind of epic
dignity.

It is in the covered market of Bologna that you encounter at
its strongest such an instinctive celebration of eating. There are
other Italian cities with markets of this kind – the great grey barn
of San Lorenzo at Florence, for instance, is calculated to induce
a kind of gastronomic madness – but Bologna, perhaps purely
because it is not crammed with avenues of stalls selling handbags,
belts and teeshirts through which you have to plunge in order to
get there, is infinitely more inviting as a bazaar. Up the little lanes
and inside the raftered and iron-stanchioned halls, the realities of
plenty and profusion are taken for granted without smothering
them in guilt or expense or ghastly good taste. The cheese shops
with their onion-shaped balls of mozzarella, yellow discs of
pecorino and geological hunks of *grana*, the salad stalls hung
with bunches of weeds and mashes, the fish slabs glistening
with *san pietro*, *branzino* and everything goggle-eyed, slithery
and tentacular, the *salumerie* decked with sausage and ham and
trotter like votive offerings hung up in a shrine, the sellers of
polenta and *fecola* and *farro*, of meats ovine, bovine and suine,
of pumpkin flowers and thistles and aubergines and beans
mottled and glistening like gemstones, of *pane integrale* and
pane tipo O, of corks and bottle openers, colanders, mandolines
and riddles, are gathered together in this dark, cool, sanded
and sawdusted *souk*, to proclaim the unwavering seriousness
involved in choosing the right ingredients without ceremonious
nonsense. It is not a Food Hall with men in tailcoats and chefs'
hats and girls in mobcaps amid acres of encaustic tilework and
fancy hampers full of Stilton and Christmas pudding and peaches
in brandy, but a place where everybody knows what they are

after and is prepared to choose, consider, discuss, reject and pick again, until they have got it to a nicety.

Even the smallest Italian town becomes linked, in the folklore of popular association, with some dish or sauce or wine or cake. Preparing to explore southern Tuscany for a book I was then writing, I made soundings at a party in Florence as to the absolutely unmissable experiences. 'Climb Monte Amiata,' said somebody, 'Have a look at the cathedral of Sovana,' said another, 'Don't forget the famous fishpond of Santa Fiora,' said a third, but all were united in their praise of The Cooked Water of Pitigliano. On no account were we to return without having sampled The Cooked Water. If we could only have brought some back with us – *magari*!

We went to Pitigliano, that strange, bleary-eyed, crag-clinging Etruscan town hidden deep in the oak forests above the Latian border, and we admired its fort of the Orsini and its churches and its synagogue and the old oven where the tenacious little community of Jews baked their unleavened bread, and we found a *trattoria* lined from floor to ceiling with simulated plywood in laminated plastic strips, and there the hostess brought to us at last the celebrated Cooked Water.

It turned out, this *acquacotta*, to be none other than a variant on good old Florentine *ribollita*, that nutritious bread pottage which is best eaten in winter as a filler against the cold. Perhaps it took its name from the pot of simmering water that hung perpetually over the fire in the poor cottages of this southern Maremma district, into which the *contadine* flung whatever food they could find to make a savoury mess for the family supper. *Acquacotta* – 'cooked water' – is made of onions, celery and tomato sweated in oil, with salt, pepper and enough boiling water sprinkled over them to create a bubbling mush. This is poured on to a dish lined with thick slices of toasted bread, and an egg is broken into the hot liquor, over which you then dredge grated cheese. Like so many Italian recipes it looks wretchedly simple on the page, but tastes sublime.

Acquacotta is easy enough to enjoy. Certain staples of the Italian table, however, are less immediately palatable, and real relish of them represents a kind of graduation for which you may award yourself a pass-with-merit or a pass-with-distinction. I am not at all sure, for example, about the much-vaunted balsamic vinegar of Modena, sold in designer cartons like flasks of expensive scent after years of maturing in ancestral barrels, but which possesses the curiously sweetish viscosity of very thin molasses. Neither am I wild about *mostarda*, which has little or nothing to do with mustard as we know it, but is essentially a selection of sickly-tasting candied fruits eaten with the plate of mixed boiled meat known as *bollito misto*. I can do without *mostarda: salsa verde*, which sounds like a Californian university ('Bobbie Jo majored in Women's Studies at Salsa Verde') will do nicely instead.

The true test of your Italian adoption arrives with *polenta*. A whole world of moral, social and political values is contained in a single dollop. I can't look at the stuff without thinking of that particularly inglorious period of the nation's history which followed unification in 1870 and culminated in the seizure of power by Mussolini and his fascist squadrons: the age of anarchist assassins, daredevil aviators, prancing Futurists, saintly Queen Margherita and gerrymandering Prime Minister Crispi, dubious colonial forays into Abyssinia and Tripoli, the first Fiat cars, *verismo* opera and the works of Gabriele D'Annunzio, whose massively fraudulent personality, specially constructed out of nothing very much in particular so as to gratify other people's overblown fancies, sums up the gimcrack, pinchbeck, penny-trumpet-and-twopenny-drum quality essential to the epoch.

In northern Italy thousands left the land for work in the new factories of Milan and Turin, or else fled abroad rather than remain tied to share-cropping estates where the agent, the lawyer, the tax-collector and the money-lender were perpetually at their throats. Racked by malaria and the nutritional disease known as *pellagra*, a form of chronic dermatitis which, at its most extreme stage, affected the brain, those who stayed turned to strike action in their desperate attempts to secure some form of change.

During the Carnival season of 1885, in the village square

of Commessaggio, west of Mantua, a gruesome charade took place. The local peasants, dressed as landed gentry, sat down to a handsomely adorned table laid with what appeared to be a sumptuous banquet. No sooner had the feast begun, with the nobs toasting one another and making orotund addresses, than a furious rag-tag-and-bobtail crowd of beggars fell upon the revellers, driving them from the piazza with cries of '*Morte, morte a tutti!*' and seizing the food and drink from the table.

The significance of the gesture was not lost on local proprietors. In a few weeks the entire Mantovano seemed alive with 'socialists' and 'agitators'. The dynamic slogan daubed on barns, stables and cowsheds and chanted by the mobs tramping the roads from village to village was '*La boje!*' a dialect phrase meaning 'The pot's boiling!' which hardly needed further elucidation. After more than a decade of worsening unrest throughout Italy, matters came to a head in the summer of 1898, when the cities were paralysed by a series of violent episodes which disclosed the flimsy framework upholding the state and its institutions. In May of that year, as rioting broke out in the streets of Milan, the government sent the Piedmontese general Bava Beccaris to restore order to the Lombard capital. Having got it firmly into his head that decisive military action was called for, the general mowed down the demonstrators with rifle fire and sabre-brandishing cavalry swept through the streets.

What sounds a sinister echo even today when you mention the name of Bava Beccaris among educated Italians is a memory of the grotesque incident which took place outside a monastery where a line of beggars stood awaiting the daily bowl of soup and crust of bread dished out by the monks. Maybe the dole included *polenta* besides. A mixture of genuine short-sightedness and panic made the general think this harmless crowd was a socialist rabble, and he ordered his guns to open fire. When the total casualty list of Bava Beccaris's operations in Milan was released, it amounted to some eighty dead and four hundred wounded. In subsequent weeks the government ordered the closure of the universities and rounded up every single important political dissident of whatever shade. As for Bava Beccaris, King Umberto awarded him a decoration for gallantry.

If I end up thinking about Bava Beccaris when I eat *polenta*, it is because the food of the peasantry was often little more than this maize porridge, which, if it did nothing much else, filled an empty belly. Rich as well as poor liked their nibble: Byron's Venetian crony, Countess Querini Benzon, who introduced him to Teresa Guiccioli, his 'last attachment', kept a piece of it steaming between her breasts as she scudded about the city in her gondola,* so that she was known as *el fumeto*, 'little smoke'. Yet the sticky yellow pap, whether eaten in blobs like mashed potato or in small oblong slabs, belongs archetypally to the humble farms of Lombardy and the Veneto, where decent bread was either a luxury or quite unknown.

Its savour is nonexistent, unless you count a certain rubberiness which derives from the consistency. What has ensured the survival of *polenta* in an age of culinary pretentiousness is its consummate versatility. It goes with absolutely everything. You can scoop up sauces with it, you can use it to clean your plate, you can eat it with liver, kidneys, duck, chicken, game and fish, you can spread honey and jam on it and sprinkle it with lemon juice and sugar like pancakes. Its quintessential featurelessness defies you to appreciate it, yet at the same time challenges you to deny its authenticity. *Polenta* seems more genuinely Italian even than *pasta*, simply because it is so intransigently resistant to adaptation. You get to like it, as if you were one of those Trollope heroines who complain to their mammas that they cannot love Lord X or the Reverend Mr B, to which the matriarch benignly replies, 'But you can *learn* to love him, my dear.' And when at last you have learned

* One of the most famous of all Venetian barcarolles, the artlessly charming 'Biondina in Gondoleta', was written in celebration of her. Liszt includes a seductive piano version of it in his 'Années de Pèlerinage'.

to love *polenta*, you will have another of Italy's secrets by heart.

Italians have an engaging way of judging you according to the degree of your determination in hunting out and sampling local gastronomic delights. No sooner had I passed the *polenta* test at a restaurant in Padua than I failed dismally a few weeks afterwards with the *stoccafisso* of Ancona. It was not strictly my fault. My liver, febrile and temperamental in ways that would gladden the heart of any French doctor, was in one of its periodic sulks, and I had reluctantly passed up the chance to sample a glass or two of the new *verdicchio* at a winemaker's *cantina* at Cupramontana. Whatever my qualms, I felt honour-bound to try the *stoccafisso all'anconetana*.

In its scrambled, knocked-about, shaken-and-stirred way, Ancona is among the sturdiest and most impressively defined of the great port cities of Italy. It lies on the end of a horn-shaped promontory thrusting into the Adriatic, with the newer parts of the town, beyond the mole and the docks, sprawling northwest along the curve of the coastline. Ancona is the place that has had it all, rather like the dead King Lear, of whom Kent remarks somewhat obtusely, 'The wonder is he hath endur'd so much.' The mediaeval maritime republic of Saint Cyriac, holding out against imperial Ghibellines, Venetians, Byzantines and Saracens, became a haven for refugees from Turkish invaders and Albanian pirates, but the popes marked it for their own and took control through a sordid combination of military arm-twisting and barefaced lies, a takeover whose realities were sealed when the papal troops symbolically chucked the entire municipal archive, some five hundred years of documents, out of the window. It was besieged twice by the Austrians, who also bombed it in the Great War, and knocked to blazes by the Allies in 1944. A massive earthquake in 1972 ravaged what was left.

Yet the city, given its dramatic layout and position, can scarcely hide its scarred, crippled beauty, and beautiful, in the louche, dashing manner of seaports, I have always found it. There is elegant gothic in Margaritone D'Arezzo's porch

to the Duomo, where the incorrupt body of Saint Cyriac*
himself lies with its mouth open inside a rococo casket, and in
the gorgeously florid merchants' houses in Via della Loggia by
the fifteenth-century Dalmatian architect Giorgio da Sebenico.
One of the loveliest Titians in the world, a cloudborne Madonna
with saints against a reeking Venetian sky, hangs in the gallery
beside brilliant Guercino, Lotto and Crivelli, and on the harbour, where the ferries sail for Patras and Dubrovnik, Trajan's
triumphal arch, with a sonorous dedication to the Emperor,
his wife Plotina and his sister Marciana, looks out towards the
amazing pentagonal Lazzaretto, combining a quarantine station,
a magazine and a fortress, built by the Neapolitan architect Luigi
Vanvitelli in 1733.

Because anything that could ever be carried in a ship's hold,
from Greek marbles and manuscripts, currants and sweet wine,
to cotton, coal and pig-iron, fetched up on the quays of Ancona,
so too did the tubs of dried cod, known as stockfish, which
was one of the prized exports of mediaeval England. The cod
were not salted but split down the centre and hung out to
dry in the keen North Sea breezes in ports like Yarmouth,
Hull and Grimsby. Thus hardened and desiccated, they became
stiff stocks, and the name clung on in Italy, where stockfish
easily metamorphosed into *stoccafisso*. Ancona is not the only
place where Italians consume dried cod – elsewhere, in its
salt incarnation, it is called *baccalà* (the ubiquitous Portuguese
bacalhau) and makes good Friday eating with oil and parsley
and little red onions – but here is where they dress it to best
advantage.

First of all you must slice thinly an onion or two, some
carrots and a stick of celery, and simmer them slowly in oil
with a sprinkling of chopped parsley. To the mixture add a

* A pious Jew named Judas Cyriacus, he told Saint
Helen the whereabouts of the True Cross, was
converted to Christianity and martyred by Julian
the Apostate. Ancona's other patrons are Saints
Liberius, Marcellinus, Primianus and Palatia.

couple of tablespoons of tomato pulp (*passato di pomodoro*) and a good pinch of marjoram, and season everything with salt and pepper. Assuming you have soaked the cod, you can start to build up a casserole dish with alternate layers of fish, peeled and sliced potatoes and the savoury vegetable mush, on top of which you should pour a little milk and a further dash of oil, before covering and cooking.

The result can scarcely fail to please. Whatever your thoughts as to the essentially prosaic nature of cod, whose sole distinction in modern England is to provide the fish-finger fallback of a million freezer compartments, this wretched gadoid will seem like an epigram from Brillat-Savarin in the context of a perfect *stoccafisso all'anconetana*. So indeed it looked to me that evening in Piazza del Plebiscito, where a sweeping exedra of shallow steps between tall brown palaces runs up to meet the half-finished façade of the church of San Domenico and a massive sub-Berninian statue of Pope Clement XII glowers down like some ugly, angry old grandmother.

The waiter had been delighted with my choice. A Brownie-point was conferred on me for unerringly picking the local dish without asking to know what was in it. While waiting, I had reached nervously for my bottle of liver pills. Italy being a country where shops actually wish to sell you their wares, chemists here are not hedged around with too many ridiculous scruples as to what they may or may not supply over the counter without prescription, and the women in the *farmacia* that morning had told me all I needed to know about the detoxifying effect of the relevant capsules and suppositories. I always opt for the capsule: there is something not altogether serious about a suppository.

When the *stoccafisso* arrived, it had a sort of bubbling unctuousness about it which under other circumstances I should have found irresistible. The scents of marjoram and tomatoes rising on the steam were as enchanting to one sense as Titian's Madonna on her curls of sunset-streaked cloud had been to another. Goddammit, I was about to eat stockfish, off which Pope Pius II, who died in the cathedral in 1464 while making ready to lead a crusade against the Turks, might well have feasted, and which Napoleon himself, who entered the city in triumph in 1797 and let the Jews out of the ghetto, would not have disdained: *stoccafisso*, a mouthful of the Middle Ages, uniting the Mediterranean and the Atlantic.

It was no earthly good. The liver took one look, as it were, and turned away in distaste. I felt as if a single mouthful must be my death-stroke. The waiter hovered expectantly, wanting to know my earliest impression of the fish I had in truth come all this way to eat. After prodding nervously at the safer-looking morsels of potato, I cried quits. The expression of dawning contempt in the waiter's face as he withdrew my full plate was like a brand upon the memory.

Perhaps it was this which made me feel determined to go back to Ancona and do it all again, properly this time. Much had changed in five years. From a glum, bomb-blasted, earthquake-battered invalid in splints of wood and metal, the city was transfigured by an almost lurid youthfulness, its *palazzi* bright with fresh stucco in washes of ochre, russet and cream, the pale golden limestone and pink brick of its ceremonious little churches gleaming like the bodies of athletes. An enchantingly out-to-lunch woman named Giò, who kept a secondhand bookshop and wore floral lycra cycling pants, a genuine eccentric (rare enough in Italy) had enlisted our signatures in her campaign to restore and reopen the ruined neo-classical Teatro delle Muse. In return she took us to see the amazing Palazzo degli Anziani, built by Margaritone D'Arezzo in the thirteenth century and much tinkered with during the intervening seven hundred years, but still containing its descending sequence of vast vaulted gothic halls which drops right down the steep hillside to the harbour.

The Piazza del Plebiscito was almost unrecognizable. On his pedestal Pope Clement looked positively benign, and the lines of shuttered palaces at either side, freshly restored, had abandoned grimness in favour of swagger. We sat down at the same restaurant, which, perhaps predictably, had now assumed an ominous air of self-regarding smartness. The menu was inscribed on crackly parchment leaves with illuminated borders, contained in a tasselled album of embossed leather. The glasses were those paper-thin, tulip-shaped goblets from which anything more than the daintiest sip is bound to crack off a lethal sliver in your mouth.

One element, however, remained unaltered. Don't ask me why, but it is never hard to remember waiters, even after five years, and this one, maybe a little balder and more rolypoly, was indubitably the same. I glanced down the menu for form's sake, though the choice had made itself ages ago. '*E per me lo stoccafisso*,' I announced with a touch of defiance. When, after the briefest of pauses, he murmured '*Ah già!*', that Italian expression which means 'But of course, you told me earlier', I knew that for the most unflattering of reasons he had recognized me and that my gastronomic lapse had never been forgiven.

For the rest of the meal he was rude in that super-irritating fashion which takes care to stay within the bounds of good manners. He ostentatiously forgot the mineral water, took care to spill a good wine on the tablecloth and dawdled unconscionably over bringing the stockfish, as if it were intended that I should perform some complicated act of contrition in the meanwhile.

Penitently therefore I ate it all, and sopped up some of the tomato sauce with my bread when the last mouthful was finished. The fish was as delicious as I could have wanted. Alas, it is unlikely that you will ever find it outside Italy, let alone beyond the Marche district in which Ancona lies, for like so many other good regional dishes, it is considered a trifle too humble and shabby for the average Italian restaurant abroad. Can you imagine English punters thrilling to the discovery that there is dried cod on the menu?

The ultimate insults, not too carefully veiled, had been saved till the end of the meal. There was apparently no pudding of any description, but a small bowl of fruit salad was at length grudgingly produced. As I began it, I saw the waiter glance at me as he took the order from the next table, occupied by two prosperous-looking elderly couples, obviously favoured habitués. Was there a pudding, they asked? But of course there was a pudding, two kinds of tart, homemade at that, which the waiter, with another sidelong smirk in my direction, hurried away to produce. And when their coffee came, it was accompanied with little *bonbonnières* in the shape of gold baskets tied with silver ribbons. As for my coffee, which arrived without sugar, he had probably spat in it.

We wandered out into the evening. The *passeggiata* had started, and the grand *corsi* running down towards the port from Piazza Cavour were crammed with young people, insouciantly elegant, preened and varnished for the unmissable vespertine rite. They spilled in and out of the lighted doorways of shops, dribbled ice-cream over the pavement, slipped their arms around each other, shouted, giggled and whispered, borne back and forth along the boulevard by the resistless rhythms of parade. I felt rather than saw their beauty as the animating principle of the city, like the warm coursing of blood under scarred skin, and cursed the occasion which drew me away from it so early. I could have done with a razzle tonight, the touch of someone unknown under my hands, and afterwards a smoke and a chat. It's how I learned to speak Italian.

15 Spontini Biscuit Box

Ancona is the chief city of the Marche – a statement which, considered in isolation, is about as meaningless as one of those sentences to be found in the right hand column of an Italian phrase book: 'I always gargle before I go to bed.' 'Underneath the washbasin there will be found a chamberpot.' 'I wish for a quire of your best whitey-brown.' 'Pick this handkerchief up and return it to the Grand-duchess.'

To say that Ancona is the chief city of the Marche is without meaning because nobody ever knows where the Marche are. The averagely knowledgeable traveller can point, more or less, towards Tuscany, Lombardy and Piedmont, probably locates the Veneto correctly, and identifies Apulia and Calabria with the heel and toe of Italy. If he or she is at all classically inclined he or she will know that Campania is the area surrounding Naples and that Lazio, besides being a football team with a rather bad reputation, embraces Rome. Umbria, thanks to the tour operators and people in search of a homelier version of the Tuscan villa with swimming pool attached, now has a higher profile, and intrepid environment-conscious ramblers know about the Abruzzi with its Marsican brown bears and the last Italian wolves.

But the Marches, where the mischief are they? The farthest anyone ever gets into them is a hop to Urbino on a tourist bus. Otherwise Pesaro and Macerata mean opera festivals and Fabriano is where the fancy drawing paper comes from that you buy in smart Milanese or Florentine art shops. It is faintly possible that those of a literary turn will remember that the poet Giacomo Leopardi passed a miserable boyhood at Recanati and that Catholics will have sought the intercession of the Madonna of Loreto. There is not much else anybody can dredge up for you about the Marche.

The Romans thought of the whole area, this central Adriatic seaboard, in terms of a vast granary. Nowadays it does not look like ideal corn country, with its bald mountains and endless plunging hillsides, but in the imperial centuries it was known as the Annonaria, because it yielded a yearly bounty in crops and cattle. The Marches were only created during the eleventh century, as territorial districts almost but not quite under papal control, around the cities of Ancona, Fermo and Camerino, over which the popes assumed full jurisdiction two hundred years later.

After that, nobody bothered much with the Marche. Apart from Raphael, who did not spend that long in his native Urbino anyway, such painters as there were get labelled '*Scuola marchigiana*' in the galleries for the sake of convenience rather than as representatives of any especially distinguished artistic tradition, and the area produced no great sculptors or architects.

Travellers, if they came at all, crossed this country en route to Ancona, or completed the last stages of their pilgrimage to the shrine at Loreto,* where the Holy House of the Virgin Mary stands within a gorgeously adorned basilica heralded by splendid colonnades. The Holy House is supposed to have flown, with the aid of angels, all the way from Nazareth to a hill in Istria, and to have touched down finally at Loreto in the year 1294. When you look at it, this humdrum brick cell illumined by candle flames in the rich, sophisticated darkness of the church, you have no difficulty whatever in believing that it is what they tell you. Faith is pointless without flying houses.

What celebrity this region ever possessed came from its abundance in two forms of human life which, in the eighteenth century at least, would have been considered fundamental components of civilized living – popes and castrati. Nicholas IV, who sent a mission to China, founded the University of Montpellier and laid the first stones of the Duomo of Orvieto, came from Lisciano near Ascoli Piceno; Marcellus II, for whom Palestrina wrote his masterly *Missa Papae Marcelli*, was born at a village outside Macerata, and the titanic and terrifying Sixtus V, who in five years created the Rome we know today, was the son of a poor family of Grottamare. Clements the Eighth, the Eleventh and the Fourteenth were all Marchesans, Pius VIII was a boy from Cingoli, and that most famous and controversial Pius of them all, Pio Nono, was Count Giovanni Maria Mastai Ferretti of Senigallia.

As for the singing eunuchs, the *musici*, the *evirati*, what exactly was it that made them so much of a local particular? Visitors to Italy always wondered whereabouts the process of castration actually took place which produced (or alas failed to produce) these prodigies of the lyric stage. Officially the gelding operation was punishable with fines, imprisonment

* One such was the poet Richard Crashaw, most baroque of the Metaphysicals, who died at Loreto on 21 August 1649, of a fever, say some, of poison, say others.

and excommunication, though *castrati* went on singing in the Sistine Chapel until the end of the nineteenth century (the last of them, Alessandro Moreschi, made a number of gramophone records). Everybody was at pains to deny that such a specialized technique was practised or even known about in the locality. The English musicologist Charles Burney, travelling across Italy in 1771, wrote exasperatedly:

> I enquired at what place boys were chiefly qualified for singing by castration, but could get no certain intelligence. I was told at Milan that it was at Venice; at Venice that it was at Bologna; but at Bologna the fact was denied and I was referred to Florence; from Florence to Rome, and from Rome I was sent to Naples. The operation most certainly is against law in all these places, as well as against nature; and all the Italians are so much ashamed of it, that in every province they transfer it to some other.

The place to which poor but ambitious Marchesan parents sent their hapless offspring for metamorphosis into beings supposedly resembling the order of angels in having no sex was probably over the Umbrian border, in the rugged old mountain town of Norcia, birthplace of Saint Benedict and his sister Scholastica. The *norcini* were, and still are, famous for their different types of ham and salami, and on some of the older pork butchers' shops up and down Italy you can still see the word *norcineria*. More sinisterly, they were regarded as experts in the quick, deft slaughter and dismembering of pigs and in the gelding of young boars. The knife that gutted a piglet could be turned easily enough to emasculating a little *marchigiano*.*

If this really was a speciality of the *norcini*, they assisted in producing many of the greatest singing stars of eighteenth-century Europe, not a few of them born in obscure villages scattered

---

* It was not unknown for audiences, listening to a particularly brilliant exhibition of the castrato's powers, to cry *'Evviva il coltello!'* – 'Long live the knife!'

across the hills of the Marche. Giovanni Carestini, who sang for Handel in *Ariodante* and *Alcina*, and whom Burney described as 'tall, beautiful and majestic . . . a very animated and intelligent actor . . . having a considerable portion of enthusiasm in his composition, with a lively and inventive imagination', came from Filottrano. From Urbania, west of Urbino, sprang the wondrous Girolamo Crescentini, whose singing enchanted the court of Napoleon at the Tuileries, and of whose tones the enraptured Schopenhauer confided to his diary 'his supernaturally beautiful voice cannot be compared with that of any woman: there can be no fuller and lovelier tone, and in its silver purity he still contrives to produce an indescribable force.' London in the 1780s went wild over Gasparo Pacchierotti of Fabriano, the most instinctively musical singer of his generation, with an unusual lack of soloist's vanity, 'unpresuming in his manners, grateful and attached to all his numerous friends and patrons', whose last public appearance was in *I Giochi d'Agrigento*, the opera by Paisiello which opened the doors of Teatro La Fenice in Venice. Stendhal tells us that he learned more in six meetings with Pacchierotti than from any book about music.

The last of this astonishing breed, in whom a unique vocal potency replaced whatever more commonplace talents they might have forfeited, was born near Ancona in 1781. Giovanni Battista Velluti lost his manhood not at the business end of a *coltello norcino*, but at the hands of a bungling doctor, who castrated him by mistake. It was a fortunate accident, and the singer went on to become the toast of Europe. 'Such sounds,' declared Napoleon, hearing him in Venice, 'I should scarcely have believed possible, save in someone who was not a man.' He was carried off to the Crimea by an amorous Russian Grand Duchess and hounded out of Milan because of his liaison with a young noblewoman. Arrested by the Austrian police for not carrying a passport, he charmed the gendarmes with an aria or two. In London, where he made his début alongside the legendary Maria Malibran, he became manager of the opera house in the Haymarket, but settled down in Italy at last as an experimental farmer near Padua.

Velluti's talent for getting into trouble never deserted him. In 1849, when he was on his way to see the doctor about a sore throat, he found himself caught up by a troop of Austrian soldiers going to besiege Venice. Their medical officer, listening to the old man's account of his symptoms, suggested that singing would probably be the best cure. The first thing that came into Velluti's head was an air by a long-forgotten eighteenth-century Neapolitan master, Tommaso Traetta. 'Good God!' cried the officer, 'my father used to say he had heard Velluti sing that piece, and that it was the loveliest sound he ever remembered.' 'Well,' said the castrato, 'I am Velluti, and now you have heard me sing it.'

The country which produced such musical dodos and quaggas is some of the loveliest in all Italy. The pen trembles in my hand as I think of it. Perhaps the beauty of the Marche has something to do with their closeness to the sea, or maybe it strikes me the more because it hasn't that lived-in, walked-over, written-about, descanted-upon quality which characterizes Tuscany and Umbria. The hills – it is all hills, for the river valleys are of the narrowest and the coastal plain is the veriest ribbon strip – move in rhythmic brown folds towards the horizon, their steep slopes feathered with olives and little coppices of oak and ash, but the prospect is purged of monotony by the presence of a strange, bony-looking mountain or two, never terribly high but loomingly primeval in appearance, as if the skin of the land had been scraped back to reveal its true making beneath. They say that the people hereabouts went on worshipping their old mother-goddess Cupra for hundreds of years after the official imposition of Christianity on the region, in caves inside these mountains, where obscene rites culminated in the sacrifice of little children. In the context of this landscape it is not hard to believe.

Perched on the spurs of these hills are tiny walled towns – forever not quite villages – built mostly of brick. In England we have no concept of the charm and versatility of brick as a building material for palaces and churches. The idea of a cathedral or a town hall or a monastery made all of soft, friable pink stocks which age has turned to cream, egg-yellow, salmon and pale rose-madder, with barely perceptible layers of frayed white pointing between them, is unknown to us simply because our light will not stand it. Italian brick needs the strong, remorseless beat of the sun, as if a sort of deliberate ageing process were being conducted, and these walls and façades had been left out to dry and turn colour in the heat.

Received historical wisdom always tells us that papal government meant bad government, and that the Marches under the popes were left to fester in provincial neglect. I'm not persuaded, more especially as each of these small brick cities has an inherent stateliness in its *mise en scène* which patently derives from the benign dispositions of bishops and cardinals building for eternity. They wanted to give their towns something to show for themselves, so the switchback road carrying you out of the valley and up towards the gateway will always lead to a triumphal arch, with the triple tiara and Saint Peter's keys atop, the arms of the cardinal or the civil governor who raised it, and an abbreviated Latin inscription in letters of bronze. There follows a long street of palaces, each with its family escutcheon in the keystone and, for what is supposedly the back of beyond, an air of comfortable self-assurance, as though neither position nor possession was ever in doubt. The churches may lack the luxury of decent frescoes, good pictures and consequential monuments, but a splash or two of gilding, a few coloured marbles around the altar of a side-chapel, or the panes of gaudy kaleidoscope glass in the doors to the sacristy relieve them from gloom.

And there is always a theatre. It may not function any longer as such; it may have become a cinema, a furniture depot, a garage or be turned over to still baser uses, yet miraculously, even in tiny Cingoli, 'the balcony of the Marches', or Castelfidardo, the accordion and concertina capital of the world, where you can hear them trying out those accursed squeezeboxes all over the town, the citizens made a cosy little space where they too might hear *Lucia* and *Traviata* and *Boheme*, just like the *signori* of Pesaro, Senigallia and Ancona, and at only half the price.

Why do I love these towns of the Marche to distraction, to

the point of wanting to disappear into their very fabric, to be made into bricks for their palaces and tiles for their roofs, or if that is not possible, at least to achieve symbiosis through eating them up, as though they had been made out of cake and marzipan in a children's tale? It has something to do with the extraordinary feeling of snugness and safety created by their layout in linked concentric rings, like the layers of a mozzarella cheese. Behind the brown ramparts, with their machicolated bastions, the streets are tacked together by tunnelled alleys and flights of steps, and you know exactly where each of them will begin and end. From the belvederes and terraces that open along the walls, you can look out across the valley and, catching the swish of traffic on the road far below, you hug yourself in the banal consolation of immobility, as if the town were a box in which you had lain in tissue paper and cotton wool for safekeeping.

There is nothing dead about these places. Without showy prosperity, they are nevertheless clean, busy, well-appointed and evidently as agreeable to live in as they seem to the casual visitor. More significantly, the impact of those crowds thronging the Corso Garibaldi of Ancona like murmurations of starlings finds its echo here in the little towns of the Marche. In Staffolo, on its conical hill to the south of Jesi, I watched the slow victory of evening over afternoon as the streets and piazzas sprang into life again with the lifting of the day's heat. Ostensibly there is nothing to see in Staffolo, yet to walk through the lanes of the walled *borgo*, with the shadows deepening and a sudden sharpness of definition in the dark outlines of roofs and parapets, jolted me with a kind of epiphany. Doubtless it was no more than a tourist illusion, strengthened by my sheer delight in being there at all, but the idea suddenly came upon me that I was in one of those places which sociologists call 'a balanced community', in which until then I had only half believed.

The people in these narrow streets seemed, in a way I find impossible to account for, to complement and make room for one another as if moving through the phases of a dance. Each of them, the old codger on two sticks, the girl in her printed teeshirt, the woman in an apron watering the geraniums growing out of a green petrol can perched on a balcony, had achieved in this instant the kind of harmony which reminded me of those images of civil concord and good government so beloved of the old painters. This was just piffling Staffolo, one among a hundred Marchesan townlets, with its gothic church and yellow Renaissance *municipio* and marble tablet to the dead of Caporetto and the Piave, and life here was perhaps as savourless, blunt-edged and *borné* as anywhere else in late twentieth-century Italy, yet this human equilibrium suddenly declaring itself in the gathering dusk, young and old, middle-aged and elderly, poised against each other without evident rancour, hatred or suspicion, gave the place a dreamlike, almost celestial perfection, like something out of the beatific visions of Blake and Traherne.

As I gaze across these hills to the intense, purplish line of the Adriatic on the eastern horizon, a hunger not to lose anything here creates a map of unfulfilled longing for a house in one of these towns, high up inside the city wall maybe, or in the attic storey of some tall *palazzo* from which I could look out into that transfiguring clarity of daylight so instantly noticeable once you get up off the *autostrada* running along the coastal plain.

For different reasons, Loreto and Castelfidardo would probably be too noisy. Apiro and Cupramontana might, on the other hand, prove a little too quiet. I'd settle for Osimo, that long red Roman Auximum, with a luxuriant Vivarini altarpiece in the museum and a white Romanesque Duomo and much gravely elegant papal architecture among its discreetly decomposing palace fronts. And in my occasional misanthropic Timon-of-Athens moods, I'd retreat to Sassoferrato, beyond the wooded gorges and shallow rock pools of the swift-flowing Sentino, where brick yields to stone and there is a sudden air of rugged, no-nonsense, upland severity, with the high Umbrian mountains brooding behind.

To come back to, there must always be Jesi, the ideal small Italian city. Lying as it does on the edge of a plateau overlooking a broad but not preternaturally interesting river called the Esino, Jesi is really several towns gathered into one. First comes a shabby, unpretending set of roads around the station, full of workshops and dusty little grocers and dark bars running eternal soccer replays on the video. East of this lies new Jesi, landscaped housing estates with little apartment blocks like Barratt Homes with lanterns at the doors and an air of modest gentrification. Up at the top of the hill beyond is a leafy suburb full of villas with answerphones at the street gates, canna lilies and yucca in the front gardens and notices which warn you, not very convincingly, to beware the unwelcome attentions of the *cane pericoloso*. It is all rather like something you might expect to find on the outskirts of Maidenhead or Pangbourne.

None of these peripheric settlements detracts in the slightest from the effect of old Jesi itself, a town slapped firmly on to the saddle of a hill shaped like a lamb cutlet and girdled by the sort of heavily turreted ramparts you thought could only be dreamed up in a Hollywood set, moulded in *papier mâché* for Robert Taylor and Maureen O'Hara to appear to best advantage in chainmail and wimple.

Implausible these bastions and baileys may seem, wholly '*ollyvoodiano*' as the Italians say, but they are as authentic as everything else in Jesi which distils the Italian hill-town to its quintessence without whimsy or pretence for the benefit of tourists, since patently it has not needed them from the start and does not specially care that in three hundred years not a single noteworthy enthusiast paused to exclaim on the place's inalienable handsomeness. Byron leaves it out of 'Childe Harold', Ruskin found nothing worth expatiating upon in its churches and palaces, Stendhal failed to imagine himself in love with any of its young girls, neither Turner nor Bonington nor Corot ever painted it, it inspired never a note of music out of Berlioz or Liszt and, as far as I know, old Edward Hutton doesn't give it the time of day.

Probably none of them ever clapped eyes on it, yet for my money Jesi is as winning, as meritorious, as free with its suggestions of beauty as anything in Latium or Tuscany or the foothills of the Dolomites. From the narrower eastern end, the rib-bone, as it were, of the chop, you are typically fanfared into the town through a giant eighteenth-century papal arch which catapults you down the long main drag, the Corso Matteotti, graced with a sequence of palaces halted here and there by small baroque church façades like semi-colons in some expansively unfolding prose paragraph. Halfway along comes a humorous little square with palm trees and an over-egged pudding of a marble fountain, on which stands the composer Giambattista Pergolesi attended by allegorical figures of Music and Song flopping woefully over the keyboard of a harpsichord. Born here in 1710, he was the most admired musician in Europe during his short life, which ended in similar circumstances to that of another precocious genius, Henry Purcell, when he caught cold one night because his shrewish wife would not let him into the house. He was only twenty-six.

The theatre they named after him, a confident neo-classical essay created during the Napoleonic period, closes one side of the prospect in the Piazza della Repubblica into which the Corso debouches. Yet lest you suppose that is that, Jesi has a trick or two left up its sleeve. For a second arch, mediaeval this time, opens into the most ancient quarter of the town, a mesh of alleys and stairways and tunnel-like lanes around three diversely-shaped squares through which you move as though threading the stages of some ritually-disposed sanctuary granting successive accretions of wisdom.

In the shadow of these brown palace fronts, these wreathed and pillared arches and white obelisks with their polite appeals to an illusion of metropolitan grandeur echoing the great vistas of Sistine Rome, what is it intended that you should learn? Probably it does not greatly matter that Pergolesi's family house was in Piazza Ghislieri, or that on the site of the old Roman forum in the year 1194, inside a huge tent, in the presence of nineteen cardinals and bishops, Constance de Hauteville gave birth to a son who was to become the Emperor Frederick II, the 'Stupor Mundi' of the High Middle Ages, or that the picture gallery in the gorgeously stuccoed Palazzo Pianetti contains no less than six canvases by Lorenzo Lotto. You might leave Jesi without any of these things, even Lotto at his most vibrantly emotive, having made the slightest impression. What the space and angles and planes within these vistas will not let you escape from is that art which only Italy has ever completely mastered, and which the rest of Europe has spent so much time and ingenuity in trying to acquire from her – the art of living in cities without hating them, without the belief that they must somehow always be hostile to the best impulses of human nature.

The epiphany of Staffolo is not a delusion after all. That perpetual Italian reluctance to leave the maternal embrace of warm brick ramparts and lose oneself in the woods and fields becomes immediately comprehensible. At night, when the long grey spine of the Corso and its pendant piazzas beyond are crammed with the amblers and hangers-out of the drifting *passeggiata*, the green pieties of modern pastoral anti-urbanism are set entirely at naught. These people are here not because they are bored or have nothing better to do and would be happier playing dominoes in the Barratt Homes at the bottom of the hill or stroking the *cane pericoloso* in the Home Counties residences along the *viali* – though such may well be the case. The city has precious little squalor and, it is safe to say, no serious dimension of violence. They do not long to be anywhere else, save perhaps at Ancona where they would simply carry on as before, only on a grander scale. They are here to renew a harmony, simple almost to banality, between the city and its people, a reciprocal affection which, inexplicably yet beyond question, settles the balance between the citizens and the place where they dwell. Walking these streets in the hottest nights of summer, I occasionally press the palm of a hand against the stucco and marble and brick, and feel that their warmth to my touch has been created not by a residual heat left behind from the day, but out of the town's love, hidden yet irrepressible, for its inhabitants.

For this very reason, you become aware, throughout the Marche, of a desire to honour the famous not just for their personal achievements but for the celebrity they have given the land. Very well, this impulse is not uniquely *marchigiano*. Certain places in Italy actually add the illustrious name to the toponym – Castagneto Carducci, Caprese Michelangelo, Riese

Pio X – and some of them, such as the village of Vinci in the
hills west of Florence, where Leonardo was born, manage to live
almost exclusively on the strength of a worldwide reputation.
Yet the pride of the Marchesans in the works of local boys and
girls is magnificently obsessive.

Go, for example, to Fano, that most agreeable of small seaside
resorts, much favoured by the Brownings, who wrote poems
about it, and Perugino, who painted two of his serenest altarpieces for the Franciscans of Santa Maria Nuova. There, among
the Malatesta tombs and the Roman arch of Augustus marking
the end of the Via Flaminia, and the cathedral of Saint Fortunatus
which was once the temple of the goddess Fortuna, and the
striped beach umbrellas on the sands, you will find, stuck
on to one of the palaces, a stone – *una lapide*, mark, not a
simple *pietra* – recording the fact that this was the birthplace
of Donna Laura Martinozzi, the mother of Maria Beatrice of
Modena, Queen of England. Donna Laura was indeed a woman
of remarkable intelligence and resourcefulness, probably the
best duchess Modena ever had, but it is somehow typical of
the Marchesan spirit that Fano should wish, amid all its other
glories, to commemorate the attainments of Mary of Modena's
mum.

They are even prouder of their saints. In this region there is
a saint under every altar of the meanest church of the smallest
village; if not an entire beatified corpse, then a member or two,
as at Recanati which possesses one of Saint Vitus's arms. There
are eight martyrs under the high altar of the cathedral of Osimo
alone, and goodness knows how many in all the towns from
Ascoli up to Urbino. They are not, for the most part, the kind of
saints you will find elsewhere than in that interesting half-inch of
The Independent Court & Social page which proclaims 'Today is
the feast day of . . .' Today in the Marche is the feast day of San
Serafino de Montegranaro, Santa Maria Goretti, San Vincenzo
Strambi, San Catervo di Tolentino, of Saint Maro the Apostle
of the Marches, of Saints Venantius and Paternian martyrs, of
the Blessed Assunta Pallotta da Force and the Blessed Antonio
Grassi of Fermo, of Saint Bernard of Offida and Saint Nicholas

of Tolentino, of San Giacomo della Marca 'artificer of the victory of Belgrade' and of San Giuseppe da Copertino 'protector of students'.

A town such as Recanati is almost embarrassed with remembered greatness. A little to the south of Loreto, which it surveys from its high, windy hilltop, Recanati expresses to perfection the triumph of brick in its beetling red ramparts, built to guard the stronghold for the Pope under the governance of ninety-seven noblemen (why always ninety-seven? why not ninety-eight or ninety-six?). In the gallery of the Palazzo Comunale hangs the most arresting of all those paintings which that poor, unsuccessful, half-crazy genius Lorenzo Lotto scattered among the Marchesans, the Annunciation he painted for the small church of Santa Maria sopra Mercanti. It is unlike those other classic Italian Annunciations, the ones you remember to have seen at Florence or Venice, Veronese's, say, which all seem to have taken place in the garden of a country house where the Virgin has been spending a quiet weekend with her books, or Fra Angelico's, in which the angel's massive rainbow pinions look so curiously menacing in juxtaposition to the slender, absorbed Madonna.

Here there is a new element, something heightened by the lurid brightness of the blue and red in Lotto's palette, which always appears slightly hysterical or hallucinatory, an element of fearful surprise. Decorum ordained that the Virgin should show humility – '*Ecce ancilla Domini*', 'Behold the handmaid of the Lord' – just as it decreed that somewhere in the picture there must be a lily to embody her purity. In Lotto's Annunciation, however, her modest reluctance is made to seem more like a terrified instant reaction to the angel's arrival, since in the background hovers God himself, pointing a hand towards her, and Gabriel, hair still bouncing in the wind, is imbued with the sense of having touched down from heaven at that very moment, as a cat scampers away in fright across the room. The unorthodoxy of this vision is majestic, enhanced by the way in which we look into the scene along a perspective avenue rather than viewing it as the customary flat tableau. This is always the last Annunciation to which the memory clings when the others have blurred.

Here is one reason why travellers seek out Recanati, but they come mostly because it was the birthplace of the poet Giacomo Leopardi, who spent his uniquely miserable childhood here in the palace of his pompous, dictatorial father, Count Monaldo Leopardi, and most of whose flawlessly-constructed but achingly melancholy poems were reactions to the imprisoning dullness of existence in this draughty provincial backwater. Recanati, you might think, could survive quite easily on its associations with one of the few first-rate poets Italy has produced. The Leopardian locations are all signposted with little yellow notices, and though his family, still in residence, will not let you see the principal rooms of the *palazzo* where he grew up, they are content to show the quite remarkably dismal library assembled by Count Monaldo, in which his poor hunchbacked son was permitted to browse, and where his early stabs at drama and poetry are preserved in forlorn-looking glass cases.

Fame sounds an 'I too am here' for other *recanatesi*. Up the hill beyond Palazzo Leopardi and into the city proper – for the Leopardi lived, as befitted them, at somewhat of a distance from the mere people – the dingy-looking opera house is named after the nineteenth-century composer and impresario Giuseppe Persiani, 'immortal author of *Ines de Castro*', whose celebrity was largely as the consort of the soprano Fanny Tacchinardi-Persiani, creator of the title role in *Lucia di Lammermoor* and, if witnesses like Gautier and Liszt are to be believed, one of those shudder-inducingly brilliant singing actresses, for a single performance from whom we would have given our eye-teeth. And as if this were not enough, on your way to look at the Lotto, you suddenly stumble across a whole room full of memorabilia of the bacon-faced star tenor Beniamino Gigli, whose 'E lucevan le stelle' is pumped out from a loudspeaker while the lights come on in a replica of his Scala dressing room, with cream pots and powder puffs and the 1940s Italian equivalent of Leichner Five and Nine tumbled across it.

The most moving evidence of the Marches' love for their own, and, more poignantly, of the Marchesans' loyalty to their *terra*, is at the tiny *borgo* of Maiolati, in the hills between Jesi and Fabriano. Here, at the end of a long and eventful career, there came to rest his old bones a composer whose name once shook the whole of Europe, but whose works at their very rare revivals nowadays are viewed more in the light of respectful archaeology than anything the ordinary music-loving public races to hear.

Gaspare Luigi Pacifico Spontini, born at Jesi in 1774, was originally intended for the priesthood (one wonders whether his parents mightn't even have considered a little trip to the gelders of Norcia), but astonished everyone with his gifts in composition, and scored an early success with an opera named (some might say ironically) *L'eroismo ridicolo*. By the time he was thirty Spontini had become the star operatic composer of Napoleonic Paris, a favourite with the Empress Josephine, the admired creator of *La Vestale, Milton* (yes, the blind bard of Chalfont St Giles as singing hero, hard as it is to credit) and *Ferdinand Cortez* (whose heroine bears the unprepossessing name of Amazilly).

The trouble with Spontini was essentially the trouble with the entire Napoleonic charade, namely that he does not appear to have had much of a sense of humour. His operas are tremendously important in the history of nineteenth-century music because they broke new ground in their explorations of the genre, because of their influence on other composers, and above all because Wagner told us they were important for being forerunners of his own works. Such was the mesmeric power of Wagner's egoism that his judgement has since been accepted all too uncritically. Interesting Spontini undoubtedly is to musicologists, crashingly tedious he appears to the untutored listener; a windbag, a noisemaker, a purveyor of tuneless musical permafrost, whose operas have all the musclebound grandiloquence of Soviet sculpture.

Whatever his wild success, Spontini was quarrelsome, toadying and a born intriguer, with a consequent gift for making enemies. When he finally left Berlin in 1842, after twenty stormy years as favoured court composer to the kings of Prussia, it was after a spell in prison for his insulting behaviour to those he believed had instigated a plot against him. Via Paris, where he was very much yesterday's news, this snobbish old reactionary, who had got himself made Conte di San Andrea by the Pope, came home at last to settle in little Maiolati, where he died in 1851.

May Gaspare Pacifico's sins be forgiven him, for with the fortune he had amassed as the blazing comet of through-composed *tragédie lyrique*, he decided to enrich the village itself. Attached to his specially designed mortuary chapel, with its splendid marble tomb, there was to be a hospital for the poor old folk of the district, tended by nursing sisters, his birthplace was to become a shrine, and a theatre was to be constructed for the performance of his works. And here, by Jove, in a village about half a yard long, it all is, at Maiolati, now named Maiolati Spontini in his honour. The white-gowned nuns will lead you through the wards where the toothless and chapfallen sit up in their beds to watch as you pass by into the chapel next door, to make a leg towards defunct genius. The theatre has not quite become the Bayreuth of the Marches, but Spontini at any rate gets a hearing, and the musically learned come to refresh their memories of *Agnes von Hohenstaufen* and *Nurmahal*. And the village carpenter will show you over the birthplace.

He is something of a character, this carpenter. As we wandered through the rooms of what is essentially a delightful neo-classical *palazzino* with 'Pompeiian' frescoes on walls and ceilings, it became clear that he absolutely refused to accept our ability to talk Italian. Whatever we said was translated into halting English and, as it were, politely recycled. 'This Spontini table', 'this Spontini bed' and so on. Incidentally it was the most elegant of beds, with a curving iron frame and painted panels in the headboard. I could die most fetchingly in such a bed.

In the last room the carpenter showed us was a display of photocopies of Spontinian manuscripts and testimonials to the composer's genius from the likes of Berlioz, Wagner and Liszt. We had already started that elaborate performance one goes through at such moments, of determining by cryptic signs and murmurs how much to offer as a tip, when the carpenter suddenly cried: 'Wait, wait! I show you!' and disappeared into a cupboard. After a minute or two, he emerged holding a large tin box covered with paper, on which was clearly written 'Huntley & Palmer's Best Assorted Biscuits', in lettering of a style not earlier than 1900.

'Spontini he go to London!' exclaimed the carpenter with a smile of utter conviction. 'They make him present. This . . . Spontini biscuit box!'

16 San Francesco and San Frediano

Many of the happiest moments in my life have been spent in other people's houses. I long ago reconciled myself to the fact that, lacking money or the prospect of an inheritance, I would never be the owner of a really nice house, but against this I place one of the greatest consolations of my existence, namely the chance held out to me by friendship to enjoy playing the cuckoo in some most delightful nests.

I think, for example, of a rococo menagerie in Northamptonshire, purchased for peanuts while it was being used as a barn for cattle, and painstakingly restored to its former stuccoed and cupolaed magnificence by a friend of mine whose eighteenth-century sympathies have made him a modern avatar of Horace Walpole and Thomas Gray, though possessed of a far gentler, less waspish nature than either. To sit under the great dome, adorned with panels representing the signs of the zodiac, the four continents and Father Time, the work of the wandering Italian stuccador Antonio Vassalli, with the light thrown clear through the high Venetian window, and a soft roll of Midland England in the landscape beyond, is one of my principal accesses to joy.

I remember also, in this connection, a house in Washington Mews, New York, once the studio of the painter Edward Hopper, a flat in Hamburg in an old Wilhelmine apartment block with tall ceilings and big windows looking out onto a tree-lined canal, a tiny cottage down a lane among fields along the Douro estuary in Portugal, an Oxfordshire vicarage, an Edwardian house in Ipswich with giant spiders in the attic, and the various dens in London – an Arts & Crafts mansion in Holland Park, a terrace in Balham, a bohemian refuge in Highbury – where I have been lucky enough to creep for shelter.

Some of the Italian places have been described in this book, as an act of gratitude, however inept, for what has been offered to me by their owners. There's something insufferable about gratitude, not so much to those who themselves feel thankful but to people who have to listen to others expressing their thanks. Sophistication implants a dislike of such sentiments. Readers of Jane Austen's *Emma* will remember the *blasée* heroine's sneering irritation at the wretched Miss Bates, always so humble and thankful for everything, even the stoutness of her old petticoat. The very last thing a girl with Emma's advantages would have wanted to profess in public was gratitude for the pleasures of life, minor as well as major.

Yet I know exactly how Miss Bates felt. Like her I can quote scripture and say that my lot has been cast in a goodly heritage. Unlike Emma, whom her creator identifies as 'clever, handsome, rich', Miss Bates and I may be only partially clever (if such a thing is possible), not especially handsome and not at all rich, yet it has been our perpetual good fortune to be surrounded and supported by those who are all three, and the time has arrived in which for me to try and pay off an old score or two of profound thanks – which is what this book, in one way or another, is really about.

A year ago, having been given a sabbatical term by my employers, I set off for Italy, to spend three months at a house on the outskirts of Florence. It had been sub-let to me by some acquaintance at a rent decidedly in my favour (they've since emphasized that they cannot afford to repeat the experiment) and during April, May and June, there I sat, industriously not writing the book (this one) upon which I had intended to work, reading all the most unimproving literature I could find in a house where books turned up in the oddest places (the log basket, the linen chest, the kitchen cupboards) and for much of the time performing that exercise for which sabbaticals were devised, the hardest act of all to accomplish, that of sitting still.

The building is a small but rambling cottage, formerly the farmhouse of a convent, and still lived in, according to immemorial country custom, by at least three households, none of whom has anything very much to do with the others. Next to it, behind a discreet box hedge, stands the *fienile*, the old hay barn for the farm, itself transformed into a little house with a patch of lawn and flowerbeds *all'inglese* beyond, on the edge of the greater garden planted by the long-vanished monks. As for the convent itself, this became, some two hundred years ago, a villa in the approved Florentine mode, but the shape of a sensible, plain-fronted, late Renaissance palazzo has endured, with an arcade of the cloister behind and the refectory to one side of it.

The monks, members of the Minimite Order founded in Calabria during the sixteenth century by Saint Francis of Paola as an extreme expression of the principles formulated by his Assisian namesake (if the original Franciscans were known as the Friars Minor, these were to be still humbler than minor, hence Minims) were brought here originally by a woman. In the later history of Florence she figures as one of the best-known female protagonists, and her story has always exerted a morbid attraction for biographers, poets, playwrights and the rakers-over of dead scandals. If ever there were an example of someone who, like Emma indeed, 'seemed to unite all the blessings of existence' and whose lot, theoretically at any rate, was cast in a goodly heritage, it was this woman, but there is no suggestion that she was ever grateful for the extraordinary hand dealt her by destiny.

Happiness in the lives of great ones is probably neither here nor there, but in any event I find it hard to believe that Bianca Capello was often sincerely or enduringly happy. Born into an impoverished branch of a Venetian noble family perched precariously upon its dignity since it had nothing else left, she ran away from Venice with a clerk in a Florentine bank named Pietro Buonaventura, with whom she had been conducting a clandestine affair. The story, from here onwards, assumes classic outlines: beautiful, ambitious and passionate, Bianca discovered quickly enough that she had hitched herself to a wimp, and was not content to remain shut up in poky tenement rooms in an unsmart district of Florence with her shrewish mother-in-law while the Venetian State put out a warrant for her arrest and enlisted the help of the Grand Duke of Tuscany himself in the search. Then a remarkable life-imitates-art episode occurred.

One afternoon, bored to death with her enforced domesticity, Bianca heard a noise of shouting and the clatter of horses' hooves coming up the street. Without a thought to her safety, she flung wide the shutters and peered out. It was none other than the Grand Duke Francesco himself, at the head of a cavalcade of courtiers. As he drew level with the house, he turned and looked up at Bianca, and in that moment she knew that she must become his mistress.

When the pair eventually consummated their affair, the Duke was initially quite content to play the statutory rôle of cuckold's patron and to give Pietro employment, but soon afterwards the slighted bank clerk was attacked and stabbed to death 'by persons unknown' on the Ponte Santa Trinità, and it seems almost certain that Francesco had a hand in the murder. Bianca meanwhile, loathed by the rest of the Medici family as a base-born interloper, became the *maîtresse en titre*, assuming so much political significance that the Venetian Republic, hastily changing its tune, hailed the proscribed runaway as 'A Faithful Daughter Of Saint Mark'.

To start with at least, Francesco was besotted by his lovely Venetian and gave her everything she wanted, including a splen-did palace in Via Maggio and the celebrated Orti Oricellari, the Rucellai Gardens, where his ancestor Cosimo's Platonic academy had held its meetings. It was when he finally married Bianca that sourness and jealousy crept into the relationship. The Duke was, after all, a Medici, with his family's vein of cold, vindictive ruthlessness, inherited subsequently by those Medici grandchildren Louis XIV of France and our own odi-ous and contemptible Charles II of England. Bianca, growing obsessed with her infertility, surrounded herself with quacks and mountebanks. One day, fretted beyond endurance by one of them, an old Jewess with a reputation as a white witch, who hung around his wife with nostrums and potions, Francesco casually knifed the beldam in the presence of his courtiers. To Bianca a more dismal ending was reserved.

At the villa of Poggio a Caiano, south-west of Florence, the first country house of modern times, built a century earlier by Lorenzo de'Medici, the Duke and his poor pinchbeck Duchess retired from the world's cold eye and diverted themselves with getting Bernardo Buontalenti, the ingenious Medicean architect, to redesign Bianca's state apartments. On 19 October 1587, the pair went out hunting, caught cold and, foolishly accepting their doctor's recommendation to cure it with iced drinks and chilled foods, died almost immediately. Francesco's brother Ferdinando, who put aside his cardinal's hat for the ducal robes and a sumptuous wedding, may not have poisoned them, as the rumour ran, but he made sure that every honour done to Bianca during her life was cancelled after death, and that her body, wrapped in a simple sheet, was dumped in the common grave for paupers in the crypt of San Lorenzo.

None of the melancholy atmosphere in this archetypal story of a girl from the wrong side of the tracks getting everything she wanted except a genuine enjoyment of it hangs over the convent of San Francesco, founded under her patronage. If the Minims have gone, the ghost of their farm, of its orchards and fields, has lingered, and while I lived here, much of the enchantment of this place for me was created by the prospect of a half-wild, barely tended domain, where only the lightest touch of the gardener's hand held back untrammelled growth among the thick hedges of bay, the file of cypresses up the steep bank onto the hill topped with an orange grove and a sequence of arbours with sudden, intensely-realized vistas of the city, or the hedge of dark bamboo along the stream below the scaly-barked ilex trees.

The pastoral illusion was further sustained by the slope of Bellosguardo rising abruptly behind the house, with fields of oats and green terraced vineyards, a Tuscan landscape of implausible perfection cancelled only by the prospect, on the other side, of the sprawling residential blocks and industrial estates of Scandicci and Galluzzo, the real Italy, as it were, breaking in upon the too-impressionable traveller. It was wonderful, nevertheless, to climb up in the early evening, into the soft upland breeze lifting the undersides of the leaves, with the scent off the fields and the swifts screaming and the towers of Florence bathed in the last muted sun beneath a clear sky, and in that most blessed time of an Italian day, to wander about the lanes between the villas amid a prospect which essentially had not altered in mood since it enraptured the Brownings and Nathaniel Hawthorne, Ouida and Augustus Hare.

Such agreeable expatriate shades hung over San Francesco itself. At some stage in the nineteenth century the convent had been divided between two owners, the American dentist to the Tsar of Russia and a celebrated German sculptor, and descendants of the union of both families keep it still. Liszt played here, Henry James came to stay, Ethel Smyth, after setting her cap at the German sculptor, fell seriously in love with his son-in-law. I never opened the iron wicket gate in the high garden wall and passed under the moss-grown statue of Saint Francis of Paola on its marble plinth without considering that in thus pleasant a fashion I was shutting myself back into an unreconstructed episode from that culture of self-banished foreigners that so immeasurably enriched the life of Florence. Both villa and park, slightly haunted, forsaken but never forlorn, always seemed to be things upon which one might have stumbled by accident, like some adventuring child in a story, by the simple act of pushing open a door in a wall.

This impression was sealed by the way in which the ordinary sounds of the city beyond failed somehow to permeate the hedge of stillness surrounding the garden. The only noise I ever noticed, presumably since I wanted actually to notice it as a congenial element in the idyll the place had conspired to create, was the occasional tolling of church bells. In Italy there is no campanology as understood in northern countries. Ringing bells as a kind of musical circus trick, the bob-major-and-triple-grandsire yelping from the perpendicular tower, is unknown, and however ethnic the magnificence of those metallic tongues heard across English fields or down a lane between Oxford colleges, I have to admit that it is something I have ceased greatly to miss when abroad.

The Italian bell is a potently individual voice, a sigh, a moan, a rebuke, a tirade, an exhortation or a eulogy. People do not ring bells in Italy, they twitch or squeeze or tug at them as if they were parts of someone's body. When you hear the tolling from a nearby church, you can almost identify the posture and disposition of the ringer from the sound, nonchalant, insolent, sturdy, vigorous or positively frantic. Should the belfry hold more than one chime, there will be no attempt to pace or synchronize them or to devise a pattern between them. Yet the effect, because it sounds like two or three individuals all trying to have their say at once, has a greater air of spontaneous liveliness than all the complex prestidigitations achieved within an English cathedral bell tower.

The essence of San Francesco was a paradox, the perpetual

contradiction between its rurality, honking pheasants in the oat fields, owls keewicking in the cypress tree beside the kitchen window, and blatant, urban Florence lying immediately outside. The little piazza beyond the garden was a nightly needle-park, and each morning yielded its scatter of empty syringes. Across the stuccoed walls on either side of the adjacent church, palimpsests of graffiti accompanied energetically depicted hardons with admiring captions and comments attached. Whenever there was a wedding, the bride and groom would be cheerfully photographed against these vigorous scratchings as if to draw fertile inspirations from them.

At the foot of the hill, across a thunderous boulevard, the real life of the town began. To tell the truth, I had never believed in Florence before I came to San Francesco, or indeed especially wanted to believe in it. The quality of perfection in everything, the impacted superlativeness of painting, sculpture and architecture, the notion of so many good and valuable things finding their origin here, were all disgusting to me. That beauty of line in the city's profile, whether viewed from the right bank of the Arno westwards towards the hills of San Miniato and Arcetri, or looked in upon from one of the belvederes and vantage points of the Boboli gardens, with Brunelleschi's dome and Giotto's tower and the mountains behind, became positively wearisome. There always seemed to me to be something heartless and saturnine about Florence, an essentially unmoving quality in what was supposed to stir the responsive emotions, a touch, one might almost have said, of idle complacency. Beautiful it undoubtedly was, but this was a beauty without animation, a dead, cosmeticized loveliness.

Travellers who write off cities as the result of a passing disenchantment are generally sending out messages about the nature of their own inadequacy, rather than making any particularly valid point about the place anathematized. I've spoken earlier of a problem or two with certain Italian towns, and in the case of Florence I was always prepared to wait a bit longer for the moment, whenever it should come, which would bludgeon me into acceptance and humbleness. I still don't care for Florence as much as for Venice or Rome or the cities of Lombardy, Emilia and Piedmont, but something has shaken me into acknowledging its truth, something I discovered while I lived at San Francesco.

For beyond the noisy *viale*, stretching down to the river, lay the Borgo San Frediano, the one quarter of the old city which has not yet entirely forfeited its individuality to improvers, developers and the urban pastoralism of the very rich. In this little rectangle of streets and squares bounded to north and south by the old Florentine fortifications and by Vio Maggio, which sweeps arrow-straight from the Pitti Palace to Ponte Santa Trinità, something like an ordinary life, without the specialness of art and the attendant awe of travellers, without hotels and glossy *vitrines* and tasselled-menu restaurants and cafés where the waiters are got up like the very cakes they serve, something ferociously resistant to smartness manages to survive. Very well, there are a good few shops in San Frediano which deal in mock antiquity, the neatly drilled wormholes in a chairback, the carefully administered knock in a cabriole leg, the distressed look industriously applied to mirrors and varnish and gilding, the implausible profusion of lacquerwork, and the still-lifes, mythologies and Madonnas which are too patently after the school of the studio. Yet even here there are people at work, not suave *antiquaires* with their tiresomely inevitable savour of corruption and backhanding, but genuine artificers, fakers at work, to be seen in the very act of brushing on the crucial gold, chiselling the rococo cornice or stitching up the French webbing.

A *borgo* was originally a small fortified post or refuge, a burgh, a borough, a bury, and in the larger Italian towns of the early Middle Ages, it was often a suburb across the river to which you might opportunely flee when driven out of your principal stronghold. In Florence the *borghi* are actually streets, Santa Croce, Ognissanti, San Jacopo and so on. I can never think of Borgo San Frediano as a single thoroughfare, however; the name, in my sense of the place as a dimension without which Florence has no substance, belongs to the entire quarter, in itself a township with manners and customs and a people of its own.

There are things to see, of course, in San Frediano. Except for its elegant red dome, the eponymous church, dedicated to an Irishman named Frigidus or Fridian who became bishop of Lucca and died in 588, is alas not one of them, being totally bare and gloomy inside. But in the church of the Carmine they have restored Masaccio's tremendous frescoes in the Brancacci Chapel and reminded us at the same time of the easy grace in the brush of Filippino Lippi, who completed the cycle fifty years afterwards. And at Santo Spirito, the last unfinished work of Brunelleschi, there is a sacristy by Giuliano de Sangallo and a whole series of deliciously not-quite-top-notch fifteenth-century altarpieces.

It is in Piazza Santo Spirito, indeed, with its faint air of tousled, knocked-about scruffiness created by the presence of a daily market selling vegetables, potplants, kitchen stuff and cheap clothes, that the spirit of San Frediano starts to take over. Pedants will insist that this is not so, and that the Irish bishop only ousts the Holy Spirit beyond the arterial thoroughfare of Via dei Serragli, but that's mere topographical nitpicking. As soon as you turn the corner out of Piazza San Felice into Via Mazzetta, past Casa Guidi where the Brownings lived, you sense the change, in the shops, the people who use them and the way in which they use them, in the notable absence of grand palaces (except in Piazza del Carmine, where they suddenly loom, yellow and unmistakable once more) and in the radiant intrusions of a light missed in the old quarters north of the river, with their groping lanes of high, teetering mediaeval barracks.

There isn't, it should be said, much room for manoeuvre in San Frediano. As elsewhere in Florence, the pavement is a thin stone ribbon for tightrope walkers, the streets are narrow enough, and cars get bunched and huddled into any available space. Yet it is precisely this sense of a quarter existing cheek-by-jowl with itself that gives warmth and momentum to life here, like some glowing, well-exercised body bursting out of clothes a sight too small for it. Other areas of the city may unplug themselves or pull down an abrupt veil of blankness and silence, but in San

Frediano there is always, whatever the impossible smallness of the hour, some twitch or murmur of continuing survival.

This straining, tumid quality of a life which is the fiercer for not possessing enough space along which to scrabble and claw its course is well seen in Via Sant'Agostino, running northwards out of Santo Spirito towards the Carmine. It is the only place in Florence where I have ever witnessed a fight. The city rather prides itself on being the repository of stolidly bourgeois virtues, and though a few cracks have been appearing in their veneer of late, as elsewhere in northern Italy, the Florentines are by and large a peaceable, well-conducted people, not given to fisticuffs or knife thrusts.

It was the more exciting, then, to witness a pair of well-dressed, middle-aged men, whom I had no reason to suppose were other than native Tuscans, slogging it out on the pavement over something as banal as a broken wing mirror. They were not drunk, nor did they have that chopped-about, roughed-up, patched-over look that professional bruisers wear like a trademark. One of them had indeed placed his briefcase on the pavement beside the car. Yet the pair, in a slow, slightly dazed fashion, as though to say 'this isn't really me, you know', kept on pushing one another backwards, administering the odd kick, pretending to walk away and then coming back for more. For several minutes nobody lifted a finger to stop them – whose business was it, after all, but theirs? – until a woman carrying a cardboard carton, evidently containing a cake, rounded the corner of Via dei Serragli. Her face suddenly transfixed by mingled horror and contempt, she put the cake down on the bonnet of the car, boldly seized her brawling husband, readying himself for another lunge at his opponent, and made a sort of citizen's arrest of him, with much angry jabbing of her fingers into his face. Somebody ironically applauded, everyone else laughed, and the three retired into the nearest bar.

If not typical of Sant'Agostino, such incidents are somehow enhanced by the street's tendency to spill bits of life all over itself like a messy eater. Oranges, radishes and little onions have rolled into the gutter off the greengrocer's stall, while an extremely dog-eared, frowzy-looking copy of Edmondo De Amicis's *Cuore* (the first, and for a long time, almost the only Italian novel written for children) has somehow detached itself from the table outside the secondhand bookshop and several pages of it are now blowing cheerfully into the faces of the rucksacked Finns coming out of the students' hostel by the church of Santa Monaca. Three soldiers in fatigues stand giggling insanely beside the doorway of the Fratellanza Militare, a boy with a billiard cue is cheerfully pretending to throttle his friend over the windowsill of the Communist recreation centre, and the crazy old woman who lives in the tiny flat next to the Public Baths has, for the umpteenth time, drenched some hapless passer-by with her slops chucked out onto the pavement.

San Frediano gets more San Frediano-ish as you near the steps of the Carmine. That greatest of all dramatic monologues and a resounding proclamation of the artist's right to live as he pleases, Browning's *Fra Lippo Lippi*, is imagined as taking place somewhere near here, when the painter, out on the razzle, comes face to face with the town watch going their rounds. Lippi was born nearby, and his poor aunt Lapaccia sent him to the Carmelite monks when she could no longer afford to feed him. The convent could not make a cloisterer of Filippo, the young lecher and wastrel, so they made the best of a bad job and let him paint instead. When Cosimo de'Medici tried to keep Fra Filippo from the women by locking him in his room until he had finished the commission on which he was working, the painter simply tore his bed sheets into strips, made a rope and was off. Cosimo, to his eternal credit, just shrugged and learned his lesson.

I think of Filippo Lippi as a San Frediano boy, even as I think of Masaccio, though he came from the town of San Giovanni in the Arno valley. He is buried here, after all, in the church that holds his most famous paintings, and when you look at them, the resilience and strength and fined-down absoluteness of outline in the faces and limbs of their *dramatis personae* belongs nowhere else but to the quarter. When he died, in 1428, he was only twenty-six.

This sense of 'lovely youth, death's early prey' is strongest in one place almost opposite the church, the shop in Piazza Piattellina which specializes in funerary portraits. When Italians die, not merely are they honoured in the *necrologie* of which I have spoken elsewhere, and in the splendid funerals with high, glass panelled hearses and enormous wreaths requiring several men to carry them, but in the *campo santo*, the cemetery itself, where onto each memorial tablet of pink marble or polished granite is stuck a small oval photograph, under bevelled glass, of the deceased as their sorrowing family might wish to remember them.

Whenever I passed the window full of these portrait mementoes, I used to dawdle purposely so as to look at them without seeming too indiscreet. It was impossible to determine whether these people were actually dead, or whether the enterprising photographer had simply commandeered a few chums and relatives to pose as models. Given the superstitiousness of Italians about things – an attitude that I entirely share – the former seemed more likely. In which case, was it not a trifle unfeeling to display them in the window?

The temptation, inevitably, was to make up life histories for them all. Some, as it were, wrote themselves: the old *contadino* in the hat from Lamporecchio who had helped Allied prisoners escape during the war, his wife in the bun and jet earrings whose *torta della nonna* was famous all over the district, the plump-jowled *ragioniere* who had dropped dead of a cardiac infarct at a Rotary Club dinner, and the dour-looking policeman shot, maybe, in the line of duty. But the smiling girl in the striped blouse, with the tumble of profligate brown curls, how had she died? What about the young couple photographed sitting beside a lake, their faces alight with a terrible joy? And the bespectacled, crewcut seminarist – had he perhaps committed suicide?

I never spent more than a minute or two in speculations of this sort, because the pavement opposite was a hang-out for kids and their bikes, and I felt too embarrassed to be seen gawping at the dead in front of the too-noisily living. Much time is spent by Italian youth in hanging out on scooters. Every village – and in essence San Frediano, being a *borgo*, is a village – has some place in which the *motorini* can draw up and the juveniles can sit about in their saddles for hours at a stretch in chat. It is, after all, good practice for the café tables and bar counters of adulthood and the benches of old age. Nothing, I fancy, will ever kill off the public sociability of Italians. If it does, that will spell the end of Italy.

Behind the scooter kids was a dim-looking bar, where perpetual moochers sat slumped in front of a nonstop soccer video, and beyond this ran Via del Leone, where one of the expatriate family at San Francesco had been solemnly enjoined, when a girl, by her nurse to walk down the middle of the street so as to avoid whatever nuisances might come tumbling from the windows. Here, and in the parallel Via di Camaldoli, there is a pavement life, created largely by people whose ground floor flats are without entrance halls, so that the front parlour opens directly onto the street. Sometimes a panel of the door has been pulled back, so that you can see the walnut veneer dining table, the gilded cornices on the china cabinet and the television on its tall platform like a household shrine. On warm evenings, rather than lurk in this stuffy, formal gloom, the family carries low-slung chairs outside and sits nattering companionably with the neighbours.

At its bottom end, Via del Leone gets workaday and business-like, a world of blue-overalled mechanics and a sort of tinkling Nibelheim, in cellars and sheds, of hammers and spanners and screws. Down towards the river, in Piazza del Tiratoio, they sell Florentine delicacies off a stall, dollops of *ribollita*, plates of Tuscan beans and sandwiches filled with chunks of lamprey, while across the square, under the walls of the grim brown school building, the dog-owners of San Frediano patiently tiptoe to and fro along the turd-strewn pavement awaiting the wished-for result.

The river widens across the bridge, and across it is thrown one of the two *pescaie* or stone weirs lying at either end of the city. On the Pescaia di San Niccolò, up by Santa Croce, sunbathers lie out along the quay between the patient fishermen, and a little community of poor Florentines sits playing cards on upturned boxes, while canoeists, their chastely perfect bodies sequined with sweat, paddle down to the edge of the weir, cast a pensive eye at the German girls turning pink on the stones and scud away again. At San Niccolò you are as solitary as you wish to be. Everyone is looking at somebody, or knows they are being looked at, and the place accordingly possesses a discreet subtext of adventure and assignation.

At the Pescaia di Santa Rosa, by San Frediano, the atmosphere is rather different, both since the stone dam is more exposed to view, and because far fewer people can be bothered to take themselves down that far. It is cleaner and airier, and I suspect the fish are more plentiful, and you go to sunbathe at Santa Rosa in preference to San Niccolò when you are genuinely not interested in staring through your shades at a well-turned buttock or thigh or in improving your Italian acquaintance through a sequence of leading questions.

Up at the higher end of the quarter, where the streets open out towards the foothills of Bellosguardo, lies my favourite Florentine piazza. It is not in the least beautiful to look at – if I wanted a square exclusively for beauty I should choose Piazza Santissima Annunziata, with its medallions of swaddled babies and equestrian statue of Grand Duke Ferdinand – but Piazza Torquato Tasso has what the others have not, namely the true life of urban, outdoor Italy, created, stage managed as it were, by those who live nearby. The bunch of cheery old winoes, slouched across its benches, used to hail me as I walked up and down the paths reading a book, with a Tuscanly-accented cry of '*Ooooh buongiornooo, Dottore!*' I am not a doctor of anything, but I'd rather be a laureate of this academy than of many more formal and self-regarding.

The currents of life here are those of that still peaceable Italy which has not traded innocence for coarseness and which manages to combine verve and energy with unforced elegance and grace of manner. My recollections of Piazza Torquato Tasso may well have smoothed away its actual uglinesses or incorporated them into that type of nostalgic pastoral vision travellers to Italy are always liable to indulge in, but its images, whatever their roots in plain prose, are now indelibly poetic for me. I think of the children catching their kite in the branches of a tree (what were they doing trying to fly a kite here in the first place?), the old man peeing reflectively in the laurel bushes, the sulky-looking girls combing their hair at the bus stop, the gawky, hulking boys playing soccer at night in the floodlit playground, the families trundling prams and dogs up and down the curving paths at the end nearest the old grandducal school, the two restaurants at which there was never anywhere to sit down, and the rattling of balls across the tables of the billiard hall.

Such mere *menus plaisirs* were a necessity after San Francesco, where there were times, especially at evening, while I sat on the terrace with a *toscanello* and a glass of *vernaccia* before supper, when the heritage might seem just a little too godly to be credible. Slipping out late after dark, I'd now and then do an investigative patrol of the quarter like one of those very nightwatchmen who catch Lippo Lippi at his jaunts, walking streets I'd not probed before and standing still for a moment on their pavements to catch the sounds from the houses on either side of me. At the end of Via della Chiesa, in which poor Walter Savage Landor died a broken, cantankerous wreck, I used to look with fascination at the gaunt mass of the Albergo Popolare, a sort of dossers' hostel set up presumably during the late 1940s and redolent of that postwar *ouvrieriste* philanthropic communism which is now almost a dead duck in Italy, but deserves honourable memorials whatever its ideological silliness. The lights were always on in the Albergo Popolare, and well into the small hours somebody would be playing the piano, real music, Beethoven, Chopin, Brahms, on what sounded like rather a good instrument, and the combination of these ballades and rhapsodies and sonatas with the inherent bleakness of the place, the cruel brilliance of fluorescent tubes, the hard metal window frames, the dingy cream paintwork of the corridor walls, brought a certain catch to the throat.

At other times I'd walk down as far as the bingo hall by the gate in the city wall at Santa Rosa. At least I assumed it was a bingo hall, since there was a caller and a row of men and women doing eyes-down at the tables in a poky little saloon with a café next to it that had decidedly seen better days. Florence of the tourists and the arts historians and the expatriates, smart Via Tornabuoni, Harry's Bar, Doney's and Cibreo, seemed to have stopped dead at this bingo hall of Santa Rosa. Across the river lay the city of the great hotels and the opera house and the railway station, of the transsexual hookers along the *viali* and the gay cruisers in the arbours of the Cascine. Just now we were in the town of the unconsidered, the never-mentioned, a place near which perhaps there had once lived that old woman about whom a Florentine friend provided a telling vignette. She refused to ride in a motorcar, and whenever her children or grandchildren proposed to take her for a walk as far as Piazza della Signoria, she would say it was for rich people and she hadn't got fine enough clothes. So she lived on, for years and years, never straying out of San Frediano, and when she died, at the age of ninety, she had still never seen the Duomo.

True or not, the story makes its point. There is a self-sufficient, not-for-the-likes-of-us snugness about San Frediano that tempts you never to cross these bridges towards art, sophistication and debauchery. Stay here with the dossers and the lamprey sandwiches, says the quarter. Yet if you do stray, it will keep one eye open for your return. Feeling especially wakeful one evening, I found good enough cause to stay out in the city until the blue of darkness started very faintly to turn pale. ''Fore God, it is so very, very late. That we may call it morning by and by.' The lights were still on in the Albergo Popolare. A blanketed form snored on a bench in Piazza Torquato Tasso. The lightest grey of morning came into the sky as I breasted the hill outside San Francesco. Over the empty square a single swallow darted to and fro, screaming crazily into the dawn. I turned the key and pushed open the door in the wall.

17 A House in Tuscany

'And if you were not here,' said Francesca, 'where would you most like to be?'

Paolo grinned, and with a kind of insolent intuitiveness which I was entirely prepared to forgive him, said: 'That's a stupid question. He'd always rather be with us.'

'Always,' repeated Francesca, laughing.

They had found me out. They must have found me out ages ago, I realized, perhaps in the first five minutes of our meeting on the rocks that morning. In their presence I felt undefended yet entirely safe. Had I sat down to use them in a novel, they would doubtless have become the menacing brace of sophisticates who, luring the green Englishman into their clutches, corrupted him in a sequence of erotic games and then abandoned him to his absurdity. Since life does not always so laboriously imitate art, their behaviour intimated no such designs. Yet I had surrendered to them from the start, I was theirs to do as they liked with, in love with them both during the few hours that we were together.

I'd wanted to spend the day completely on my own, not because I was tired of the friends whose seaside flat on the Ligurian coast I shared, but because these little gestures of revolt, however contrived, are always necessary on holiday. So I got up very early that morning and slipped out of the house while some of the grey indistinctness of dawn still hung about the streets, and set off to walk along the path which teeters above the beetling red cliff from Monterosso to Vernazza in the Cinque Terre.

The smell of morning in the lands of the south, before the heat comes and destroys it all and the cicadas get into full throttle, is something you never forget, because it is really a sort of tease, an implication that all these scents of leaves and dew-washed grass and the bark of pine trees and the dusty shoots of wild thyme and marjoram, are what you could have for much longer if you weren't after the sunlight as well. I felt an extraordinary freedom and exhilaration, of a kind I only ever feel in such places and when absolutely alone.

> I'm happy. It's sublime,
> This perfect solitude of foreign lands!
> To be, as if you had not been till then,
> And were then, simply that you chose to be . . .
> . . . Possess, yourself,
> A new world all alive with creatures new,
> New sun, new moon, new flowers, new people – ah!
> And be possessed by none of them! no right
> In one, to call your name, enquire your where,
> Or what you think of Mister Some-one's book,

Or Mister Other's marriage, or decease,
Or how's the headache which you had last week,
Or why you look so pale still, since it's gone?
– Such most surprising riddance of one's life
Comes next one's death; it's disembodiment
Without the pang.

She knew all about it, did Ba Browning.

The path wound down for a moment into a grove of lemon trees, and the arc of the hillsides framed a prospect of the sea, over which the haze of a hot day was starting to gather. There was a track leading through a cane-break to a stretch of rocks which I felt inclined to follow. I can't swim for toffee apples, but I love nothing better than to be in the water or beside it, so I spread my towel, stripped off and gingerly let myself down into the waves, with many a grasp and fumble for adequate footholds and the nightmare scenarios always dreamed up on these occasions, in which the current sweeps me away before I have completed my masterpiece, and I am found weeks later, like poor Shelley along these very shores, fish-nibbled.

On a flattish piece of rock I stretched out to dry. In the preceding days my skin had passed through the obligatory lobster pink phase of the hyperborean's earliest embarrassing encounter with the sun, and I had turned a flattering terracotta. I stuck a peppermint lozenge into my mouth for concentration and started reading Spenser's *Faerie Queene*, through which I have been steadily ploughing beside the Mediterranean for the past decade. The battered old Penguin has yellowed with salt water, and its pages, blotched with Clarins Lait Solaire, are interleaved by old bus and *vaporetto* tickets, restaurant bills, grains of sand, flowers and people's addresses. It makes ideal beach reading because such is the self-contained nature of its cantos that you do not have to worry about losing the thread of the story. There is something infinitely relaxing, what is more, about the steady roll, wave upon wave, of the Spenserian stanza:

Sleep after toil, port after stormy seas,
Ease after war, death after life, does greatly please.

After a while I looked up and saw, standing a little way off, a man watching me. He was not the most beautiful man I had ever seen – that was a fisherman on the island of Delos whose image still burns the memory – but as near as dammit. His face, under the coarse bunches of black hair, and his lean, smooth body like a runner's, had a patina of experience, of knowingness of which I felt instantly jealous. When the woman who was with him got up as well, and I saw that she was just as beautiful, and with what seemed even stronger hints of character in the glance she so steadily fixed on me, I began to blush and then burst out laughing. Then she called: 'We wanted to know what you were reading,' and they came over and sprawled themselves in the hollows of the rocks and we started to talk.

I showed them the book. 'Like Tasso or Ariosto,' I said.

'Better?' said the man, with a wary, slightly cynical hoisting of one side of his mouth, which did duty for a smile.

'No, just different.'

'English, you mean.'

'Exactly.'

They both laughed. 'Which do you prefer?' she asked, 'Tasso or Ariosto?'

The assumption that I had read either poet was flattering enough, but the idea that she meant to discuss their merits seriously was beyond my wildest expectations. I said I preferred Tasso because he suited my northern sobriety, and that I liked the inset stories of Rinaldo and Armida and Tancredi and Clorinda. Yes, she rejoined, but weren't there a lot more inset stories in Ariosto? They both liked Ariosto better; he was more – how should she put it? – *fantasioso*, *stravagante*, Tasso they found *troppo triste*.

So there we lay, three brown gymnosophists dividing the merits of *Gerusalemme Liberata* and *Orlando Furioso* between the odd Marlboro and Tic-Tac and swig at the water bottle, with the stone warm against our backs and under our thighs. They were called Paolo and Francesca – which was the occasion for some further poetical name-dropping – and the pair of them were doctors from Udine who were spending the remnants of a holiday on the coast before leaving in September for the Sudan, where they were to take up work in a hospital for famine victims.

They were the kind of Italians I always dream of meeting but so seldom encounter, who can talk with a lethal sharpness of perception about any subject under the sun, and who can manage abstractions without having self-consciously to intellectualize their vocabulary to give the subject a ponderousness it doesn't need. Their medical experience scarcely impinged on the conversation. They were far more interested in books and pictures and music, so much so, indeed, that I wondered what sort of resources they would fall back on in the upper reaches of the Nile.

We had quite simply picked each other up, and if there is anything I like it is picking people up for whatever purpose, which is easier in Italy than elsewhere. Slowly I began to luxuriate in the situation, the glaring brilliance of light across the nap of the blue water, the warmth of my oiled skin, the uncompromising attractiveness of my two companions, the sudden fluency of my Italian in measuring itself against concepts and hypotheses which under any other circumstances would have floored it, and the great fields of memory, vicissitude and observation we seemed to cross in our talk.

I didn't mind that they appeared more grown up than I was. It is safer to feel a bit like a child in moments like these, however coyly self-conscious you may actually be, but Italians in any case make me feel like a clumsy five-year-old, so I wasn't in the least surprised at envying these their gracefulness of pose and fluidity of gesture. What's more, I was relieved that neither of them felt the temptation to patronize me. To begin with, I found their ardour of engagement with whatever I said almost disturbing. Their sincerity was as incredible as their shared handsomeness, yet it was this direct, unembarrassed manner in glance and tone which enabled me to apprehend them as a couple.

When at a certain point Francesca jumped into the sea, bobbed up and down for a moment and then got out again, I watched Paolo looking at her as she sat back on her haunches shaking the spray out of her curls on to the dry surface of the rock like a mermaid. His stare was solemn, all-inclusive, betraying not the least hint of uncertainty or desire to possess more in her than he held already. Something in the way she sat twisting her wetted hair, and throwing her head back now and then while she did so, told him that she knew his gaze was upon her without needing to return it.

Feeling my heart begin to race, I went through the parade of reaching for a cigarette and lighting it. Because I no longer have the slightest urge to marry, I am the more interested in married couples and the way they behave towards each other. I've often thought of writing a quasi-anthropological series of notes on such relationships, but the humbug and sanctimoniousness with which so many otherwise intelligent people end up discussing marriage has put me off. In England I seldom find myself able to imagine husbands and wives making love. In Italy I think of it all the time, and I started now to think of Paolo and Francesca – who, by the way, were married – alone together without me there.

Yet the consideration made me resentful. In a way which had nothing whatever to do with simple Italian good nature, the pair had contrived that, for the time being at least, I should appear indispensable to them. Sensing this, I suddenly heard myself say in English:

' "Ready to be anything in the ecstasy of being ever".'

'What's that?'

'It's from one of our old *prosatori*, Sir Thomas Browne. And he was a doctor as well. "*Pronto ad essere qualsiasi cosa nell'estasi di essere per sempre.*" '

'*Che bello!* And is that what you feel, Jonathan?'

'Yes, in this moment.'

Paolo took a long drag on his cigarette and repeated the phrase, as I had lamely and inaccurately translated it. "*Pronto ad essere qualsiasi cosa nell'estasi di essere per sempre. Bene, bene.* And what exactly, in this moment, would you wish to be?'

For the rest of that day we spoke about nothing else. Or, that's to say, we managed to relate everything we talked about to this single idea of imaginative displacement, of the soul leaving the body during sex, of envy and jealousy being forms of emotional creativity, of the desire, when one is in a restaurant, always to have what other people are eating, precisely because they, and not you, are eating it. We talked about these things as we shared our respective picnics (mine exiguous, theirs prodigal, almost a hamper – 'we shan't eat like this in the Sudan') and as we climbed the track towards the friend's house they had borrowed, little more than a hut with a large bed in it, a kitchen and a terrace with a pergola overlooking the bay of Vernazza, and as we clanked cheerfully to and fro in the preparation of supper. Damned if I was going back to Monterosso until the last train. Something beyond my generally carnivorous approach to new friendships had told me I should not see them again, and when dusk fell I began to think dismal thoughts.

'Stop looking sad,' said Francesca, catching me at it. 'You're the kind of person who invents sadness for yourself.'

'How the hell do you know?'

'I don't. I'm a doctor who diagnoses things, and diagnosis isn't the same as knowledge. That's why patients are just as good as doctors at saying what is wrong with them.'

'You're right,' I said, 'I'm afraid of happiness. Something dreadful always happens afterwards. Happiness to me is like epilepsy or a fever or the sort of thing that turns people into werewolves. I always want to be somewhere else when I feel happiness coming on.'

'Like now, eh?' said Paolo, his lips oily with pasta.

'Yeah.'

'And if you were not here,' said Francesca, 'where would you like to be?'

'If not with you,' I answered, 'then there's a house . . .' I paused. They couldn't honestly be interested. A moth batted itself against the lamp which hung from the beam. From the top of the hill came the rattling of the express train plunging through the tunnels on its way down to La Spezia.

'Go on,' said Paolo.

'There's a house . . . it's on the road south from Florence

to Arezzo. That's to say, not on the road exactly, but along a valley which you enter through an arch. It's called L'Arco della Camicia, the Arch of the Shirt, don't ask me why. You follow the track which leads up through the olive groves, past a little cemetery behind high walls and a hedge of cypress trees and orchards where I used to see them ploughing with a pair of white oxen. One night, when I was walking up in the moonlight, I saw a porcupine running along in front of me.

'Farmers have never taken over the valley entirely, and the thick oak woods come right down the far side towards a hidden stream. There are houses here and there, some of them the old *case coloniche* of undressed stone and roofs whose red tiles are blotched with mosses and houseleek, others more brash and vulgar, with fortress fences and slavering guard dogs, and up at the head of them all a big yellow seventeenth-century villa of no special beauty beyond what the surrounding landscape gives it.

'The track makes a sudden turn, and there on the grassy slope, with the woods behind it, stands my house. I mean, it's not *my* house, but well, you understand . . .'

I stopped, embarrassed. Francesca said serenely: 'Let us not be too precise, Jonathan,' and from being five years old, I felt about two.

'It's the oldest,' I went on, 'in the valley. There's a tall, square tower, which must have been built in the days of the Countess Matilda, before Guelphs and Ghibellines were ever heard of and Tuscany was called Tuscia and, stuck on to it in an extemporized fashion typical of the whole place, are a series of what I suppose were once barns and stables when it was a farm. There's a big gloomy room at the back, with an iron grille across the window and a colossal fig tree outside, which I call the Fidelio Room, because it looks like a set for the gravedigging scene in the opera, and a sort of back kitchen with a bread oven hollowed out of the wall, where they roast a sucking pig at New Year over a brushwood fire.

'It isn't, at first glance, outstandingly attractive, a house of the sort that gets into the design magazines, that photographers do fancy double-spreads on, that photogenic Beautiful People are shown posing in amid the impedimenta of a self-consciously Simple Life. Tuscany is littered with places of that kind, but Il Castellare – which is what it's called – really isn't one of them. Downstairs it is poky, extremely dark, freezing cold in winter and always a bit smelly, though the smell is a kind of cocktail whiff compounded of garden, dog, old breakfasts, petrol, books and drains.

'I suppose, if I had to compare it with anything, it would be an Irish country house, the sort described in Irish novels.' Paolo and Francesca looked a bit blank. Even their apparently vast literary cognizance, in a country where you can find almost anything in translation, hadn't yet taken Molly Keane and Somerville and Ross on board, so I went on: 'It's a bit as if a tribe of extremely erudite and sophisticated gypsies had taken over the place. Which is true, since in one sense it's a great caravanserai full of travellers, and you never know whom or how many you'll sit down to dinner with that night. Everything is tattered and battered and beaten and wormy, things get broken, things fall apart, the roofs leak, the gutters fall off, the water comes and goes and sometimes disappears altogether, so that there are daily walks with pitchers to the fountain like Isaac and Rebecca. A colony of termites lives under the tiles of the tower, and each night, sleeping up there, you get used to shaking the latest fall of dust and pigeon-shit out of the bed. In summer housemartins fly through the windows of the cavernous *salotto* and build their nests in the crooks of the rafter above the chimney-breast.

'Existence there becomes a kind of archaeology. If things get tidied, it isn't in that reproachful fashion intended to suggest that houses are for show rather than use, but because they are in people's way. The book you didn't quite finish the year before will turn up on top of the bathroom cupboard with the playing card you left in it as a marker, the shoe you lost will mysteriously reappear under the walnut tree beside the swimming pool, its surface a sargasso flotsam of feathers, twigs and dead butterflies, its floor carpeted with yellow moss. The house in some sense always remembers that you were there, though in case it should not you have got into the habit of making superstitious tributes to its indwelling spirit, a flower or a nut or a bunch of grass pushed into a cranny of the stonework as an earnest of your determination always to return.

'At dawn, as the light creaks through the low, narrow windows of the tower, and you wake to the strange, orgasmic moaning of the doves whose little feet rattle up and down the tiles over your head, the valley becomes shrill with birds – magpies, jays, hoopoes, finches – an impertinent loudness unafraid of the hunter, for on this side at least there is the *divièto di caccia*.

'And at night, when they have all gone to bed and the crickets sing and a mosquito coil glows on the terrace wall, you sit alone, staring into the darkness as if to will the nightingales to start. They are like divas warbling through their solfeggio exercises, these nightingales. Every cliché made by poetry about them is true, and composers' imitations give you only the palest shadow of this music. First a single bird essays a little run of a few notes, a sketch, as it were, on which to improvise. Then another tries the same. The leader, meanwhile, has moved into more complex divisions: sequences of high, piping single tones alternating with throaty, gurgling trills and quick volleys, followed by amazing roulades like showy cadenzas for the wonder of a theatrical audience. Thus they'll go on, four, five, six of them in the thick blackness of the wood, unseen divinities, until morning.

'The ultimate sound of Il Castellare, the benign ghost of the house, is talk, endless currents and surges of engulfing, unstoppable talk, the better because there is nothing whatever to regulate it. You can always escape if you want, find a tree to curl up under, shut the door of the study and light a cigar, clamber into the tower and read a book, but the best conversation in the world will invariably succeed in drawing you back. In the long dining room, with the olive brands spitting in the fire and the rickety candelabra threatening eternally to crash into the middle of the table, or on the terrace, where the mongrel scraps with the cat under your chair, you can be the enthusiast, the anecdotalist, the lecturer, the biographer, critic, gossip, casuist and bore as you choose. There's always the possibility that you will not be asked again, but you'll just be forgotten if you never open your mouth to speak. There is plenty of silence at Il Castellare, but it is not studied or admired there as a conscious virtue whenever there's an opportunity for argument or laughter.

'I think I like this house best because it is one of the very few places on earth where a complete apprehension of happiness doesn't frighten me. In its beaten-down, knocked-about, omnium-gatherum, rag-tag-and-bobtail way it has rewarded me with things my guiltiest impulses could never enable me to repay. Now and then it seems to me like one of those castles in chivalric romances where the wounded knight retires to be healed before being turned out again into the world.'

Francesca laughed. 'Like a hospital!'

'Yes, but I'd rather think of it as a castle. With that tower . . .'

Why had I told them all this? The detail could hardly make an impression. Even though what I said was true, it was a kind of selfishness, a further attempt to solicit their affection, a meretricious picking-up of sympathy. I could see from Paolo's manner that he accepted it as such, but was glad of it nevertheless.

'You'll always want,' he said, 'to be somewhere else, no? Not just in another place, but in another body. Maybe when you're in love, it is not with the person, but with the image of yourself as that person. To renew your own life in other people's.'

'"Ready to be anything in the ecstasy of being ever"', I repeated. It was all I could find to say.

There was a silence between the three of us. He had his arm around her, and they turned away to look into the night. Idiotically I wanted them both to invite me to go with them to the Sudan. I felt it was what they ought to be asking me. Instead Paolo simply said: 'Stay with us, Jonathan. Don't go. Like that it's more comfortable.'

18 Ending up in Umbria

'It was the 15th January, 1304, and Giacomo, returning from Chiusi, whither he had gone to defend the rights of the hospital, was on his way home to Pieve; attacked and brutally murdered, his body flung into a ditch at the foot of a wild pear tree and covered with branches and thorn twigs. A shepherd found it, who was amazed at the sight, in the very depth of winter, of the pear tree, the branches and the thorns all in flower. A miracle having been proclaimed, the body of the Blessed Giacomo was claimed by Chiusi, Castel della Pieve and Perugia; and, that a quarrel might be avoided, a wise man proposed that the corpse be laid upon a cart, tied to two bullocks, not broken to the yoke, and that these be left to draw where they would.

'The bullocks, becoming mild as twin lambs, thereupon took the road to La Pieve, crossing through the town as if making towards Perugia, when, almost at the Vecciano gate, they stopped before the hospital, knelt down, and vain indeed was every effort to move them. Therefore the Blessed Giacomo was buried there in the chapel of San Giovanni Battista that now bears his name, and from that moment onwards all the *pievesi* held him in great reverence. His feast is celebrated even to this day on the last Sunday in August, and it is the custom then to bring to the solemn mass those flowers called "the flowers of the Blessed Giacomo".'

The body of the Blessed Giacomo Villa lies on top of the altar in the little church dedicated to him outside Porta Santa Maria on the southern edge of Città della Pieve. They keep the martyr's bones in a silver urn, and since he studied law in Siena and defended the legal privileges of the *pievesi* against all comers, they hail him now as the Protector of Lawyers. Città della Pieve, endowed with so much beauty, the birthplace of Pietro Perugino, is yet rather poorly off for saints – poor, that is, in an Umbrian sense, since it only has two, which for Umbria is pretty piffling. Even more than the Marche, this is Italy's *terra santa* with a vengeance. The most famous of the saints, Francis of Assisi, Benedict of Norcia, Rita of Cascia, rescuer of lost causes and impossible demands, are the mere distinguished icing on a giant cake. Todi, for instance, shelters about fifty, including Pope Martin I, who for some reason is the patron of Russian sailors on the Black Sea, the Blessed Jacopone, poet, mystic and madman, and Filippo Benizzi, most glorious of the Servites, whom the Florentines tried in vain to recapture for their city since he was born there. Saint Valentine was an Umbrian, the first bishop of Terni, before becoming the heavenly sponsor of lovers, and so was Saint Clare, who led women to follow the Franciscan rule and whose name has been, as the newspapers like to put it, 'romantically linked' – though always in the best possible taste – with that of Francis himself.

The point about Umbria is that you can imagine saints spring-
ing out of this landscape, their early visions and trances shaped
by the outlines and contours of its hills, the shadows of its
woods and the splashing of its mountain rivers, each meditative
absence from the world a retreat into its craggy fastnesses and
bald uplands, and every road and field a spot for the sudden
working of a miracle.

I never feel this presence in Tuscany. Not merely has that
region lost its numinous qualities by becoming too banalized
with superlatives and panegyrics, but its prospects are, if anything, too blatantly winning, too 'notice-me' in their appeal
to the onlooker. Sophistication is starting to corrupt me amid
Tuscan shades, and I very much fear that unless matters are
taken in hand I shall grow cynical and disenchanted with a
country where I ought instead to be counting my blessings.

Perhaps I only prefer Umbria because it is quieter, less
comeatable than Tuscany, or maybe the English have not yet
made a colony out of it. Maybe I just affect to like it more because
fewer people know about it, apart from a quick dash to Perugia,
Assisi and Orvieto, and a favourite vice among travel writers is to
trash the familiar in favour of the obscure. Yet there is something
in its unsmartness, in its lack of ostentation and gesture, in the
sense that, if not grindingly, bitterly, resentfully poor, it has
nevertheless had to do everything on the very simplest of terms,
which endears it to me as a place where I might fancy dying.

In which of the little cities of the region might one choose to
end it all? Città della Pieve would answer as well as any. I used to
see it from the train on the line going south to Orvieto and Rome
and long to get off, a city perched with such clean definition
of line on a small hill overlooking the dusty vale beneath, and
appearing like one of those distantly realized places which act
as eyecatchers in the landscapes of Poussin and Claude, both of
whom must surely have passed this way. Umbrian towns have
this look so strongly imprinted upon them because of the way
in which they are made to seem intrinsic to the geology of the
slopes and summits from which they rise. They do not stand
on the hills, they grow out of them, and far from profaning

the holiness of the landscape with their intrusions, they have become essential to its existence.

Città della Pieve is all made of a very light, crumbly pink brick, like madeira cake soaked in red wine, and if I were to die there, it would be for choice in one of the rooms at the top of Palazzo Fargna, in the square which opens out off Via Garibaldi, a high, confident, ineffably patrician eighteenth-century marquis's palace with curious projecting corners topped by rounded cornices. I should have taken my last walk down Via Vannucci to look at the Adoration of the Magi with which, in 1504, Perugino covered an entire wall of the oratory of Santa Maria dei Bianchi, and thrown a final glance into Vicolo Baciadonna (Kiss-the-woman Lane), reputedly the narrowest alley in Italy – what used in mediaeval England to be called 'a gropecunt' – and stood for a moment staring out across the plain, its trees and grasses stirred by the wind that in Umbria is never still.

If I wanted to die in happy obscurity, I think I should choose Trevi, topping a hill above the left bank of the Tiber, which cuts the region neatly in half. Early evening would be the ideal time for death to arrive, with the long twilight shadows across the street leading up to the small oblong piazza where the old men sit in their hats and the water flows sweet and crystalline from the rusty taps in the steep streets. I'd find a quiet bench under the trees in Viale Ciuffelli and watch the kids eating their ices and hanging out in the last of the sun, their features touched with something older than Roman, perhaps even than Etruscan, a beauty of aboriginal Italy.

Spello would be the nicest of all. I can't think of anywhere in Italy in which I've felt safer, more *coccolato* as the Italians say, more cocooned within an embrace of walls and streets. Spello possesses that phagocyte quality of the ideal Italian town, in which you can see layer upon layer of historical occupation not quite properly absorbed within the fabric of brick and stone. There are Roman arches and mediaeval windows and Renaissance doorways and Baroque cornices eternally on the verge of disappearing within one another, yet never altogether extinguished. I'd take a long time over dying in Spello.

There would be one more paper to submit to the Accademia Constantiniana on whether the poet Propertius did not after all have some Hispelline family connection, one more hat to throw into the ring in the never-ending argument as to the authenticity of the reputed Giotto in Sant'Andrea, one final bottle of Bianco d'Arquata to knock back, and at Spello I should choose to be gathered at breakfast on the terrace of the Albergo Bastiglia, since there can be few sights lovelier than the fields far below gradually revealed through a thinning mist.

Let's not talk like this, you tell me. Why not? Umbria, perhaps because of what its saints have taken and given, has something in its very bones which defies mortality, which asserts that we live even in the earth of some village *campo santo* or inside a silver urn on top of a church altar. It is the part of Italy which will somehow be allowed to go on existing when an ecological cataclysm has done for the rest, if only for this enduring touch of primal innocence, this air of a place that has known, yet remains untainted by the knowledge.

Therefore, an Umbrian *memento mori* is more cheerful than otherwise, a celebration rather than an elegy, and few things, in this connection, are jollier than the Mummies of Ferentillo. You would not expect there to be anything much at Ferentillo. It lies on the river plain, under the glowering, beetle-browed crags of the Nera valley, south-east of Spoleto, and has a positively deadbeat look to it, as if the sprawling grey village had chucked itself face downwards on the ground and refused ever afterwards to get up. With understandable scepticism, you prepare to take the road down to Terni, the town where they made the revolver with which Lee Harvey Oswald shot J.F. Kennedy, when all of a sudden a rust-pocked yellow sign says '*Mummie*'.

Don't go on, for if you do you will have missed one of the grand bizarreries of Italy. Instead, do as the sign says, head straight for the village church, and ring the custodian's bell. He is – or was, and I feel always should be – an old man with a dead-white cadaverous face and the tremulous tones of some foot-dragging, knobbly-boned retainer out of a Gothic novel.

Clanking his chatelaine of keys he opens the door to the crypt, and then . . .

Heaven knows by what accident they discovered that the air in this crypt of Ferentillo had the miraculous property of preserving dead bodies more or less entire. They are distinctly withered and desiccated, these mummies, and their flesh, having shrunk on the skeletons, has turned a sort of manilla-envelope colour, but everything is there in its elemental nakedness, and a ghastlier display of poor bare, forked humanity you never saw.

The treasures of this collection, as it were, are three Chinese, two men and a woman (why is it their teeth, more than their eyes, which identify them as Orientals?) who died of cholera on a journey to Naples in the 1880s. There is a lawyer who was shot in a local feud over a farm, and a villager whose gun backfired and made a hole in his stomach during the same struggle, a policeman, a bearded dwarf, a woman who died in childbirth, shown complete with her baby, and a Papal gendarme together with his gun, standing upright inside a grandfather clock case.

I suppose these corpses would be the more tolerable were they lying on their backs, swathed in bituminous bandages at the bottom of hieroglyphic-decorated sarcophagi. As it is, their stick-thin nakedness, inside the glass cases, is so completely without dignity that even as you shudder, there arrives a temptation to giggle. In fact none of them is quite as ghoulishly terrifying as the mummified owl which suddenly seems to come flapping at you from a corner among a pile of skulls.

I went to see these mummies on my way to a certain city in Umbria where I was meant to be writing a guidebook. It was not a place to which ordinarily I should have wanted to write a guide, though there is much there which is beautiful, and the citizens, like all Umbrians, cherish their city with the sort of loving care which suggests that they are afraid lest all of a sudden it get up and run away from them. The opportunity to spend four or five days here, being fed and watered at the expense of an Italian publisher and seeing everything, open or locked, that the town might have to show me was not to be scorned, so I buried my reluctance easily enough and addressed myself to pottering about among churches and ruins and galleries, than which, considering all things, there can be few more agreeable exercises.

My mentor in this operation was an elderly professor of art history whom the publisher had instructed me to contact on my arrival. Professor Bernardoni was not at first either an inspiring or an especially welcoming figure. He had a curious handshake, the apparently unwilling submission of two damp fingers, and his pale, habitually sad face (I can hardly ever recall him smiling) was animated, during our early meetings at least, by an expression of pained disapproval. Evidently he was not happy at the notion that a strange Englishman, possibly very ignorant and stupid, should presume to address the task of boiling down the city's historic bones into an easily-digestible soup, and made it clear that the publisher's freak in sending me here was decidedly not to his liking.

He lived in a corner of what was clearly his family's palace, *la casa gentilizia*, and our first interview was conducted in a tall, shuttered study, stacked to the ceiling with books. Cultivation in Italy is not worn on the sleeve. A truly erudite Italian, a Muratori or a Croce, is an earthly marvel, and Professor Bernardoni was doubtless not far short of this. The volumes stuffed and jammed into the shelves and strewn about the floor in piles had all been read, and the fact that there were obviously too many of them for him to move comfortably around the room was immensely reassuring. I took a couple of old exhibition catalogues off a chair to sit down, knocking to the ground as I did so an edition of Pontormo's diary which I hastily put back to a tea-tasting noise of disgruntlement from the professor.

As we spoke, or rather as he spoke and I supplied the occasional lame answer or embarrassed nod of assent, a tremendous sense of the *déjà vu* began to overcome me. Where, long ago, had I experienced similar feelings of humble insufficiency? Then I realized that what in essence was taking place in this darkened bookroom in an Umbrian palace on a hot morning in the middle of July was a species of tutorial examination such as I had not known since university. I was being tested on my fitness for the task in hand before being allowed to proceed one step into the town. To complete the impression, the professor would now and then scribble a little note or two. Maybe it was only the name of some gallery curator or inspector of ancient monuments with whom I needed to be placed in touch, but it felt more as if he were writing down observations which would satisfy him, or not as the case might be, that I was worthy even of coming near so holy a thing as this city was to him.

For there was no doubt that beyond everything else he loved this place. A bachelor, cared for by a family apparently so large (he had eight brothers) that the suggestion of infinity in the frescoed corridors of the palace was no mere illusion, he had lavished all his affection on his native ground. It wasn't a question of knowing when things were built and painted, knocked down and put up again, or a matter of authentications and signatures and catalogue descriptions. Anyone may be an expert, but the professor was far more than that. He knew the city as something to which these walls and cobbled lanes and fountains and leaping arches were merely a coat or a skin, the body which had flourished and suffered and changed, but which, under his care and that of others like him, would survive the most thoughtless of knocks from the modern world.

The professor was not alone in this. When subsequently, having passed the first phase of my examination, I was permitted to go out and explore, I discovered the simple truth, however sentimental it must sound to the jaundiced reader, that the citizens carried their town with them as a kind of extra organ from which a whole series of specialized emotions derived. The man who opened up the church with the mediaeval frescoes of the life of Saint Agnes did so with a genuine anxiety that I should believe – as indeed I was quite prepared to believe – that there was nothing like them for grace and beauty in the rest of Italy. The little bespectacled priest who displayed the diocesan collection of ecclesiastical vestments, drawer after drawer of silken copes and jewel-encrusted dalmatics, kept crying out as he did so '*Ma guarda che meraviglia, ma guarda che bello!*' as if, having never seen these things before, he had come upon them by accident while turning out the cupboards. The cathedral sacristan, unlocking a family chapel for me to look at the eighteenth-century stucco decoration, said firmly: 'Now don't tell me that they've got anything finer than this down in Rome, if you do I shan't believe it.' On the walls of the fortress, one of the archaeologists excavating the site of a neolithic shrine nearby talked to me for a moment about the dig and then, in answer to some inane question of mine as to whether he enjoyed his work, said, cheerfully aggressive: 'Look, those bastards in charge of all this pay us peanuts, right? The region's dirt poor as it is. But if they offered me a job anywhere else I wouldn't take it, okay, because of this' – he gesticulated towards the great surges of Umbrian hill country lying beyond – 'and this' – he pointed to the city below us, lucid and articulate in the clarity of morning light – 'Understand?'

From time to time as I wandered to and fro in my 'chiel's amang ye takin' notes' fashion, trying to think of original ways in which to describe a Gothic rose window or the interior of a sixteenth-century palace, I would meet Professor Bernardoni. His head perpetually tilted to one side, he would offer me his guarded greeting, ask me, in his bleat of a voice, a few pointed questions about dates and styles, then, stretching out two dead fingers for me to clutch, would go on his way.

Yet his manner, I detected, had grown warmer towards me. The professorial examination was not over, there were still several papers, as it were, to be sat, but, perhaps only by my plodding determination to examine the city from top to bottom, I had somehow made him believe I was serious. What was more, I was beginning to love the place on my own account, without needing the advocacy of the townsfolk to recommend it to me. I liked the theatricality of its open spaces, the way in which the curtain always seemed to rise after the overture when you entered one of the squares, and the people leaning out of windows or standing at doorways looking as if ready to break into a chorus. I liked the singularity of its details, the half-buried Roman arch across the western entrance to the central piazza, the big rococo fountain dominating its farther end, the nineteenth-century loggia at the highest point of the municipal cemetery, whose arcade sheltered the 'good families' with swelling periods of Italian funerary prose bursting off their memorial slabs.

I liked above all the unselfconscious good manners of everyone in the city, from the woman in the grocer's who sold me a jar of black truffles as a present to my brother to the waiters at the hotel, from the limping custodian of the civic museum to the girl in the cake shop wrapping me up a packet of almond biscuits. Though it often seems as if Italy is the only country left in Europe where courtesy is still an instinct rather than something acquired as a class indicator, the Umbrians are beyond competition for sweetness and affability, and the people of ——— are in this respect little short of gods.

By the time my last evening arrived, I had become aware that not just the professor but everyone else, the town itself, was sifting and appraising me, wondering whether I would do. Meeting me in the street that morning, he had asked me, rather to my surprise, if I would join him and a party of friends at dinner, and there at length we sat, under the lime trees in a little square with a dribbling fountain in the middle, eating the local form of pasta, which is shaped like small flat shoelaces, and drinking the rough, sandpapery wine of the nearby hills.

There was the engineer Damiani, a man with a face like a sheep and a way of unwinding his sentences in syntactical loops which made him sound like a kind of Italian Henry James (in the novelist's later manner). There was the engineer Damiani's wife, whose wildly exaggerated declamatory style, rhapsodizing on everything from the seaside villa they were preparing to buy near Orbetello to the constituents of that evening's salad, would have been exasperating had it not been obvious that she had devised it as a means of coping with her husband's harmless but inescapable pomposity. There was an artist who made sculptures out of old washing machines and bits of motorcars, a cheery old widow whom everybody called by her surname – Testasecca – because of the obvious mileage you could extract from its faintly ribald overtones, and a little man named Nino who had appointed himself the life-and-soul, laughed louder than everyone else, plied us all with wine and went through an elaborate pantomime of generosity when the bill arrived, which was decent of him since, as the professor managed to tell me under cover of the fuss, he was not in the least well off.

Bernardoni himself sat at the head of the table, a figure without arrogance or presumption and somehow the more credible for his complete lack of physical elegance. Though the dinner was not in any sense given in my honour, it was plainly the last paper of the exam. These people, the engineer prosing on about the Byzantine exarchs, his wife calling everything *squisito* or *fantastico*, La Testasecca helping herself to another snort of wine, and Nino teasing her by pretending to jog her elbow, had been gathered together as the final syndicate before whom I must pass muster. Unusually for such a gathering, I managed to exchange more than a word or two with each of them, and I felt Bernardoni's scrutiny raking me as I did so, even if he seemed to be talking to somebody else at the time.

When the bill was paid and he said 'Bene, bene. Andiamo ragazzi,' I knew that 'Bene, bene' was, if not my *summa cum laude*, at any rate some indication of a pass. Everybody said their goodbyes, and the professor then decided to walk with me a little way down the hill before going home. He grew surprisingly communicative, telling me all about the late Signor Testasecca who, although he had made his money in cement, had yet developed an eye for mediaeval Umbrian masters, and asking me to forgive Nino for his bumptiousness, since the poor fellow didn't get out much these days and couldn't have much of a social sense.

When we reached a little piazza with a statue of some heavily-whiskered *risorgimentale* hero in the middle of it, brandishing his sword against the night, the professor halted to bid me farewell. In the few days of our acquaintance I had grown immensely fond of him, of that slightly crabby air of someone reluctant to suffer fools gladly, of his pedantic crotchets, his shambling modesty and weary politeness. He gave me the pair of fingers for the last time and I touched them with becoming reverence. Then at last he smiled, a boyish, indulgent grin. 'You'll come back to us, won't you, if there's anything you need to know,' he said, 'but I expect you've already discovered most of what you want.'

It was not until he had gone that I grasped the devastating ambiguity of his last remark. The distinction was exactly the kind he would have made, between what was necessary for me to know and what I desired to find out. Alone in the square, in a silent town half emptied of its inhabitants for the summer, I felt defenceless in my ignorance. Maybe I had not passed Bernardoni's exam after all, and knew nothing worth knowing about the city, about Umbria, about Italy. What was there to do except begin again? I looked up at the statue, all epaulettes and grandiloquence, so confident of what he had to do, so determined in the doing of it, and decided that perhaps I'd better not drop dead just yet.

INDEX OF PLACES